INDIA IN PRIMITIVE CHRISTIANITY

INDIA IN PRIMITIVE CHRISTIANITY

ARTHUR LILLIE

1909

GYAN

Published by

Gyan Publishing House
5, Ansari Road
Daryaganj, New Delhi-110002
Phone: 011-47034999, 9811692060
E-mail: books@gyanbooks.com

Distribution Network
gyanbooks.com
India, USA, Canada, UK, Australia, France

ISBN : 978-81-212-9576-5 (PB)
First Published, 1909

2nd Impression 2023

Printed at: Gyan Press, Delhi.

INDIA IN PRIMITIVE CHRISTIANITY
Author: ARTHUR LILLIE

INDIA IN PRIMITIVE CHRISTIANITY

After Daniell.

THE RATHAS OF MAHÂBÂLIPUR.

India in Primitive Christianity

BY

ARTHUR LILLIE
(Late Regiment of Lucknow)
Author of "Buddhism in Christianity," "Buddha and Buddhism," &c.

"Ye gave the Nazarite wine to drink and commanded the Prophet saying, 'Prophesy not.'"—TATIAN.

1909.

CONTENTS

PAGE

CHAPTER I

S'IVA

His legends being older and not in Sanskrit he has been neglected—Found in India by the Aryans when they crossed the mountains—S'iva as the Cobra, and Durgâ the Tree (pestilential Indian jungle) probably the oldest gods in the world.—S'iva as the Phœnician Baal. —Esoterically a noble Pantheism fighting with the Polytheisms around.—The S'iva-Durga cultus rises everywhere far above other religions and also sinks lower—Invents the Yogi and the Yoga philosophy—Invents the Hypostases—Great importance of Gaṇes'a in the history of civilisation. 9

CHAPTER II

BAAL

Tree and Serpent Worship carried by the Phœnicians everywhere—The religion of the Indian jungle—Baal in Palestine—The "Star of Chiun" (S'iva)—The Mahâdeos and Masseboth—Special blood-thirstiness of the Phœnician divinity—Holy of Holies of Jewish Temple, and "Sanctuary of the S'iva-linga" in India 27

CHAPTER III

BUDDHA

Born of a Virgin—Genealogies—The "Flower star" in the East—Asita and Simeon—The Four Presaging tokens—The Prince leaves the palace—The Bo Tree —Buddha preaches—Early biography altered—Mâyâ Devî is Durgâ—Dasasatanayana, S'iva the "thousand eyed," blesses him when he leaves the palace—Other changes 46

PAGE

CHAPTER IV

THE WISDOM OF THE OTHER BANK

Fine mysticism of Buddhism—The man who was born blind—The Tevigga Sutta—The Sinner—The Penitent Thief—"God revealed in the form of Mercy"—The Death of Buddha 69

CHAPTER V

KING ASOKA

King Asoka—Rock inscriptions—Only reliable records of early Buddhism—Not an atheism—Immortality—Dharma Râj—Kingdom of Justice—Helps to expose a portentous fraud—Buddhaghosa and the Ceylon records—King Wijayo—Date altered by Buddhaghosa one hundred years—Fictitious "Second Convocation" —Mahindo, Asoka's son, visits Ceylon—Vast literature of S'iva-Buddhism palmed upon him—Brief of modern English missionaries in their attack on Buddha 84

CHAPTER VI

THE MAHAYANA

New gods—All of them S'iva—A mask of Buddhism on some of them—Dhyâni or Heavenly Buddhas—Dhyâni Bodhisatwas—Conversion of the relic cairn of early Buddhism into S'iva's Lingam disguised as a Chaitya—Chaitya worship at Mathurâ—S'iva-Buddhism a worship of S'iva with "Left-handed" Tântrika rites—It is to be found in all Buddhist kingdoms—Rapid survey - - 107

CHAPTER VII

AVALOKITESWARA

The great Monastery of Nalanda—The "High Priest of all the World"—Is he the modern Pontiff of Tibet?—S'iva supposed to be incarnate in each successor—S'iva and Durgâ worshipped in all Buddhist rituals—Great revolution effected by King Kanis'ka—Strong remonstrance on the part of the "High Priest of all the World"—He declares that the encroaching cultus is pure S'ivism and Nihilism 120

PAGE

CHAPTER VIII

THE CAVE TEMPLE AND ITS MYSTERIES

Maurice on Temple Worship—Description of Cave temples—Worship the same in Egypt and Persia—Immense labour employed in constructing them—Cave mysteries everywhere an object of dread—Cicero on them—Eleusis—Lucian on the Tree Festival at Hieropolis—Bacchantic Festivals derived from S'iva as Somnâth (lord of Soma the first intoxicant)—These festivals still secretly celebrated in India 131

CHAPTER IX

ARCHITECTURE

Mr. James Fergusson—The "Sangharâma of Kasyapa"—Was it Elora?—Points of contact—Kailâs—Importance of the head of Avalokitishwara—Found on all S'ivan buildings ancient and modern—Buddhist arch the head of the Cobra—Serpent not worshipped in Buddhism until union with S'ivism—Fergusson on the Lingam—Calls it a "Dagoba"—Believes the Kailâs temples at Elora and the Mahabalipur Rathas to have been intended for dormitories of Buddhist monks—Proposition contested—Strange discovery that Avalokitishwara's head is very plentiful on both these old groups of rock-detached temples 141

CHAPTER X

THE ESSENES

Was Essenism due to Buddhist Missionaries?—Testimony of Asoka—The μοναστήριον, compared with the Sangharâma—"Apostles of the Bloodless Oblation"—Tertullian on the similarity between the rites of the Christians and the Mithraists—Testimony of Philo—Thirty thousand mokns go from Alexandria to Ruanwelli in Ceylon and are hospitably received on the occasion of the consecration of the great temple there. B.C. 170 162

CHAPTER XI

THE ESSENE JESUS

Was Jesus an Essene?—Nazarites or Nazareens—Baptised by the Nazarite John—A secret society—"Inquire who

PAGE

is worthy ! "—Essene Bread Oblation—Miracle of the Loaves—Probably an Essene Passover gathering—The Codex Nazaræus—The earliest gathering of Christians at Rome, Essene water-drinkers and vegetarians—The Gospel according to the Hebrews—Gospel of the Infancy 176

CHAPTER XII

MORE COINCIDENCES

Twelve Disciples—Love one another—Buddhist Beatitudes —The Sower—Blind Guides—Early Buddhism, a religion of joy—Buddhist baptismal rites—Other coincidences 200

CHAPTER XIII

RITES

The Abbé Huc on the close similarity of Christian and Buddhist rites—Confirmed by Fathers Disderi and Grueber—Reverend S. Beal on a Buddhist liturgy—Mr. Fergusson holds that the various details of the Christian basilica have been taken from the temples of the Buddhists—On which side was the borrowing ?—Arguments *pro* and *con* 219

CHAPTER XIV

PAULINISM

St. Paul a puzzle—Was he an ascetic mystic, or the author of the theory of the "Atonement," "Original Sin," etc., in fact of priestly Christianity ?—Up to the date of Irenæus there is no trace of his writings, nor even of his teachings—Did he convert Peter and James as described in "The Acts ?" James, Peter, John the Evangelist and Matthew all Nazarites—also Paul—Were they all instrumental in making the water-drinking Essenes drink wine ?—Valentinus—"Left-handed gods"—Early Zodiac of S'iva 225

CHAPTER XV

TRANSUBSTANTIATION

Gibbon on the rites of the Agapae at Alexandria—Professor Horace Hayman Wilson discovers similar rites in the

PAGE

Indian books—The S'rî Ka Chakra in the Devî Rashya—The Sacrifice of the Year-god in the Kalî Ka Purâna—Its analogy with the Roman Catholic Eucharist—Both sacrifices make-believe—Startling points of contact with the great Mystery-play in Tibet—Description of the "Sacrificial Body of the Dead Year"—Stabbed and cut to pieces—Great scramble for the fragments—New Year as in Alexandria represented by a baby covered with flour 235

CHAPTER XVI

CEYLON

Hiouen Tsiang, the Chinese traveller, on the religion of the Island in his day—"Followers of the Great Vehicle"—Bishop Copleston combats this—Three hundred "Great Vehicle" monks at Kânchapura—Wytulian heresy—Kappooism—S'iva as Saman Deva Râja supreme in the Island—Dewales and Buddhist Viharas in the same enclosures—Cure of the sick officially handed over to the Kappooists—Sekkraia (Sîva as Indra) a man, half man, half stone—S'ivan "Mystery"—The "Inebriating Festival of the Buddha"—Legend—Temple women—Kattragam or Karttikeya—His power and popularity 245

CHAPTER XVII

ALEXANDRIA

Adi-Buddha described by Hodgson—Abrasax described by Matter—Close points of contact—Mithras—His death and burial at Easter—Abrasax,—an individual, and also the whole body of the faithful, like Sangha, and also St. Paul's "Christ"—Points of contact between Kattragam and the Logos of Philo—Abrasax has two serpent legs—So has Padmapâni in the sculptures of Jemalgiri—Close analogies between Sekkraia and Serapis—Each is half man, half stone—Description of the advent of the Son of Man in the Gospels quite different from what was expected, but quite in harmony with S'iva's Pralaya 263

PAGE

CHAPTER XVIII

OPHIS AND THE SERPENTS

Serpent symbol everywhere in S'iva-Buddhism—Unknown in early Buddhism—Legend of Buddha burning the palace of the Nâga King—On a bas relief of the Sanchi Tope—The Serpent and the Lotus leaf—Valentinus—Dhyâni Buddhas—Saktis or Wives of the Dhyâni Buddhas—Gnostic Aeons—They also have their Saktis—Violent attack of Tertullian on these Saktis—Valentinus and Fourth Gospel—Valentinus and Serpent worship—The Gnostic Christos a Serpent—Cainites and Naasseni—The "Thousand-eyed (Dasasatanayana)" in Alexandria 276

CHAPTER XIX

DESCENT INTO HELL

New evidence—Five bas reliefs of the Amarâvatî Tope—They illustrate Buddha's Descent into Hell—Details of Amarâvatî Tope imitate details of an early tope—Tree Worship—Tree stem a lingam—Cairn Worship—Cairn a lingam—Roman Catholics maintain that their rites give the life of Jesus in epitome—Question examined—Not the life of the Jesus of the first three gospels—A "willing victim"—Suffers at night—Herod Antipas, the "King of the Jews"—An originality of Luke—Why brought in—His dress the same as that of a Catholic Bishop—The "Amice," the Hoodwinking rag of the Freemasons—The spear thrust—Blood and water—Baby New Year, in Alexandria and Tibet—Covered with flour—Tertullian on "Eleusinian dissipations" 282

LIST OF ILLUSTRATIONS

PLATES.	PAGE
FRONTISPIECE (RATHAS OF MAHÂBÂHPUR)	
1.—DURGÂ AS THE SERPENT MANASÂ	10
2.—TRAILINGA ÎSHWARA	41
3.—S'IVA DANCING	26
4.—THE BUDDHIST VIRGIN AND CHILD	49
5.—BUDDHA PREACHING	68
6.—THE CHAITYA LINGAM	109
7.—CHAITYA LINGAM WORSHIP	112
8.—SAMANA DEVA RÂJA	113
9.—THE HEAD WITHOUT A JAW	129
10.—A CAVE TEMPLE	133
11.—KAILÂS	147
12.—A MADRAS GOPURA	152
13.—THE PYRAMID, MAHABALIPUR	154
14.—BUDDHIST MONASTERY	166
15.—BUDDHIST MONKS	219
16.—BUDDHIST HIGH ALTAR	222
17.—S'IVA'S TRISULA OR TRIDENT	230
18.—ZODIAC OF S'IVA	231
19.—S'IVA WITH ANTELOPE	230
20.—SEKKRAIA	249
21.—BALI DEVIL-DANCER	251
22.—SESH DISGUISED AS BUDDHA	253
23.—DURGÂ AS A GIANTESS	260
24.—GNOSTIC GEMS	264

PLATE. PAGE

25.—THE BURNING OF THE NÂGA'S PALACE - - 275

26.—WORSHIP OF THE SILVER TREE-STEM - - 284

27.—LINGAM WORSHIP - - - - - 284

28.—THREE SCENES IN THE INEBRIATING FESTIVAL - 285

29.—THE CUP - - - - - - 285

30.—PYRAMID OF WOMEN - - - - 286

MINOR ILLUSTRATIONS

THE HEAD IN THE ARCHWAY - - - - 156

THE TEMPLE AND PALACE - - - - 158

S'IVA'S HEAD IN CEYLON - - - - - 261

SERPENT AND BASKET - - - - - 281

INTRODUCTION.

THE first edition of this work, issued in 1893, had an unexpected success, especially abroad. In France, the eminent Sanskrit scholar, M. Léon de Rosny, reviewed it very favourably in the "XXme Siêcle" in a long article that gave a digest of the subject.

He said: "The astonishing points of contact (ressemblances étonnantes) between the popular legend of Buddha and that of Christ, the almost absolute similarity of the moral lessons given to the world, at five centuries' interval, between these two peerless teachers of the human race, the striking affinities between the customs of the Buddhists and of the Essenes, of whom Christ must have been a disciple, suggest at once an Indian origin to Primitive Christianity."

And in Germany the eminent scientist, Ludwig Büchner, also reviewed it in one of the periodicals summing up thus: "There is no longer any question of the close relationship, in form and contents, of the two greatest and most successful religions of the world." This article has been reproduced in the volume entitled "Last Words on Materialism."

But the subject had already been ventilated on the continent.

In the "Revue des Deux Mondes," 15th July, 1888, M. Émile Burnouf has an article entitled "Le

Bouddhisme en Occident." M. Burnouf holds that the Christianity of the Council of Nice was due to a conflict between the Aryan and the Semite, between Buddhism and Mosaism :

"History and comparative mythology are teaching every day more plainly that creeds grow slowly up. None come into the world ready-made, and as if by magic. The origin of events is lost in the infinite. A great Indian poet has said, 'The beginning of things evades us ; their end evades us also. We see only the middle.'"

M. Burnouf asserts that the Indian origin of Christianity is no longer contested : "It has been placed in full light by the researches of scholars, and notably English scholars, and by the publication of the original texts. . . . In point of fact for a long time folks had been struck with the resemblances, or rather the identical elements, contained in Christianity and Buddhism. Writers of the firmest faith and most sincere piety have admitted them.

"In the last century these analogies were set down to the Nestorians, but since then the science of Oriental chronology has come into being, and proved that Buddha is many years anterior to Nestorius and Jesus. Thus the Nestorian theory had to be given up. But a thing may be posterior to another without proving derivation. So the problem remained unsolved until recently, when the pathway that Buddhism followed was traced step by step from India to Jerusalem."

A small work that had such a reception would by-and-by require a second edition, but intermediately an obstacle had come in the way, a very serious obstacle. Looking over the "Buddhist Records of the Western World," by the Reverend Samuel Beal, I came across a passage in which he declares that there was a complete union between Buddhism and the followers of S'iva, brought about by Nâgarjuna about A.D. 100. I had been partially on this track myself. Mr Beal asserts that Quan Yin in Chinese means Avalokitisvara (S'iva looking down), and Mr. Beal asserts that in China Quan Yin is an Hermaphrodite God.

At first I did not attach much weight to the theory. But when I thought of bringing out a second edition to my work, the "Influence of Buddhism in Primitive Christianity," I found that it complicated my task.

The main postulate of my work was that the monks and mystics in Egypt and Palestine were in close touch with the Buddhist monks in India. How did S'iva-Buddhism affect them? Immensely. The task at first appeared too much for me. But I found a great difficulty in throwing over the matter altogether, and I subsequently got leisure to take it up in earnest.

One flash of light quickly came to corroborate Mr. Beal.

I found that the Left-handed Tântrika rites, the devil-dancing, and the worship of S'iva as Bhairava, were in every Buddhist kingdom. This did not seem so very important at first. The worship was accounted for everywhere locally. In Tibet it was due to the Bons, in China to Dragon-Worshippers, in Ceylon to the aboriginal Nâgas. These were mere remains of local superstitions, mere barnacles outside the ship. I accepted the interpretation.

But soon many points suggested themselves to completely overthrow it. In each Buddhist kingdom was a hierarchy as strongly organised and as persistent as the hierarchy at Rome. That is the testimony of the Roman Catholic bishop, Bigandet. Now a hierarchy is an institution specially framed to resist all change instead of effecting changes. Why should all these hierarchies accept radical changes suddenly and simultaneously. One writer suggests that

Buddhism desired to gain over the poorer classes of India by bringing Durgâ into their Pantheon. But Buddhism was already the religion of the poorer classes. It was the religion of the Yellow races and the low caste Sûdras. It gave to these peace, honesty, prosperity instead of Eastern slavery and interminable Indian warfare. It changed wastes into waving rice fields. It established the first hospital for healing the sick instead of handing them over to the interested sorceries of greedy devil dancers. It revealed to the Sûdra the spiritual life which the haughty Âryan had steadily kept from him. Plainly the great change called Mahâyâna could not have come from the outside.

But it might have come from a Supreme Curia like the Court of Rome. The Dalai Lâma claims to be the head of the Buddhist hierarchies. In ancient days he bore sway in the splendid monastery of Nalanda near Buddha Gaya. He was called the Âcharya (Teacher). He is alluded to in the Mahâwanso as the "High Priest of all the World." When the Buddhists were turned out of India at the revival of Brahminism, it is alleged that the great Buddhist establishment from Nalanda took refuge first in Kashmir and then in Tibet. Avalokitishvara (S'iva) guided them on their journey. And Avalokitishvara, becoming incarnate in the Dalai Lâma, still inspires Buddhism: China, Nepal, and I believe Burma, still treat him as their Pope. Such a supreme Authority coerced by a monarch so powerful as Kanis'ka, might have forced a change as revolutionary as the Mahâyâna upon the minor churches. The task was quite beyond a few ignorant devil-dancers working separately and at far distances one from the other.

Many other points tend to the same conclusion.

Avalokitishvara and his wife Durgâ have the chief place in the litanies and prayers of the Viharas.

The great seven days' festival of India the Durgâ Pûjah, under various names "Perahar," the "Festival of the She-devil Devî," etc., is the chief festival of most Buddhist countries.

The healing of the sick by the casting out of devils which was the chief outside function of the Buddhist monks, has now in Buddhist countries been taken from them and handed over to the unadulterated followers of Bhairava. The vow to worship the Chaitya is the chief solemn promise exacted from the Buddhist postulant at his baptism, or Abhisheka.

This Chaitya is a sham relic-dome made purposely like S'iva's Lingam. A model of it is given to the postulant with his beads and alms bowl.

Now it must be remembered that the main subject of this book is the question of the influence of Buddhism on primitive Christianity. The first edition was directed chiefly to an attempt to show the many points of resemblance between the water-drinking vegetarian celibates of Galilee who had for their main point of attack the superstition of the bloody altar, and the water-drinking vegetarian celibates of India, who had for their main point of attack the same superstition. It was suggested that the analogy was so close between them that they must have been in close communication. This at once suggests enormous difficulties. If there was this close communication, evidences of the great change which brought back to India the recking altar and Bacchantic intoxicants would soon find their way to Alexandria and the West. This was the difficulty that faced me when I thought of preparing a new edition of this work. I saw that I would have to make an elaborate study of the religion of Serapis and of the gnostic and early Christian sects. I saw that I must get clearer ideas of the channel by which India was in communication with the West. The result is now before the reader.

I soon found strong evidence that Ceylon was the high road along which Buddhism had come. The early Christian controversies might be said to be a battle between Persian Dualism, the philosophy of the authors of the later Jewish scriptures, and the pantheism of S'iva. In the following pages the reader may gain some knowledge of how it affected the doctrine of eternal rewards and punishments, the rite of Transubstantiation, the destruction of the Kosmos by the advent of the great Judge, the Trinity and Logos ideas. As in Ceylon the Western World in those days believed themselves to be a prey to millions and billions of evil spirits, who everywhere and at all times sought their destruction. Cures could only be effected by charms and spells and the "casting out" of these devils.

And the gods of S'iva-Buddhism seemed really to have invaded Alexandria. Serapis was a servile copy of Sakkraia, a god, half man, half stone; and Kattragam had analogies with the Logos of Philo and Abrasax, the Time-god, sacrificed at the end of the year.

But a more startling discovery was behind, which, if authenticated, would place my theory of a S'iva-Buddha union on a basis that cannot be easily shaken. I came across a passage in the writings of the Orientalist, Horace Hayman Wilson, showing that he was much struck with the close analogy between certain gross rites amongst the Vâmâcharîs, or left-handed Tântrika rites of the followers of S'iva as detailed in the Devî Rashya and the alleged improprieties of the Agapæ, as described by Gibbon. I give these rites as described in the Indian work, and also in the Kâlî Ka Purâna.

But this discovery led to others. In Nepal, according to Mr. Brian Hodgson, and in Ceylon, according to Spence Hardy, the Buddhists are very reticent about their esoteric mysteries, as Mr. Hodgson calls them, and initiatory rites; but a Miracle Play from Tibet, entitled the "Sacrificial Body of the Dead Year," when read side by side with the Kâlî Ka Purâna, quite opened my eyes. In a word, it was quite plain that the slaughter of a victim to represent the dying year, had been part of the mysteries which the followers of S'iva had forced upon the blameless water-drinking ascetics, who hailed Buddha for a teacher. The records of Ceylon told much the same story. The initiatory rite there is called the "Inebriating Festival of the Buddha," and to bring in the Bacchantic element, a version of Buddha's descent into hell has been invented, detailing how he took part in this festival as a man named Mâga; and how he made the Nâgas drunk, and cleared hell both of its victims and its fiends. This might of course only be a Sinhalese fable, but I have discovered five bas reliefs amongst the Amarâvatî marbles on the staircase of the British Museum which tell the same story in stone. This shows that at an early date it was current in the Buddhism on the mainland of India. Brian Hodgson shows that the worship of Bhairava or S'iva in his aspect as the God of Evil was part of the baptismal initiation as detailed in the esoteric Sûtras, which were sent for safety from Magadha to Nepal. These Tântras, setting forth the worship of the Left-handed gods, the Târâ Tântra or Worship of Durgâ, the Mahâkâla Tântra or worship of S'iva as Time, the terrible Kâla Chakra Tântra, the Nâga Pûjah (Worship of Serpents), etc., amount to seventy-four in the Buddhist library of Nepal alone.*

S'iva-Buddhism reached Alexandria, and it may be asked how it affected the religion of Christ. I answer, In no way, if by Religion of Christ something

* Hodgson, "Religion in Nepal," p. 38.

distinct is understood from what is now called Christianity. The Nazarine water-drinkers of the Church founded at Jerusalem by Christ's genuine apostles to the last refused to adopt the Bacchantic Change which Tatian summed up in the terse indictment: " Ye gave the Nazarite wine to drink, and commanded the prophet, saying, ' Prophecy not.' "

The Church of Rome boasts that their sacramental rites picture in brief the life of Christ. I examine this theory and show that it certainly does not apply to the Jesus of the first three Gospels whatever it may do to the " Mystery " of the Gnostic Year God. Tertullian tells us that the followers of Valentinus called some of their rites " left-handed."

CHAPTER I

S'IVA.

His legends being older, and not in Sanskrit, he has been neglected.—Found in India by the Âryans when they crossed the mountains—S'iva as the Cobra, and Durgâ as the Tree (pestilential Indian jungle) probably the oldest gods in the world.—S'iva as the Phenician Baal.—Esoterically a noble Pantheism fighting with the Polytheisms around.—The S'iva-Durgâ Cultus rises everywhere far above other religions, and also sinks lower. Invents the Yogi—and the Yoga philosophy.—Invents the Hypostases.—Great importance of Ga es'a in the history of civilisation.

As the Indian god S'iva has much to do with our present inquiry, first of all we must try to get a better knowledge of him. Professor Horace Hayman Wilson tells us that Saiva literature has been very little presented to the Hindus. The legends are not in Sanskrit.

From the earliest times the thunderstorm has been used to image God's voice and God's anger. We see Thor with his "hammer" knock down the enormous cloud-giant, Hrungner. In the First Book of Samuel, Yahve "thunders with a great thunder" and defeats the Philistine enemies of the chosen race. In Hesiod the "vaulted sky, the Mount Olympus, flashed with the terrible bolts" of Zeus in the Titan warfare. This symbolism naturally suggests itself when we look up to the "vaulted sky"; but in the Rig Veda it takes a different turn. Indra the

Thunderer vanquishes his enemy Vritra, but often he seeks him in a "Cavern," a bottomless pit.

"He (Indra) has burst in the doors of that cavern where Vritra detained the waters shut up in his power. Indra has torn to pieces Suchna (Drought viewed as God) with his horns of menace."

"By him has been opened the bosom of that vault, yea, that vault without boundaries. Armed with the thunderbolt, Indra, the greatest of the Angiras, has forced the stable of the Celestial Cows."*

That the chief god inimical to the Âryans was S'iva there can be no doubt. His special symbol is the Mahâdeo, and Dr. Muir has unearthed two passages of the Rig Veda that blurt out this truth brutally.

"May the glorious Indra triumph over hostile beings. Let not those whose god is the S'is'na approach our sacred ceremony."

"Desiring to bestow strength on the struggle that warrior (Indra) has besieged inaccessible places at the time when irresistibly slaying those whose god is the S'is'na he by his force conquered the riches of the City with a hundred gates." †

The S'is'na is the Mahâdeo, sex worship in *puris naturalibus*.

Another symbol under which S'iva is attacked is that of a serpent. He is "Ahi," of the Rig Veda. Serpents even in modern times kill about 24,000 people every year in India. It is most probable that S'iva and Durgâ as two snakes were the earliest of Indian gods. Every year Durgâ figures as a snake at the Nâgapanchami Festival, and is prayed to to preserve her votaries against snake bites.

"He (Indra) has struck Ahi, who was hiding in the body of a mountain. He has struck him with that resounding weapon forged by Twashtri (the Vulcan of

* Rig Veda (Sect. II. Hymn IX. v. 3.)

† Muir's "Sanskrit Texts," IV., pp. 345, 346.

PLATE I.

5

DURGÂ AS THE SERPENT MANASÂ.

the Vedas), and the waters like cows ran towards their stable. . . . . He has struck the first born of the Ahis."*

But Ahi or Vritra has a wicked wife, "Nirriti the insurmountable." This is plainly S'iva's wife, Durgâ (the Tower of Strength).

"May Nirriti whose force is so formidable never come near to smite us, Nirriti the insurmountable. May she perish with the thirst that she herself instils."

A French Orientalist thinks that she was a personification of the terrible Indian fever. This is, of course, the basis of the tree worship in an Indian jungle.

But another name, a very important one, was rendered prominent by that active Orientalist, Colonel Tod, namely Bal. When he was staying in Saurashtra he noticed this name in many temples. There was Balpur (the City of Bala), Balnath (the Lord Bal), and the plateau of the Sahyadri mountains was called Mahâbaleshwar (the Great Ishwara, Bala or S'iva).

Colonel Tod believed that this God, Bala, was the Baal of the Phenicians, and through them the Bal, Sit, or Typhon, the earliest god of Memphis and lower Egypt. In Babylon he was Bel with his wife Ashtoreth. The names Bala and Bali are philologically the same, being based on the word Balishwara. In the Râmâyana S'iva is termed Bali, and in the Rig Veda he is named Bala.

"God who wieldest the Thunderbolt, thou hast burst in the cavern where Bala kept the celestial cows."

"The Maruts support Indra when that God armed with the lightning and strengthened by our offerings, smites the soldiers of Bala, as Trita dispersed the guards."

Inscriptions dating as early as 4,000 B.C. have induced Professor Sayce and others to claim for Assyria the lead in early religious ideas. But Colonel

* Lect. II. Hymn XIII., v. 2.

Tod believes that the religion of S'iva was spread abroad at a very early age, before the Phenicians came in with their Baal worship. Recent discoveries have confirmed Colonel Tod.

It has been discovered that Indian teak was used for building purposes in Babylon, and Indian muslin was known there, and called "Sindhu," the early name for India.

Another singularly able Orientalist, Mr. Paterson, wrote thus in the "Asiatic Researches"*

"The doctrines of the Saivas seem to have extended themselves over the greatest portion of mankind. They spread amongst remote nations, who were ignorant of the origin and meaning of the rites they adopted, and this ignorance may be considered as the cause of the mixture and confusion of images and ideas which characterised the mythology of the ancient Greeks and Romans.

"In fact, foreign nations could only copy the outward signs and ceremonies. They could not be admitted beyond the threshold of the temple. The adytum was impenetrable to them.

"Kal and Kâlî assumed various names. Kal became Kronos, Moloch, Saturn, Dis, Pluto, and Typhon. Kâlî became Hecate, Proserpine, and Diana who was worshipped with bloody sacrifice at Tauris. It was to the barbarians that the Greeks were referred by their own writers to understand the names and origin of their deities.

"S'iva in his character of the creative power became the Zeus triopthalmos (the 'three-eyed,' a special characteristic of S'iva) Jupiter and Osiris. His consort Bhavânî, became Juno, Venus, Cybele, Rhoea the Syrian goddess, the armed Pallas, Iris, Ceres, and Anna Perenna. The multiplication of deities arose from the ignorance of foreign nations as to the source

* Vol. VIII.

of the superstition which they adopted, and the original meaning of the symbols.

"They supplied their want of information by fables congenial to their own national character and manners: hence arose those contradictions which made their theology a labyrinth of confusion."*

And now what is S'iva?

The first answer would be that he is the God of Destruction, who moves about amongst the tombs in the guise of an old and emaciated Yogi, a mere scaffolding of the human building. Around his neck is twisted a Naja Tripudians, the most deadly of snakes, but he wears also a larger necklace composed of human skulls. His waist-cloth is a tiger's skin. Vipers are his ear-rings. In one of his hands he holds the Pâs'a, the terrible noose of the Thugs, his ardent worshippers. In another hand hangs a bleeding head; a third holds the Gada, his terrible mace of war. But more awful than all, in his fourth hand is the Trisul, the three pronged pitchfork, with which he pushes about human enterprises and mars them chiefly. Ashes made of very disagreeable ingredients cover him.

> Is that the King of Dread
> With ashy musing face
> From whose moon-silvered locks famed Gunga springs?

The religions invented by man have reached the most abject depths of baseness. The religions invented by man have reached superb heights of human exaltation. It is a strange paradox that at this early date the religion of S'iva-Durgâ capped both ends of this long line of human speculation. It gave to the world the foul left-handed Tântrika rites; and was also the forerunner of Patanjali, Buddha, Isaiah, Jesus, Fenelon, and Mirza the Sufi. For there sat the Indian Yogi, calmly contemplating this great problem:

* "Asiatic Researches," Vol. VIII.

What is man, and what are his relations to the universe around him ?

That the Indian Yogi was in existence when the Âryans reached India is proved from the Zend Avesta : for in the fourth Fargard, the Persian Âryans denounce his solitary dreamings in an Indian forest :—

" Verily I say unto thee, O Spitâma Zarathustra, the man who has a wife is far above him who begets no sons ; he who keeps a house is far above him who has none ; he who has children is far above the childless man ; he who has riches is far above him who is poor.

" And of two men he who fills himself with meat is filled with the good spirit much more than he who does not do so.

" It is this man who can strive against the onsets of the death fiend ; that can strive against the winter fiend with the thinnest garments on ; that can strive against the wicked tyrant and smite him on the head ; can strive against the ungodly Ashemaogha (heretic) who does not eat."

S'iva is Darkness—the Lord of Hell, a region that seems to have sprung from him and his cave. But from him has also came the idea of Kailâs and its jewelled buildings. That was still the Hindu Paradise at the date of the Râmâyana. And S'iva's rude stone denotes life as well as death,—earthly life, heavenly life.

Also he is sometimes represented with three heads. Trailinga Ishwara, as Creator, Protector, Destroyer. This fancy has been stolen by the Brahmins who call Brahma the Creator, and Vishnu the Protector. But the central head of his statue, say the one at Elora is not that of Brahma, for it has Ganga (a head of the Ganges) in its top knot. Trailinga Ishwara dates very far back, for a considerable portion of Madras is called Telinga after him. And Mr. Crawford tells us that in Java and the Islands it appeared to be the name of the islanders for India. And Sîva has one more attribute, the most formidable of all. S'iva is Mahâkâla (Remphan, Kronos, "Great Time.") In the Râmâyana, Valmiki informs us that S'iva has "emasculated all the gods." And when winter tourists in India sneer at a white-dusted yogi in the bazaar, they little guess what he represents. He bears the white ash of the innumerable gods, stars, systems races of men that the Great Yogi, Mahâ Kâla, has burnt up.*

Man's religion may be called the "Non-ego as viewed by the Ego." It is the relation that the thinking individual believes himself to hold with the infinite universe around him. What mind-picture did the facts of life present to the early races of India, driven by the hardier Âryans into jungles and wastes where serpents and fevers were very plentiful, and food very scarce? They were pronounced to be Pariahs. They were forbidden to look into any sacred book, death being the penalty. Indra, Agni, Varuna and other gods had poured down on the Indian soil colleges of holy men to perform certain rites that pleased these gods; and folks gained in return happiness and comfort. But such joys were not for the yellow-faced Turanian. Even the Nirvâna promised after many dreary rebirths was refused to him.

But whilst matters were running along in this manner S'iva's Yogi was sitting in his jungle seeking the Bodhi, or transcendental knowledge. It came to him in a form which we might call the critical faculty. He examined the divine claims of the priests, and found them contradicted by experience. Agni ate up greedily the flesh of the bullocks, the rice and the ghee, placed on his altar, but did not give in return

* "Catechism of the Shaiva Religion," by Sabhapati Mudalyar, p. 73.

wealth, health, or immunity from the accidents and sorrows of life. Indra, when requisitioned, refused, as often as not, to strike with his vajra the bellying cloud and deluge the baking earth with fruitful showers. Soon an early philosophy arose. It was called the Sankhya, and had two schools, two Bibles. One, that of Patanjali, is called Seshwara Sankhya, the Sûtras or maxims of S'iva, the Great Serpent Sesh. The other that of Kapila, is called the Nirîswara Sankhya, and it denies the existence of God altogether. These tractates are immensely old. Professor Manilal Mabhubhai* Dvivedi says that in the Yoga Patanjali talks as if he were only an editor, and Colebrooke believes Kapila to be a mythological personage.

We will copy down from Colebrooke a digest of the two prominent philosophies of the followers of S'iva, the first derived from the Yoga S'âstra of Patanjali, and the second from the Karica of Kapila. Says Colebrooke :—

"God, Îs'wara, the supreme ruler according to Patanjali, is a soul, a spirit distinct from other souls ; unaffected by the ills by which they are beset ; unconcerned with good or bad deeds and their consequences, or with fancies and passing thoughts. In him is the utmost omniscience. He is the instructor of the earliest beings that have a beginning (the deities of mythology), himself infinite, unlimited by time."

Kapila on the other hand, according to Colebrooke, denies an Îs'wara (ruler of the world by volition), alleging that there is no proof of God's existence unperceived by the senses, not inferred from reasoning, nor yet revealed. He acknowledges, indeed, a being issuing from nature who is intelligence absolute, source of all individual intelligences, and origin of other existences successively evolved and developed. He expressly affirms that the truth of such an Îs'wara

* "Translation of Yoga Sutras," p. 1.

is demonstrated, the creator of worlds in such sense of creation: for "the existence of effects," he says, "is dependent on consciousness, not upon Iswara."*

As I shall have to show that the second or Atheistic Sankhya had so much to do with the great change of Buddhism, I will add another detail, taking advantage of an able essay by Ludwig Büchner.

"A consistent pessimism is the main feature of the system." "Happiness is a mere illusion, and all conscious life, pain and suffering."†

Suffering man is involved in a vortex of rebirths. It is only after tasting old age and death and other infirmities time after time for thousands of years, that the saint can gain repose in complete annihilation.‡

S'iva is the God of Destruction as well as life. Periodically he destroys the entire Kosmos—gods, men, and whirling stars. The white ashes of his followers represent the charred remains of these portentous destructions, as I have shown. The idea was plainly invented as an answer to the high-blown pretensions of the Brahmin polytheism—"Yes, there are gods, Brahma, Indra, Vishnu, etc., but S'iva sweeps them all away"; and oddly enough, the Brahmins seem to have accepted the theory.

It is also plain that the callousness of the god is another gird against the Brahmin priesthoods, who urged that sacrifices and other savage rites alone could move him. The Yogis held that the Great All was unknowable, unthinkable, omnipresent, inert, eternal.

The theory of this Pralaya, or destruction of worlds, suggests the origin of the Nirvâna of Buddha, in the sense of annihilation. According to his biography, he came to earth to give immortality to mankind,

* Colebrooke's "Essays," Vol. I., p. 251.

† Büchner, "Last Words on Materialism," p. 119.

‡ *Ibid.*

but the Pralaya sweeps away gods, men, and stars. This made immortality out of the question. And the Mahâyâna movement plainly also got from the Sankhya philosophy its atheism, cosmism, pessimism, and the idea of the grievous, prolonged tortures of its metempsychosis. Early Buddhism had pronounced that by joining Buddha's fold these torments could be made at once to cease.

But the Yogi of S'iva in his jungle gave to the world another gift. He said practically this—A god mysterious and callous, who dwells in the great Temple of Darkness, may be said to be incomprehensible to all except minds of his own fathom. The Absolute must be treated as the Absolute. It could not create anything for everything is already perfection. It could not supervise and direct mortal affairs, for those affairs were by absolute wisdom already arranged. A mind inscrutable and boundless can have no will to produce anything but what is like himself boundless and perfect.

But in the world some men are more wise, some more strong, some more virtuous than others. Could we not, as a workable postulate, deify what seem to be the attributes of this mighty mystery? Could not we imagine a God of Wisdom, a son of God, and call him Gaṇes'a? Could we not imagine a God of Strength and call him Karttikeya? The result was the Avesthâ idea, which, according to Professor Horace Hayman Wilson, was translated "Hypostasis" in Alexandria. Gaṇes'a was the son of Sîva, the "Word" of God, the Creator of the World; and two great feats are plainly his. As Gaṇes'a he gave to India much of its civilisation. As Janus, which Orientalists all affirm is the word Gaṇes'a a little altered, he gave civilisation to ancient Rome.

I insert a quotation from the works of Sir William Jones.

"The titles and attributes of this old Italian deity are fully comprised in two choriambick verses of Sulpitius; a further account of him from Ovid would here be superfluous:—

> Jane pater, Jane tuens, dive biceps, biformis,
> O cate rerum fator, O principium deorum!

Father Janus, all beholding Janus, thou divinity with two heads and with two forms. O sagacious planter of all things and leader of deities.

"He was the God we see of Wisdom whence he is represented on coins with two, and on the Etruscan image found at Falisci, with four faces, emblems of prudence and circumspection. Thus is Gaṇes'a, the God of Wisdom in Hindustan, painted with an elephant's head, the symbol of sagacious discernment.

His next great character (the plentiful source of many superstitious usages) was that from which he is emphatically styled the Father, and which the second verse before cited more fully expresses; the origin and founder of all things. Whence this notion arose, unless from a tradition that he first built shrines, raised altars, and instituted sacrifices, it is not easy to conjecture. Hence it came, however, that his name was invoked before any other god; that in the old sacred rites corn and wine, and in later times incense also, were first offered to Janus; that the doors or entrances of private houses were called Januæ, and any previous passage or thoroughfare in the plural number Jani, or "with two beginnings;" that he was represented as holding a rod as guardian of ways, and a key as opening not gates only, but all-important works and affairs of mankind; that he was thought to preside over the morning or the beginning of day; that, although the Roman year began regularly in March, yet the eleventh month named Januarius, was considered as first of the twelve, whence the whole year was supposed to be under his guidance, and opened with great solemnity by the Consuls inaugurated in his fane, where his statue was decorated on that occasion with fresh laurel; and for the same reason a solemn denunciation of war, than which there can hardly be a more momentous national act, was made by the military consul opening the gates of the temple, with all the pomp of his magistracy. The twelve altars and twelve chapels of Janus might either denote according to the general opinion that he leads and governs twelve months, or that, as he says of himself in Ovid, all entrance and access to the principal gods must be made through him. They were, to a proverb of the same number. We may add that Janus was imagined to preside over infants at their birth or the beginning of life.

"The Indian divinity has precisely the same character. All sacrifices and religious ceremonies, all addresses even to superior gods, all serious compositions in writing and all worldly affairs of moment are begun by pious Hindus with an invocation to Gaṇes'a, a word composed of "Isa," the Governor or leader, and "gana" a company of deities, nine of which companies are enumerated in the Amaracosha. Instances of opening business auspiciously by an ejaculation to the Janus of India (if the lines of resemblance here traced will justify me in so calling him) might be multiplied with ease. Few books are begun without the words "Salutation to Gaṇes'a," and he is first invoked by the Brahmins who conduct the trial by ordeal, or perform the ceremony of the Homa, or sacrifice by fire. M. Sonnerat represents him as highly revered on the Coast of Coromandel, where, the Indians, he says, "would not on any account build a house without having placed on the ground an image of this deity which they sprinkle with oil and adorn every day with flowers. They set up his figure in all the temples, in the streets, in the high roads, and in the open plains at the foot of some tree, so that persons of all ranks may invoke him before they undertake any business, and travellers worship him before they proceed on their journey." To this I may add from my own observation that in the commodious and useful town that now rises at Gaya, under the auspices of the active and benevolent Thomas Law, Esquire, Collector of Rotas, every new built house agreeably to an immemorial usage of the Hindus has the name of Gaṇes'a superscribed on its door; and in the old town his image is placed over the gates of the temples."*

I pause here to notice an important point. Colebrooke, Sir William Jones, Horace Hayman Wilson, and the old giants, all held that the mythologies of Greece and Rome were derived from India, but since Oriental studies have become professorial, some authorities subscribe to the wild theory of Max Müller, that when the Âryans passed from Bactria across the Hindu Kush, "the great mountains closed for centuries their Cyclopeian gates," † and India became a sort of undiscovered America until the arrival in India of Alexander the Great.

Now it seems to me that it would be quite impossible for any writer to compose a paragraph which would more completely pulverise Max Müller's fancy about the "Cyclopean Gates" than that of Sir William Jones. The Professor holds that the Greek and Latin languages were sisters to the Sanskrit before the separation at the Hindu Kush. He holds, too, that the Greek and Latin mythologies were sisters to the Indian mythology; but when the Âryans crossed the mountains, all connection ceased. And yet we find in Italy a wide knowledge of the best Indian religious ideas

* Sir William Jones "Works," Vol. III., p. 329.

† Max Müller "Chips from a German Workshop," Vol. I., pp. 8-12.

and customs. This knowledge could not have been obtained before the Âryan separation, for Gaṇes'a is a non-Aryan and non-Vedic god. It was not obtained subsequent to Alexander's expedition, for Gaes'a stretches away to the earliest and haziest traditions of Italy, to the time when Kronos his father battled with Zeus.

Learned professors who have never been to India study the Indian books, but not the Indians themselves. We must try and throw ourselves into very early times, when there were no letters of the alphabet, and folks had to rely on their rhapsodists and "bhats" for history; and the said rhapsodists had to make the dull framework of facts into a pleasant romance to obtain a hearing.

Let us suppose that the votaries of one religion think they have triumphed over another, and a pleasant allegory suggests itself. The god of the triumphing religion may be represented as a dwarf who comes to the god of the second religion, and humbly asks to be allowed as much land as he could pace with three of his poor, inconsiderable, dwarfish steps. Then comes the *denouement.* The dwarf becomes a giant and his three steps cover hell, earth and the vast region lit up by the stars. Every Indian would know what this was intended to mean quite as well as if it were written down in the unpoetical, systematically dull, language of Hallam.

How was such an attack to be met in days when there were no letters of the alphabet and no books.

An answer to this question comes from the S'iva Purâna. It is a legend of great importance to our inquiry.

At a place called Merlya Loka a number of very holy Brahmins had collected together with their wives. They lived in a collection of rude huts called an Â'sram, and they performed daily the most severe and painful exercises of ascetic Brahmanism, to gain magical powers. The people around flocked to them, with their ailments and troubles. All admitted that such holy men had never been seen in those parts. They were stern men, no doubt, especially towards the followers of S'iva, wicked men who neglected and derided the holy Vedas.

But one morning a strange circumstance occurred. One of them looking up whilst seated cross-legged under a tree, saw at the edge of the jungle a woman of exquisite beauty. She seemed to wish him to come towards her, although why he thought this he would not have been able to explain. She held in her hand an Indian lute. Suddenly on this she played a few bars. Such melody had never been heard before. He got up almost unconsciously and moved towards her. He was seeking to bridge earth and heaven. Perhaps Indra had sent one of his beautiful Apsaras to help him.

But the odd thing was that all the other ascetics had much the same experience. They wandered away into the leafy glades after the same Apsara. What occurred there is not narrated in the S'âstras. The next day they were in an angry mood, and specially angry with a magician whom in a body they visited and accosted with these stern words :—

"Ugly fiend, what trick is this that thou hast played?"

The person thus designated was a dwarf, certainly ugly, and as certainly endowed with very rare and magical faculties. He was named Tripurasura. He lived in a hut alone, and was quite independent of the other ascetics. Indeed, he intercepted many of the offerings of the poor people around, folks who thought that he was a greater magician than they were.

"Ugly fiend," said Tripurasura, with a laugh,

"go to, the story of an ugly fiend has to be narrated to me and explained to me, worthy masters!"

"What dost mean, O deformed one?"

"I am told that an 'ugly fiend' persuaded certain grave ascetics to follow her into the paths of wantonness."

"Vile slanderer!" cried the ascetics.

"Did ye not recognise the woman with the gaping mouth, Durgâ, who feeds on little babies?"

"These words are silliness, O man of falsities!" said the Brahmins, now thoroughly alarmed.

"And all this time," pursued the malicious dwarf, with a chuckle, "where were the Brahmins' wives? and where was the Apsara's husband, S'iva, the progenitor of many?"

With shrill voices the Brahmins' wives treated this as a most pernicious insinuation. But women sometimes quarrel, and by-and-by it came out that a young man as handsome as Kâma had visited them when the Brahmins were away in the forest.

The Brahmins were now furious, and desired a summary vengeance. They held that a Brahmajnâni (as initiate in the mysteries of Brahma), was superior to any tricky fiend whatever. They performed new incantations and sacrifices, and produced a tiger whose mouth was like a cavern, and his voice like thunder amongst the mountains. This they sent against the god S'iva. He seized the tiger and squeezed it to death, and he still wears its skin as a kummerbund.

Nothing dauntèd, the Brahmins tried new incantations. This time they determined to send something that he could not kill. They selected the Ânanta Nâga, the Serpent of Eternity. S'iva played to it a tune on his flute to charm it, and wound it harmlessly round his neck, where it still remains. The Brahmins now thought of a new plot. It was to send the dwarf, Tripurasura, against the god. He was vain-glorious, and a little flattery might easily turn his head. He had, moreover, a terrible club charged with horrid spells by Vishnu himself. But S'iva seized the club, dashed out the dwarf's brains with it, and then danced in triumph over the dwarf's body. The club, as the Gada, figures in his hand in all his images.

A fourth plot of the Brahmins had a success that they did not anticipate. They united all their magical potencies to dismember the god, as Ouranos was dismembered by Saturn. In this they succeeded. But an astounding development took place. The severed Mahâdeo, flaming and burning, began to traverse the world and burn up the cities; and Durgâ followed it, uttering the piercing lamentations that re-echo still in the temples. The amazed Brahmins fled for help to Brahmâ, who advised them to sacrifice to Mahâdevî, and to pray to her to calm the fury of S'iva, before the Traipura (earth, hell, and the sky) was burnt up.

There are two terminations to the story.

One is that it was settled that the S'iva-Durgâ symbol should be set up as chief object of worship in every temple in India. The second termination was that a search was made for the remains of the charred Mahâdeo. It was at last found, and then by miraculous multiplication thirty-nine portions of it were detached. Of these twenty-one were distributed amongst that number of temples on earth, nine were delegated to the temples of heaven, and even dark Pâtâla got its portion, a solitary one, of the precious flesh. But this version of the story has a corollary which would be unintelligible unless we bear in mind S'iva's bull vitality, his marriage, his mutilation, his asceticism, his necklace of skulls, items which represent the sum of human life as seen through the yearly journey of the sun. In the Mahâkâla Sanhita S'iva dies at the end of the year, but at once springs up again as a baby, who becomes a giant almost immediately, under the title of Bâles'war.

And the moral of the story is clear enough. The Brahmin satire described Vishnu as a dwarf compassing the Traipura (earth, heaven and hell) with his portentous strides. "Just so," said the followers of S'iva, "but it was as the Evil Spirit (Asura)," and S'iva vanquished this Dwarf, Traipura Asura. "See the club which he holds as a trophy." And the dwarf has certainly got the worst of the fight. A missionary in Madras, Miss Wilson Carmichael, tells us that thirty millions of S'iva stones (the Mahâdeo, as it is called) are now being adored in India, and that the followers of Sîva number a hundred million. And the gods of the Brahman polytheism, Agni, Brahmâ, Indra, Vishnu, have been placed on a shelf to give way to a monism, with S'iva nicknamed "Brahma" (neuter).

THE TEMPLE SONG.

Giver of joys untold
Thou trampledst on the wondrous dwarf of old,
His club made weird by Vishnu's might
Became thine honoured trophy in the fight,
O dancer in the wondrous halls of gold!

In Perunturrai's shrine
The saints assemble round the Lord divine,
Nilkanta,* when the mountain whirled around
To mark the land and fix the ocean's bound
He drank, to save us, all the poisoned brine.

Past days and present days
Thou art, great Mahâkâla, and thy gaze
Measures the future that thou hidst from all,
New joys, new pangs, surprises that appal,
For Time is Fate with Fate's remorseless ways.

Charred cities fame of old
Mark out thy fateful path; and we behold
At night thy diamonds streak across the sky,
Thy coils great Sesh enfold infinity,
O dancer in the wondrous halls of gold!

* Blue Throat!

PLATE 3.

S'IVA DANCING.

CHAPTER II

BAAL

Tree and Serpent worship carried by the Phenicians everywhere —The religion of the Indian jungle—Baal in Palestine—The "Star of Chiun" (S'iva)—The Mahâdeos and Masseboth—Special blood-thirstiness of the Phenician Divinity—"Holy of Holies" of Jewish Temple, and "Sanctuary of the S'iva-Linga" in India.

COLONEL TOD tells us that somewhere near Baroda he came across some followers of Durgâ living in caves in abject poverty. They were called Aghoras, or Murdi Chors (man-eaters), and fed on human flesh of the most putrid description, sometimes coming down and begging the body at a funeral. Their goddess they called Aghora Îswarî Mata (Lean Famine), and they pictured her as hungry and as insatiate as themselves.

This spectacle is immensely interesting.

We see the religion of Durgâ in its earliest form.

Early man had three stages of progress :—

(1) The cave man, whose sole food came to him by hunting and battle.

(2) The shepherd, who by the invention of tents could move about from place to place seeking new pastures for his flocks and herds.

(3) In the third stage man had learnt to till the ground and build houses.

The Egyptians and Babylonians, when they emerge in real history, had selected vast plains watered by great rivers as sites for their cities. In a word, they had reached the third stage of progress, the agricultural. Between them and the starving Indian Aghora in his dripping cave there might be hundreds, possibly thousands, of years. And yet their religion was the religion of the Indian Aghora.

Let us try and picture to ourselves the condition of the earliest cave man in an Indian jungle. When we remember that man's first idea of a god is that of a malignant and hurtful being, we cannot be surprised that two special divinities soon suggested themselves.

(1) At the period when the rainy season is over and the burning sun strikes upon the rotten vegetation, Indian jungles are ravaged by a terrible fever called the jungle fever. It is almost certain death to expose oneself to it.

(2) The second danger comes from the cobra (*Naja Tripudians*), a snake whose poison mingling with the blood kills the victim in a few hours. In civilised modern India something like 24,000 Hindus perish every year from this snake. India is a vast triangular plain. In these days it was choked with jungles. The poor Aghora had to hunt for his food, bare-footed, in unhealthy seasons as well as healthy seasons. Soon came to him his first idea of a god, a cannibal witch,* symbolised in the form of a tree. She was Nirriti, of the Rig Veda, the fever-breath of the Indian forest.

But the deadly snake likewise did not escape observation. He became at once a male god, the Seshanâg, S'iva the husband of Durgâ ; the two seemed to work together. Both were propitiated with the gift that the starved and hungry Aghora most valued—raw meat, the warm blood of beasts and babies.

A third divinity very soon suggested itself: a stone; and at this point all that we shall say of it is that it was utilitarian. It was not carved or fashioned in any way; man did not know how to carve or fashion anything. In his cave dwelling it was a lump of the bed rock, and on this he poured the warm blood of the victim. The stone represented Durgâ as well as S'iva. These three objects of worship were started many thousand years ago.

What was the date of the early Indian cave men? How can we fix that? Cave dwellers before they could become shepherds had to invent the tent.

One fact suggests an enormous gap between the Aghora and the builder of cities. When the great Âryan shell burst in Bactria the fragments, the separate Âryan clans, must have been in a pastoral state of development at most. One fragment, Greece, as we see, learnt agriculture from the wife of S'iva or Kronos; one fragment, the Italian, learnt it from S'iva's son Janus, or Ganeśa; one, the Babylonian, learnt it from Rhea, or S'iva's wife Durgâ.

But Professor Max Muller tells us that thousands of years must have elapsed before the ancient Bactrian language could have changed to pure Greek or pure Latin; and Janus, let us say, and Ceres, must have given their instructions in some more modern tongue than the Bactrian, or they would not have been understood.

Of only one thing we can be quite certain, and that is that the epoch of the cave-dweller must be judged by the figures, almost of geological computation.

Kronos, or S'iva, taught Thebes, Babylon, Tyre, Jerusalem, agriculture. Another lesson he taught them: the religion of the Aghora.

That consisted, as we have seen, of three special points:—

(1) The worship of a cannibal witch in the form of a tree.

(2) The worship of a snake, the Naja Tripudians.

(3) The worship of a rough unhewn stone.

Now this in a word was the exact religion of Thebes, Babylon, Athens, Tyre; and the cannibalism of the witch survived everywhere in vast human sacrifices.

THE TREE.

The following legend comes from the Skanda Purâna:—

Durgâ was once very angry with S'iva, accusing him of dalliance with the Apsaras. Refusing to be pacified she fled to the jungles, and seating herself in the hollow trunk of a Sami tree, she performed Tâpasya, or ascetic practices, for nine years. Immense magical powers came to her in her wrath, and flames burst forth which scattered all the animals and shepherds living near the place, and threatened ruin far and near. Sacrifices were made to her and, pacified by these, she determined to restrict this combustion to the Sami tree. She lives in it as Samirama, the goddess of the Sami tree. It was settled that the Araṇî, the wooden drill that lights the sacred fire, should always be from this tree, and that her festival as the Tree goddess should take place once a year, on which occasion she would bestow abundant wealth and corn to all her worshippers.*

This legend is plainly written to account for Indian tree worship to appease the goddess of Indian fire and Indian fever.

This festival of Durgâ is still the leading festival of India.

Let us now consider Tree-worship in Palestine.

"In early times," says Robertson Smith, "tree worship had such a vogue in Canaan that the sacred tree, or the pole its surrogate, had come to be viewed as a general symbol of Diety."

* "Asiatic Researches," Vol. IV.

Mrs. Philpot, in her work on Tree-worship, says the same thing. " There is no country in the world where the tree was more ardently worshipped than it was in ancient Palestine. Amongst the Canaanites every altar to the god had its sacred tree beside it, and when the Israelites established local sanctuaries under their influence, they set up their altar under a green tree, and planted beside it, as its indispensable accompaniment, an Ashêra, which was either a living tree or a tree-like post, and not a 'grove,' as rendered in the Authorised Version."

But in some texts the Ashêra is confused with the goddess Ashtoreth in person, as the Sami Tree in India and Durgâ are deemed one.

Another point of contact between Israel and India is remarkable, namely, the reaping festival. The Jews are commanded to go out for nine days into the woods " when they have gathered the fruit of the land," and to " cut down the boughs of goodly trees, branches of palm trees, and boughs of thick trees, and willows of the brook," and to live in booths of trees seven days.

In India, in the Deccan, during the festival of the tree, the Peishwa and all his followers move out into camp. The whole population marches in solemn procession towards the Holy Tree. Elephants and camels, Sepoys and noblemen, are all dressed out in gorgeous array. The Peishwa in person plucks a few leaves from the tree after the prescribed sacrifices are completed. Cannon and muskets are discharged and all decorate themselves with stalks of the jowri or rice plant.

Mrs. Philpot holds that the Israelites got this Tree worship from the followers of the Assyrian Astarte, but why go so far afield? Ezekiel (xx. 8, 13.) tells us that the Israelites were thoroughly imbued with the religion of Egypt, and that they " rebelled " against Jehovah in the wilderness, which phrase means, no doubt, that they still preserved Egyptian rites and Egyptian ideas. Lower Egypt, where they had been confined, worshipped Bal, or Typhon, with its serpent worship and tree worship. "Trees," says Maspero, "were the homes of the various divinities."

Says Jeremiah :—

"They have built also their high places to Baal to burn their sons with fire for burnt offerings to Baal, which I commanded not, nor spake it, nor came it into my mind."

Many critics hold that the earliest god of the Israelites was really this Baal, the chief point of discussion now being, When did Jehovah worship come in.

"Amos," says Professor Dozy, "tells us that the so-called Tabernacle, the Mosaic Sanctuary, was dedicated to Saturn (Chiun or Chievan, *i.e.*, Baal), so that a sanctuary of Baal stood at Shiloh just as a feast of Baal took place at the Gilgal.

"The same is shown by the fact that the place where the ark stood in Samuel's days, known afterwards as Kirjath Jearim was formerly called Kirjath Baal or simply Baal (1 Chron. xiii. 6).

"The strongest proof, however, that the worship of Baal went hand in hand with that of J.H.V.H. and existed as lawful worship till David's time is the fact that the name Baal occurs in several proper names. Among others in those of the sons of Saul and David, *viz.*, Eshbaal, Meribaal, Baalyahad. The Compiler of the Books of Samuel, who disliked this, changed these names into Ishbósheth, Mephiboseth, Elyadah, but in parallel passages of the Chronicles the original names are preserved." *

Dr. Oort attacks this as "extravagant." He points out that the passage in Amos mentions not one but three objects of worship, a tent, a Chiun, and a star. He concludes that there is no proof at all that Chiun

* Cited in Dr. Oort's "Worship of Baalim," p. 7.

had anything to do with the planet Saturn. In writing thus confidently he little expected a bolt from the blue.

For Orientalists marking the controversy saw at once its immense importance. Chiun, in its more correct reading "Chievan," is almost the French "Chivin," their name for S'iva. He is called in different parts of India "Shiva," "Shivin," "Chivin." The French call him "Chivin." And the three objects that are supposed to confound Dr. Dozy confirm him instead. The Tabernacle is the Vahan or pavilion carriage of S'iva, and the six-rayed star is also most important. S'iva's symbol is an equilateral triangle; Durgâ's is the same turned upside down. The two joined form the six-rayed star of Amos. That is the S'iva-Durgâ combination.

And when Dr. Oort tells us that Chiun had nothing whatever to do with Saturn we are a little amazed.

In Acts vii. 43, we read, "Yea, ye took up the Tabernacle of Moloch and the star of your god Remphan." The author of "the Acts" knew what was meant, and in point of fact he is quoting the Septuagint, which altered "Chiun" into "Remphan."

And Jehovah's great anger against "Ashtoreth, the goddess of Sidon," and the "pillars" and "groves," does not harmonise with the early books. We are told (2 Kings xviii. 24) that "Hezekiah removed the high places and brake the images and cut down the groves and brake in pieces the brazen serpent that Moses had made."

Does it seem likely that Moses would have made a brazen serpent almost immediately after he had received a stupendous command from the Almighty never to make the likeness of anything in the heaven above or the earth beneath?

Professor Maspero shows a curious point of contact between the worshippers of Ba'al, in Syria and the worshippers of S'iva, in India. Each tribe, each city, each people had its special Baal, Baal Sur, Baal Sidon, as in India Andhikîśwara is the S'iva in Andheke's cave, another is in Perumterrai, and so on.

"Each of these Baalim, as they were called, had his Astarte, Ashera, Sanit." "Astartis," says the Professor, "presided over love, generation, war, and in consequence over the different seasons of the year, that when nature is restored to youth and that when she seems to die. Gods and goddesses they dwell on the tops of mountains, the Lebanon, Hermon, Sinai, Kasios. They love forests and springs. They reveal themselves to mortals in high places (bamoth). They dwell in trees, in unhewn stones (betyles) and even in fashioned columns (masseboth)." *

But when we have shown the Indian Durgâ in Palestine and Egypt as the provider of plenty at the tree festival, we have only got halfway to the real difficulty. Why, at that festival did she also figure as a cannibal witch?

Says the "Encyclopædia Britannica":—"Among the nations of Canaan the victims were peculiarly chosen. Their own children and whatever was nearest and dearest to them were deemed the most worthy offerings to their god. The Carthaginians who were a colony of Tyre, carried with them the religion of their mother country and instituted the same worship in the parts where they settled. It consisted in the adoration of several deities, but particularly of Kronus; to whom they offered human sacrifices, and especially the blood of children. If the parents were not at hand to make an immediate offer the magistrates did not fail to make choice of what was most fair and promising, that the god might not be defrauded of his dues. Upon a check being received in Sicily, and other alarming circumstances happening, Hamilcar without any hesitation

* Maspero, "Hist. Ancienne des Peuples d'Orient," p. 340.

laid hold of a boy and offered him on the spot to Kronus. The Carthaginians another time upon a great defeat of their army by Agathocles imputed their miscarriages to the anger of the god whose services had been neglected. Touched with this and seeing the enemy at their gates, they seized at once three hundred children of the prime nobility and offered them in public for a sacrifice. Three hundred men, being persons who were somehow obnoxious, yielded themselves voluntarily and were put to death with the others . . . There were particular children brought up for the altar as sheep are fattened for the shambles; and they were bought and butchered in the same manner. It is remarkable that the Egyptians looked out for the most specious and handsome person to be sacrificed. The Albanians pitched upon the best man of the community."

When we read of this awful butchery, we see at once a wild paradox, a monstrous inconsequence. A tree charged with ripe fruit suggests a festival of thanksgiving, but why should it be smeared and fouled with all this human blood. Durgâ is a cannibal witch, and I say that we must go back to the Indian Aghora and his jungle, at a time when human flesh was choice food. In those days the fever tree suggested frantic propitiations.

Mrs. Philpot and Professor Sayce carry Tree-worship back to Eridu on the Persian Gulf, B.C. 4,000.

But Assyria was badly off for trees and had to get her teak from India. Why should not the Indian Tree goddess have come with the Indian tree? In the Rig Veda, Bala has a wife, "Nirriti the Insurmountable."

"May Nirriti so formidable by her power, Nirriti the Insurmountable, never draw near to smite us. May she perish with the thirst that she causes."*

* Lect. III., Hymn VI.

THE SERPENT.

Monsieur Buffon thus describes an ancient forest :—

"All along the swampy banks of the river Niger or Oroonoko, where the sun is hot, the forests thick, and men but few, the serpents cling among the branches of the trees in infinite numbers. They carry on an unceasing war against all other animals in their vicinity. Travellers have assured us that they have often seen large snakes twining round the trunk of a tall tree, encompassing it like a wreath and thus climbing up and down at pleasure."

The French naturalist goes on to say that the fabulous stories of gigantic serpents may have had some solid truth. Pliny talks of a serpent one hundred and twenty feet long. In India is a serpent that attacks large tigers and buffaloes. These animals it swallows whole; and it takes, we learn, almost as many months to digest a big buffalo as Ravan's brother Kumbhakarna took to digest his gigantic meal.

This description of a forest by the French naturalist gives probably a good picture of an Indian jungle when the earliest Aghora was living in a cave near it. What wonder that he sacrificed to the Serpent Manasâ (one of the earliest forms of Durgâ), and prayed her to protect him from her too numerous brood.

Turning from India to the Delta of the Nile, we find that a city sprang up there which had for its god Typhon, or 'Bal; then Typhon had for wife Echidna, a serpent, and was himself furnished with one hundred serpent heads. The pair are certainly Seshanâg and Manasâ.

The Creator of the universe was the serpent god and "Kneph, and Egypt," says the anonymous author of "Ophiolatreia," "was the home of this peculiar worship." Gau gives a drawing of one of the columns of a cave temple at Derri. It was four-sided, with for capital four heads of Isis, and with Typhon's serpent body repeated four times along the shaft. This would make Typhon her first husband. In "Ophiolatreia," Horus is called a serpent god. Thermuthis was the name of the snake chiefly worshipped. It is a cobra, the Naja Hage. We learn from Diodorus Seculus that the kings of Egypt wore high bonnets that terminated at top in a round ball, and the whole was surrounded with figures of asps. The priests likewise had upon their bonnets these serpents.

Says the author of "Ophiolatreia," "The worship of the Serpent, next to the adoration of the Phallus, is one of the most remarkable, and at first sight, unaccountable forms of religion the world has ever known. Until the true source from whence it sprang can be reached and understood, its nature will remain as mysterious as its universality, for what man could see in an object so repulsive and forbidding in its habits as this reptile to render worship to, is one of the most difficult problems to find a solution to. There is hardly a country of the ancient world, however, where it cannot be traced pervading every known system of mythology.

* * * *

"Whether the worship was the result of fear or respect is a question that naturally enough presents itself, and in seeking to answer it we shall be confronted with the fact that in some places, as Egypt, the symbol was that of a good demon while in India, Scandinavia, and Mexico it was that of an evil one."

All this is very important: indeed, far more important than the anonymous author of "Ophiolatreia" seems to suspect. In point of fact India viewed the serpent from two opposing points. First it was an object of wild terror when rude tribes like the Aghoras died in thousands from its bites. Ahi was a terrible god at the date of the Rig Veda. But by whatever name and under whatever symbol you describe the Supreme God, the god of the savage will in process of time gain in wisdom and gain in loving-kindness. Ahi became Sesh. At first "in distributing the regions to the different gods," says Colonel Moor, "Seshanâga had the regions under the earth allotted to him."* That is, he was S'iva living in his bottomless pit. Then Sesh with his thousand heads grew so popular in India that the followers of Vishnu were obliged to try and steal him. One thing is certain, serpents are more petted in India than elsewhere. Purchas, in his "Pilgrims," tells us that a king in Calicut (the city of Ḳâlî) built cottages for live serpents, whom he tended with particular care. He executed any one who in his dominions destroyed a snake.

Says Mr. Rivett Carnae :—

"I find from my notes that one Kunbi whom I questioned in old days when I was a Settlement officer in camp in the Nâgpur Division, stated that he worshipped the Nâg and nothing else; that he worshipped clay images of the snake, and when he could afford to pay snake catchers for a look at a live one he worshipped the living snake; that if he saw a Nâg on the road he would worship it, and that he believed no Hindu would kill a Nâg or cobra if he knew it was a Nâg. He then gave me the following list of articles that he would use in worshipping the snake.

(1) Water; (2) Cleaned rice; (3) Gandh pigment of sandal wood for the forehead and body; (4) Flowers; (5) Leaves of the Bail tree; (6) Milk; (7) Curds; (8) A thread, or piece of cloth; (9) Red powder; (10) Saffron; (11) Abir, a powder composed of fragrant substances; (12) Garland of flowers; (13) Buttemah, or grain; (14) Jowarri; (15) Five

* Moor, "Pantheon," p. 180.

lights; (16) Sweetmeats; (17) Betel leaves; (18) Cocoa-nut; (19) A sum of money, according to means; (20) Flowers offered by the suppliant, the palms of the hand being joined.

We see from this that Indian Serpent worship had two stages. The serpent was first of all a grim bogey, and then a benign being. In Egypt we see only the second stage. We must remember also that Egypt was inundated yearly by the Nile which would kill most of the snakes. Plainly the derivation comes from India.

Other coincidences I give for what they are worth. The city of Typhon was Memphis, where dwelt the Pharoah of Exodus, and if it be true that the Israelites, as Dr. Erasmus Wilson assures us, had dwelt four hundred years in Lower Egypt, we may credit them with carrying away some of the local superstitutions across the Red Sea. At the Nâgapanchami festival in India, Durgâ figures as Manasâ the Serpent, and it is curious that the first god objectivised after the Exodus takes the form of the curative brazen serpent erected by Moses to cure the bites of the "fiery" serpents. Miss Wilson Carmichael gives another point of contact. The natives of Madras once a year leave a number of hand-prints and finger-prints on their doors, marking them with S'iva's white paste made of cow dung and the ashes of the vilva and asoka. In India this is done that the snake Manasâ may spare the houses of her votaries. This suggests the marking of the houses in Exodus.

SEX-WORSHIP.

We have considered two out of the three special characteristics which I have put forward as tracing S'iva Worship to the early cave man. We now come to the third—sex-worship; and it is time to mention a fourth characteristic, namely, bull-worship. This, of course, cannot be traced as far back as the cave man, for it implies that the pastoral age had been reached. But when Saivism went abroad on its strange missionary career, this bull-worship was very prominent. We must all defer to an Indian authority as shrewd as Colonel Tod. He held that this bull worship was the strongest evidence in Palestine, Egypt, etc., of S'ivan derivation.

"What are Bal and the Brazen Calf to which especial honours were paid on the 15th day of the month but the Baliswar, and the Bull Nandi of India?"*

Colonel Tod explains that the Hindus divide the month into two pukhs or fortnights. At the beginning of the second pukh called the Amava, the bull Nandi is worshipped on the fifteenth day of the month. Now we learn from 1 Kings xiii. that Jeroboam made a golden calf and sacrificed to it on the fifteenth day of the month at Beth-el. Colonel Tod connects the two incidents.

Now although, as I have said, we cannot carry back bull worship to the date of the Aghora who lived by the chase alone, we may, I think, inferentially carry it back to the Rig Veda. Bala there figures living in his cavern with his "wives," "cows," "Devaputras," and if Âryan bards were like other bards, and used what was before their eyes to express their ideas, the Asura whose wives were "cows" must have been a bull. Indra is praised in one hymn for having "killed the wives whom the Black one had rendered pregnant." S'iva or Bala was the Black One, and his followers are called in the Rig Veda "Black, noseless Dasyus."

But Devî is certainly a cow when S'iva is a bull.

Of this union Sir William Jones writes thus:—

"Bhavânî (Durgâ) now demands our attention, and in this character I suppose the wife of Mahâdeva to be as well the Juno Cinxia or Lucina of the Romans

* "Travels in Western India," p. 54.

PLATE 2.

TRAILINGA ISHWARA.

व्याघ्र यायी

DURGÂ AS EUROPA.

(called also by them Diana Solvizona, and by the Greeks Ilithyia), as Venus herself, not the Idalian queen of laughter and jollity . . . but Venus Urania, so luxuriantly painted by Lucretius, and so properly invoked by him at the opening of a poem on nature; Venus presiding over generation, and on this account exhibited sometimes of both sexes (an union very common in the Indian sculptures), as in her bearded statue at Rome, in the images perhaps called Mermathena, and of those figures of her which had the form of a conical marble "for the reason of which figure we are left," says Tacitus," in the dark." The reason appears too clearly in the temples and paintings of Hindustan, where it never seems to have entered into the heads of the legislators or people that anything natural could be offensively obscene, a singularity which pervades all their writings and conversation, but is no proof of depravity in their morals. Both Plato and Cicero speak of Eros or the Heavenly Cupid as the son of Venus and Jupiter, which proves that the monarch of Olympus and the goddess of Fecundity were connected as Mahâdeva and Bhavânî. (Works Vol. III., p. 367).*

This moderation of tone, and this spirit of abstract justice on the part of a distinguished legist contrasts with certain clerical petulancies.

Bishop Heber calls this worship "uncleanness and abomination." In fact he considers the 200,000,000 Hindus in India as "vile" as the poor Buddhists of Ceylon, who to the grosser vision of the laity, seem the most peaceable and loyal of His Majesty's subjects.

> What though the spicy breezes
> Blow soft on Ceylon's Isle,
> And every prospect pleases,
> And only man is vile. . .

* Each Indian god had an emblematical animal. Brahmâ had Brahmî, a swan, hence Sita. S'iva's animal was a bull, hence Durgâ the Indian Europa. See Plate p. 14.

But to visit on the heads of the Indians the blemishes of a form of worship which was universal at one time, and especially conspicuous and objectionable in Palestine of old, and not very nice at the head-quarters of Christianity in the Middle Ages, is scarcely just. The "Jew's harp" symbol, as it is called, is said to be on the portal of the cathedral of Toulouse, and also on other churches; and Nelson's friend, Sir William Hamilton, has described practices, not mere carnival fooleries, but proceedings at the solemn festivals of St. Cosmo and St. Damiana which bring down the "abomination" to very modern times.

The Aghora, the early savage, lived in a cave. Fever swept away some of his companions. Snakes killed others. He had an idea of a god, not a very lofty one, but the best obtainable. Vaguely he imaged to himself a potency that could oppose death; and he chose a stone to represent him, a plain stone. The idea was utilitarian, and by-and-bye it developed. In enlarging his cave he left a lump of the bed-rock to represent the "Mahâdeo," and the larger this object the less his labour. It is impossible to know how soon sex worship intervened. Mr. R. F. Burton, in a paper entitled "Certain Matters connected with the Dahoman," read before the Anthropological Society, shows that the crave for offspring is very strong with savages like the Dahomans, and the practices of sex worship very gross. Certainly, if births do not correct the death rates, the tribe promptly dwindles, and with savages, for labour and battle, strong men are required. But it is difficult to prove that this sex worship is spontaneous and not derived. The Aryans, when they first reached India, were in a rude state of development, and they fell foul of the Indian sex-worship at first instead of adopting it.

Mr. Grant Allen has shown the close analogy between S'iva and Yahveh, each being symbolised by a stone on which the oil, wine and ghee of the linga pûjâ was poured, and each being famous for opening the wombs of elderly Sarahs, Hannahs, Rebekahs.* The Holy Places were all Mahâdeos. A "Rock" accompanied the Israelites in the desert.

"Of the Rock that begot thee thou art unmindful," says Deuteronomy (viii. 18). Grant Allen thinks that the "ark" carried always a S'iva stone inside.

In the Temple of S'iva there is one holy chamber which contains the Shiva Linga, the most exalted form of Mahâdeo. No one but an Ati Shaiva Brahmin can enter this.† Two special forms of adoration are exacted in the "Sanctuary of the Shiva linga." The first is the Pari-i-dakshina. "I will compass thine altar, O Lord," said David. The second is the "Salutation with eight members." "And Balaam bowed his head and fell flat on his face" (Numbers xxiii. 31). I have alluded already to the S'iva Temple Dance. "Let them praise him in the dance," says Psalm clxix.

In the Sepher-Toldoth-Jeshu it is announced that there was a stone in the temple on which was inscribed the inexpressible name of God. It was placed in the Holy of Holies by David.

There is a controversy about this book, but the statement is partly confirmed by passages in the Old Testament :—"Jacob set up a pillar and anointed it with oil and poured a drink-offering on it, and called it Beth-el, the 'House of God.'" Plainly he worshipped it like the Indian Mahâdeo. (Genesis xviii. 22 ; xxv. 7, 14.)

Later on David selected a site for Solomon's Temple, and apparently this stone was chosen, this "House of God" (1 Chron. xxii. 1, 4). It was believed in the

* Grant Allen, "Evolution of the Idea of God." p. 73.

† "Catechism of the Shaiva Religion," by Sabhapati Mudahya, p. 53.

Talmud to figure in the Holy of Holies, and to be nscribed with the inexpressible name J.H.V.H. It was called the Shemhamphoras. Do we not here seem to get the "Sanctuary of the Shiva linga?"

And in many other points the worship of Baal and S'iva seems identical. The Israelites burn incense to the brazen serpent (2 Kings xviii. 4). There is mention of a "box" with perfumes and oil (1 Sam. x. 1); also of the "flowers," the "lamps" and the "tongs" (2 Chron. iv. 21). "A people that sacrificeth in gardens" (Isaiah lxv. 3) suggests the sacredness of the "Temple Gardens" of a S'ivan pile.

Noteworthy also is the "Prophet disguised with ashes" (1 Kings xx. 38).

The Yogis of S'iva are distinguished thus all over India, the god being imaged as a white-dusted Yogi. The Book of Numbers gives a receipt for this white ash:—

"Burn the heifer with her dung" (Numbers xix. 5).

The Indian white ash has also cow-dung for the chief ingredient. One more point is remarkable. The ashes of S'iva "can blot out all the greater sins."* In Israel the ashes were collected outside the camp to purify "the congregation and the children" (Numbers xix. 2, 17). In Hebrews (ix. 13) it is announced that these "ashes of an heifer sprinkling the unclean sanctify to the purifying of the flesh."

And the earliest Indian account of the Creation of the Fourteen Worlds is very remarkable. At first on the top of Kailâsa, S'iva's mount, appeared a bare tree trunk in a triangle, the lingam and the Yoni. This equilateral triangle is still S'iva's special symbol; and that of Yahveh is a similar triangle, with the upright letter Yodh in it.

* "Catechism of the Shaiva Religion," by Sabhapati Mudahya, p. 74.

It is plain too that the earlier Jewish divinity represented a god that supervised what men call evil as well as what they call good :—

Says Yahveh : " I make peace and create evil."

And S'iva's Hermaphrodite element appears as well as his Pantheism : " The Lord created Adam male and female."

Then, too, the priests who danced to the sound of the tabret and cut themselves with knives remind one of modern Sadhus in India. All this is of considerable importance as it points to a well-worn pathway between India and Palestine.

And why was the serpent viewed as a beneficent Divinity by Moses, and the Author of Evil in the fragment called the " Jehovistic " interpolation, in chapters ii., iii., and iv. of Genesis ? It seems an attack on the Serpent and Tree Worship of the earlier times.

CHAPTER III

BUDDHA

Born of a Virgin—Genealogies—The "Flower Star" in the East—Asita and Simeon—The four presaging tokens—The Prince leaves the Palace—The Bo Tree—Buddha preaches—Early biography altered—Mâyâ Devî is Durgâ—Dasasatanayana (S'iva the "thousand eyed") blesses him when he leaves the palace—Other changes.

BUDDHA was born at Kapilavastu, in the Lumbini Garden, B.C. 550.

Kapilavastu—the City of Kapila. This is the translation of the word. Much has been made by some Orientalists of this. The City of Kapila, the author of the *Nirîśwara*, or Atheistic Sankhya philosophy, is evidently, it has been urged, a non-existent place, and Buddha a non-existent person. He is a myth invented to shadow forth the dissemination of Kapila's atheism. But nothing is certain except the unexpected. The non-existing city has suddenly turned up, covering miles of jungle.

Sir Alexander Cunningham, the great Indian archæologist, was of opinion that the site of Kapilavastu was Bhuila, in the Basti district. But the real site is now no matter of doubt. It is between Gorukhpore and the Himalayas.

In 1893, a pillar was discovered in the Nepal Terai, the mighty forest that surrounds the great Himalayan range. Deciphered, it proved to be one of the columns of King Asoka, who covered India with his stone inscriptions, B.C. 257. It announced that on this particular spot was the *stûpa* of Kanaka Muni, one of the seven great mortal Buddhas. In the year 1896 Major Waddell pointed out, in the "Journal of the Asiatic Society of Bengal" that according to the testimony of Hwen Thsang, the celebrated Chinese traveller, this *stûpa* was only seven miles off from Buddha's birthplace, the traveller having paid it a visit. This brought Dr. Führer into the field, and he was soon rewarded with the discovery of an inscription identifying the celebrated Lumbini Garden where Queen Mâyâ gave birth to her distinguished son. Then came a second triumph. Choked up in the luxurious jungle by colossal ferns and creepers, emerged a dead city of *stûpas*, and monasteries, and villages and buildings. More important still was another column set up by King Aoska. This is the translation of it:

"King Piyadasi (Asoka) the beloved of the gods, having been anointed twenty years, himself came and worshipped, saying, 'Here, Buddha, Sakya Muni, was born!' And he caused a stone pillar to be erected, which declares, 'Here the Venerable was born.'"

I propose now to give a short life of Buddha. It has points of contact with that of Jesus, whose great importance will be dwelt on by and by.

PRE-EXISTENCE IN HEAVEN.

The early Buddhists, following the example of the Vedic Brahmins, divided space into Nirvritti, the dark portion of the heavens, and Pravritti, the starry systems. Over this last, the luminous portion, Buddha figures as ruler when the legendary life opens. The Christian Gnostics took over this idea and gave to Christ a similar function. He ruled the Pleroma.

"BEHOLD A VIRGIN SHALL CONCEIVE."

Exactly 550 years before Christ there dwelt in Kapilavastu a king called Śuddhodana. This monarch was informed by angels that a mighty teacher of men would be born miraculously in the womb of his wife. "By the consent of the king," says the "Lalita Vistara," "the queen was permitted to lead the life of a virgin for thirty-two months." Joseph is made, a little awkwardly, to give a similar privilege to his wife (Matt. i. 25).

Some writers have called in question the statement that Buddha was born of a virgin, but in the southern scriptures, as given by Mr. Turnour, it is announced that a womb in which a Buddha elect has reposed is like the sanctuary of a temple. On that account, that her womb may be sacred, the mother of a Buddha always dies in seven days. The name of the queen was borrowed from S'ivism. She was Mâyâ Devî, the Queen of Heaven.

Queen Mâyâ was chosen for her mighty privilege because the Buddhist scriptures announce that the mother of a Buddha must be of royal line.

Long genealogies, very like those of the New Testament, are given also to prove the blue blood of King Śuddhodana, who, like Joseph, had nothing to do with the paternity of the child. "King Mahasammata had a son named Roja, whose son was Varaoja, whose son was Kalyana, whose son was Varakalyana," and so on, and so on.*

How does a Buddha come down to earth? The sign of Capricorn in the old Indian Zodiac is an elephant issuing from a Makara (leviathan), and S'iva's son had an elephant's head. It symbolises the active god issuing from the quiescent god in his home on the face of the waters. In consequence, Buddha comes

* Dipawanso, see "Jour. As. Soc.," Bengal, Vol. VIII., p. 925.

PLATE 4.

THE BUDDHIST VIRGIN AND CHILD.

down as a white elephant, and enters the right side of the queen without piercing it or in any way injuring it. Childers sees a great analogy in all this to the Catholic theory of the perpetual virginity of Mary. Catholic doctors quote this passage from Ezekiel (xliv. 2):

"Then said the Lord unto me: This gate shall be shut, it shall not be opened, and no man shall enter by it; because the Lord, the God of Israel, hath entered in by it, therefore shall it be shut."

A DOUBLE ANNUNCIATION.

It is recorded that when Queen Mâyâ received the supernal Buddha in her womb, in the form of a beautiful white elephant, she said to her husband: "Like snow and silver outshining the sun and the moon, a white elephant of six tusks, with unrivalled trunk and feet, has entered my womb. Listen, I saw the three regions (earth, heaven, hell), with a great light shining in the darkness, and myriads of spirits sang my praises in the sky."

A similar miraculous communication was made to King Śuddhodana:

"The spirits of the Pure Abode flying in the air, showed half of their forms, and hymned King Śuddhodana thus:—

> Guerdoned with righteousness and gentle pity,
> Adored on earth and in the shining sky,
> The coming Buddha quits the glorious spheres
> And hies to earth to gentle Mâyâ's womb."

In the Christian Scriptures there is also a double annunciation. In Luke (i. 28) the Angel Gabriel is said to have appeared to the Virgin Mary before her conception, and to have foretold to her the miraculous birth of Christ. But in spite of this astounding miracle, Joseph seems to have required a second personal one before he ceased to question the chastity of his wife (Matt. i. 19). Plainly, two evangelists have been working the same mine independently, and a want of consistency is the result.

When Buddha was in his mother's womb, that womb was transparent. The Virgin Mary was thus represented in mediæval frescoes.*

"WE HAVE SEEN HIS STAR IN THE EAST."

In the Buddhist legend the *devas* in heaven announce that Buddha will be born when the Flower star in seen *in the East*."†

In the "Lalita Vistara" two serpents, Nanda and Uponanda, show their forms in the sky, and rain down baptismal water on the young infant. "Nanda," says Colonel Tod, "is a favourite title of S'iva in Saurasthra."

Amongst the thirty-two signs that indicate the mother of a Buddha, the fifth is that, like Mary, the mother of Jesus, she should be "on a journey"‡ at the moment of parturition: this happened. A tree (palasa, the scarlet butea) bent down its branches and overshadowed her, and Buddha came forth. Voltaire says that in the library of Berne there is a copy of the first gospel of the Infancy, which records that a palm-tree bent down in a similar manner to Mary.§ The Koran calls it a "withered date-tree."

In the First "Gospel of the Infancy" it is stated that, when Christ was in His cradle, He said to His mother: "I am Jesus, the Son of God, the Word whom thou didst bring forth according to the declaration of the angel Gabriel to thee, and my Father hath sent Me for the salvation of the world."

* See illustration.

† Lefman, XXI., 124; Wassiljew, p. 95.

‡ Beal, "Roman History," p. 32.

§ "Oeuvres," Vol. XL.

In the Buddhist scriptures it is announced that Buddhạ, on seeing the light, said: "I am in my last birth. None is my equal. I have come to conquer death, sickness, old age. I have come to subdue the spirit of evil, and give peace and joy to the souls tormented in hell."

In the same scriptures * it is announced that at the birth of the Divine child, the *devas* (angels) sang thus:—"O Purusha, the equal to thee exists not here; where will a superior be found?"

CHILD-NAMING.

"Five days after the birth of Buddha," says Bishop Bigandet, in the "Burmese Life," "was performed the ceremony of head ablution and naming the child" (p. 49).

We see from this where the ceremony of head ablution and naming the child may have come from. In the "Lalita Vistara," Buddha is carried to the temple. Plainly, we have the same ceremony. There the idols bow down to him as in the First Gospel of the Infancy the idol in Egypt bows down to Jesus.

HEROD AND THE WISE MEN.

It is recorded in the Chinese life† that King Bimbisâra, the monarch of Râjâgriha was told by his ministers that a boy was alive for whom the stars predicted a mighty destiny. They advised him to raise an army and go and destroy this child, lest he should one day subvert the king's throne. Bimbisâra refused.

At the birth of Buddha the four Mahârâjas, the great kings, who in Hindoo astronomy guard each a cardinal point, received him. These may throw light on the traditional Persian kings that greeted Christ.

* See Turnour's "Pali Legendary Life."

† Beal, "Romantic History," p. 103.

In some quarters these analogies are admitted, but it is said that the Buddhists copied from the Christian scriptures. But this question is a little complicated by the fact that many of the most noticeable similarities are in apocryphal gospels, those that were abandoned by the Church at an early date. In the Protevangelion, at Christ's birth, certain marvels are visible. The clouds are "astonished," and the birds of the air stop in their flight. The dispersed sheep of some shepherds near cease to gambol, and the shepherds to beat them. The kids near a river are arrested with their mouths close to the water. All nature seems to pause for a mighty effort. In the "Lalita Vistara" the birds also pause in their flight when Buddha comes to the womb of Queen Mâyâ. Fires go out, and rivers are suddenly arrested in their flow.

ASITA.

More noticeable is the story of Asita, the Indian Simeon.

Asita dwells on Himavat, the holy mount of the Hindoos, as Simeon dwells on Mount Zion. The "Holy Ghost is upon" Simeon. That means that he has obtained the faculties of the prophet by mystical training. He "comes by the Spirit" into the temple. Asita is an ascetic, who has acquired the eight magical faculties, one of which is the faculty of visiting the Tawatinsa heavens. Happening to soar up into those pure regions one day, he is told by a host of devatas or heavenly spirits, that a mighty Buddha was born in the world, "who will establish the supremacy of the Buddhist Dharma." The "Lalita Vistara" announces that, "looking abroad with his divine eye, and considering the kingdoms of India, he saw in the great city of Kapilavastu, in the palace of King Śuddhodana, the child shining with the glitter of pure deeds, and adored by all the worlds." Afar through the skies the spirits of heaven in crowds recited the "hymn of Buddha."

This is the description of Simeon in the First Gospel of the Infancy, II, 6: "At that time old Simeon saw him (Christ) shining as a pillar of light when St. Mary the Virgin, His mother, carried Him in her arms, and was filled with the greatest pleasure at the sight. And the angels stood around Him, adoring Him as a king; guards stood around Him."

Asita pays a visit to the king. Asita takes the little child in his arms. Asita weeps.

"Wherefore those tears, O holy man?"

"I weep because this child will be the great Buddha, and I shall not be alive to witness the fact."

The points of contact between Simeon and Asita are very close. Both are men of God, "full of the Holy Ghost." Both are brought "by the Spirit" into the presence of the Holy Child, for the express purpose of foretelling His destiny as the Anointed One.

DISPUTATION WITH THE DOCTORS.

More remarkable still is the incident of the disputation with the doctors.

A little Brahmin was "initiated," girt with the holy thread, etc., at eight, and put under the tuition of a holy man. When Viśvâmitra, Buddha's teacher, proposed to teach him the alphabet, the young prince went off:

"In sounding 'A,' pronounce it as in the sound of the word 'anitya.'"

"In sounding 'I,' pronounce it as in the word 'indriya.'

"In sounding 'U,' pronounce it as in the word, 'upagupta.'"

And so on through the whole Sanskrit alphabet.

In the first Gospel of the Infancy, chap. xx., it is recorded that when taken to the schoolmaster Zaccheus

"The Lord Jesus explained to him the meaning of the letters Aleph and Beth.

"(8) Also, which were the straight figures of the letters, which were the oblique, and what letters had double figures; which had points and which had none; why one letter went before another; and many other things He began to tell him and explain, of which the master himself had never heard, nor read in any book.

"(9) The Lord Jesus further said to the master, 'Take notice how I say to thee.' Then He began clearly and distinctly to say Aleph, Beth, Gimel, Daleth, and so on to the end of the alphabet.

"(10) At this the master was so surprised that he said, I believe this boy was born before Noah."

In the "Lalita Vistara" there are two separate accounts of Buddha showing his marvellous knowledge. His great display is when he competes for his wife. He then exhibits his familiarity with all lore, sacred and profane, "astronomy," the "syllogism," medicine, mystic rites.

The disputation with the doctors is considerably amplified in the twenty-first chapter of the First Gospel of the Infancy:

"(5) Then a certain principal rabbi asked Him, hast thou read books?

"(6) Jesus answered that He had read both books and the things which were contained in books.

"(7) And he explained to them the books of the law and precepts and statutes, and the mysteries which are contained in the books of the prophets—things which the mind of no creature could reach.

"(8) Then said that rabbi, I have never yet seen or heard of such knowledge! What do you think that boy will be?

"(9) Then a certain astronomer who was present asked the Lord Jesus whether He had studied astronmy.

"(10) The Lord Jesus replied, and told him the number of the spheres and heavenly bodies, as also their triangular, square, and sextile aspects, their progressive and retrograde motions, their size and several prognostications, and other things which the reason of man had never discovered.

"(11) There was also among them a philosopher, well skilled in physics and natural philosophy, who asked the Lord Jesus whether He had studied physics.

"(12) He replied, and explained to him physics and metaphysics.

"(13) Also those things which were above and below the power of nature.

"(14) The powers also of the body, its humours and their effects.

"(15) Also the number of its bones, veins, arteries, and nerves.

"(16) The several constitutions of body, hot and dry, cold and moist, and the tendencies of them.

"(17) How the soul operated on the body.

"(18) What its various sensations and faculties were.

"(19) The faculty of speaking, anger, desire.

"(20) And lastly, the manner of its composition and dissolution, and other things which the understanding of no creature had ever reached.

"(21) Then that philosopher worshipped the Lord Jesus, and said, 'O Lord Jesus, from henceforth I will be Thy disciple and servant.'"

Viśvâmitra in like manner worshipped Buddha by falling at his feet.

THE FOUR PRESAGING TOKENS.

Soothsayers were consulted by King Śuddhodana. They pronounced the following :—

"The young boy, will, without doubt, be either a king of kings or a great Buddha. If he is destined to be a great Buddha, four presaging tokens will make his mission plain. He will see—

" (1) An old man.
" (2) A sick man.
" (3) A corpse.
" (4) A holy recluse.

" If he fails to see these four presaging tokens of an avatara, he will simply be a Chakravartin" (king of earthly kings).

King Śuddhodana, who was a trifle worldly, was very much comforted by the last prediction of the soothsayers. He thought in his heart, "It will be an easy thing to keep these four presaging tokens from the young prince." So he gave orders that three magnificent palaces should at once be built—the Palace of Spring, the Palace of Summer, the Palace of Winter. These palaces, as we learn from the "Lalita Vistara," were the most beautiful palaces ever conceived on earth. Indeed, they were quite able to cope in splendour with Vaijayanta, the immortal palace of Indra himself. Costly pavilions were built out in all directions, with ornamental porticoes and burnished doors. Turrets and pinnacles soared into the sky. Dainty little windows gave light to the rich apartments. Galleries, balustrades, and delicate trellis-work were abundant everywhere. A thousand bells tinkled on each roof. We seem to have the lacquered Chinese edifices of the pattern which architects believe to have flourished in early India. The gardens of these fine palaces rivalled the chess-board in the rectangular exactitude of their parterres and trellis-work bowers. Cool lakes nursed on their calm bosoms storks and cranes, wild geese and tame swans; ducks, also, as parti-coloured as the white red and blue lotuses, amongst which they swam. Bending to these lakes were bowery trees—the champak, the acacia serisha, and the beautiful asoka tree, with its orange-scarlet flowers. Above rustled the mimosa, the fanpalm, and the feathery pippala, Buddha's tree. The air was heavy with the strong scent of the tuberose and the Arabian jasmine.

It must be mentioned that strong ramparts were prepared round the palaces of Kapilavastu, to keep out all old men, sick men, and recluses, and, I must add, to keep in the prince.

And a more potent safeguard still was designed. When the prince was old enough to marry, his palace was deluged with beautiful women. He revelled in the "five dusts," as the Chinese version puts it. But a shock was preparing for King Śuddhodana.

This is how the matter came about. The king had prepared a garden even more beautiful than the garden of the Palace of Summer. A soothsayer had told him that if he could succeed in showing the prince this garden, the prince would be content to remain in it with his wives for ever. No task seemed easier than this, so it was arranged that on a certain day the prince should be driven thither in his chariot. But, of course, immense precautions had to be taken to keep all old men and sick men and corpses from his sight. Quite an army of soldiers were told off for this duty, and the city was decked with flags. The path of the prince was strewn with flowers and scents, and adorned with vases of the rich kadali plant. Above were costly hangings and garlands, and pagodas of bells.

But, lo and behold! as the prince was driving along, plump under the wheels of his chariot, and before the very noses of the silken nobles and the warriors with javelins and shields, he saw an unusual sight. This was an old man, very decrepit and very broken. The veins and nerves of his body were swollen and prominent; his teeth chattered; he was wrinkled, bald, and his few remaining hairs were of dazzling whiteness; he was bent very nearly double, and tottered feebly along, supported by a stick.

"What is this, O coachman?" said the prince. "A man with his blood all dried up, and his muscles glued to his body! His head is white; his teeth knock together; he is scarcely able to move along, even with the aid of that stick!"

"Prince," said the coachman, "this is Old Age. This man's senses are dulled; suffering has destroyed his spirit; he is contemned by his neighbours. Unable to help himself, he has been abandoned in this forest."

"Is this a peculiarity of his family?" demanded the prince, "or is it the law of the world? Tell me quickly."

"Prince," said the coachman, "it is neither a law of his family, nor a law of the kingdom. In every being youth is conquered by age. Your own father and mother and all your relations will end in old age. There is no other issue to humanity."

"Then youth is blind and ignorant," said the prince, "and sees not the future. If this body is to be the abode of old age, what have I to do with pleasure and its intoxications? Turn round the chariot, and drive me back to the palace!"

Consternation was in the minds of all the courtiers at this untoward occurrence; but the odd circumstance of all was that no one was ever able to bring to condign punishment the miserable author of the mischief. The old man could never be found.

King Śuddhodana was at first quite beside himself with tribulation. Soldiers were summoned from the distant provinces, and a cordon of detachments thrown out to a distance of four miles in each direction, to keep the other presaging tokens from the prince. By-and-bye the king became a little more quieted. A ridiculous accident had interfered with his plans: "If my son could see the Garden of Happiness he never would become a hermit." The king determined that another attempt should be made. But this time the precautions were doubled.

On the first occasion the prince left the Palace of Summer by the eastern gate. The second expedition went through the southern gate.

But another untoward event occurred. As the prince was driving along in his chariot, suddenly he saw close to him a man emaciated, ill, loathsome, burning with fever. Companionless, uncared for, he tottered along, breathing with extreme difficulty.

"Coachman," said the prince, "what is this man, livid and loathsome in body, whose senses are dulled, and whose limbs are withered? His stomach is oppressing him; he is covered with filth. Scarcely can he draw the breath of life!"

"Prince," said the coachman, "this is Sickness. This poor man is attacked with a grievous malady. Strength and Comfort have shunned him. He is friendless, hopeless, without a country, without an asylum. The fear of death is before his eyes."

"If the health of man," said Buddha, "is but the sport of a dream, and the fear of coming evils can put on so loathsome a shape, how can the wise man, who has seen what life really means, indulge in its vain delights? Turn back, coachman, and drive me to the palace!"

The angry king, when he heard what had occurred, gave orders that the sick man should be seized and punished, but although a price was placed on his head, and he was searched for far and wide, he could never be caught. A clue to this is furnished by a passage in the "Lalita Vistara." The sick man was in reality one of the Spirits of the Pure Abode, masquerading in sores and spasms. These Spirits of the Pure Abode are also called the Buddhas of the Past in many passages, as I shall shortly show.

In the Southern scriptures it is explained that the Spirits of the Pure Abode dwell in the heaven of Brahma.* I may mention, too, that in a valuable inscription, copied from an old column in the island of Ceylon by Dr. Rhys Davids, it is announced that in the reign of the king who erected it, the Buddha devatas "talked with men"† in the great temple. Here we have plainly the Buddhas of the past, of the "Lalita Vistara." The disciples of the "Carriage which drives to the Great Nowhere" have senselessly interlarded this book with certain "Bodhisatwas of the Ten Regions," which, figuring side by side with the "Buddhas of the Ten Regions," confess the cheat. When the "Great Vehicle" movement dethroned the Buddhas of the past, it substituted Bodhisatwas (mortals who have reached the last stage of the metempsychosis) and transferred the old saint-worship, the sacrifices, processions, relic expositions, etc., to them.

For another valuable fact we are indebted to the Southern scriptures. They announce that the answers of the charioteer were given under inspiration from the unseen world.† On the surface this is plausible, for we shall see that the speeches of the charioteer were not always pitched in so high a key.

And it would almost seem as if some influence, malefic or otherwise, was stirring the good King Śuddhodana. Unmoved by failure, he urged the prince to a third effort. The chariot this time was to set out by the western gate. Greater precautions than ever were adopted. The chain of guards was posted at least twelve miles off from the Palace of Summer. But the Buddhas of the Ten Horizons again arrested the prince. His chariot was suddenly

* Turnour, "Journ. Beng. As. Soc.," Vol. VII., p. 798.
† "Journ. As. Soc.," Vol. VII., p. 364.
‡ Spence Hardy, "Manual," p. 157.

crossed by a phantom funeral procession. A phantom corpse, smeared with the orthodox mud, and spread with a sheet, was carried on a bier. Phantom women wailed, and phantom musicians played on the drum and the Indian flute. No doubt, also, phantom Brahmins chanted hymns to Jâtavedas, to bear away the immortal part of the dead man to the home of the Pitris.

"What is this?" said the prince. "Why do these women beat their breasts and tear their hair? Why do these good folk cover their heads with the dust of the ground. And that strange form upon its litter, wherefore is it so rigid?"

"Prince," said the charioteer, "this is Death! Yon form, pale and stiffened, can never again walk and move. Its owner has gone to the unknown caverns of Yama. His father, his mother, his child, his wife cry out to him, but he cannot hear."

Buddha was sad.

"Woe be to youth, which is the sport of age! Woe be to health, which is the sport of many maladies! Woe be to life, which is as a breath! Woe be to the idle pleasures which debauch humanity! But for the five 'aggregations' there would be no age, sickness, nor death. Go back to the city, I must compass the deliverance."

A fourth time the prince was urged by his father to visit the Garden of Happiness. The chain of guards this time was sixteen miles away. The exit was by the northern gate. But suddenly a calm man of gentle mien, wearing an ochre-red cowl, was seen in the roadway.

"Who is this," said the prince, "rapt, gentle, peaceful in mien? He looks as if his mind were far away elsewhere. He carries a bowl in his hand."

"Prince, this is the New Life," said the charioteer. "That man is of those whose thoughts are fixed on the eternal Brahma (Brahmacharin). He seeks the divine voice. He seeks the divine vision. He carries the alms-bowl of the holy beggar (bhikshu). His mind is calm because the gross lures of the lower life can vex it no more."

"Such a life I covet," said the prince. "The lusts of man are like the sea-water—they mock man's thirst instead of quenching it. I will seek the divine vision, and give immortality (the Amrita) to man."

In the "Lalita Vistara" the remedy for age, sickness, and death is immortality.* In Dr. Rhys Davids' "Buddhism," the remedy for death is death. If the apologue was composed outside of Bedlam, it is plain that the "Lalita Vistara" gives us the correct version. If a prick with a dagger is the amrita, why go through all the tortures of yoga to gain it?

King Śuddhodana was beside himself. He placed five hundred corseleted Sakyas at every gate of the Palace of Summer. Chains of sentries were round the walls, which were raised and strengthened. A phalanx of loving wives, armed with javelins, was posted round the prince's bed to "narrowly watch" him. The king ordered also all the allurements of sense to be constantly presented to the prince.

"Let the women of the zenana cease not for an instant their concerts and mirth and sports. Let them shine in silks and sparkle in diamonds and emeralds."

Mahâ Prajâpatî, the aunt who, since Queen Mâyâ's death has acted as foster-mother, has charge of these pretty young women, and she incites them to encircle the prince in a "cage of gold."

But the heavenly legions have not forgotten their son. One day, when the prince reclined on a silken couch listening to the sweet crooning of four or five

* "Un fruit de vie, de bien être, et d'immortalité," Foucaux, p. 185.

brown-skinned, large-eyed Indian girls, his eyes suddenly assumed a dazed and absorbed look, and the rich hangings and garlands and intricate trellis-work of the golden apartment were still present, but dim to his mind. And music and voices, more sweet than he had ever listened to, seemed faintly to reach him. I will write down some of the verses he heard.

Mighty prop of humanity
March in the pathway of the Rishis of old,
Go forth from this city !
Upon this desolate earth,
When thou hast acquired the priceless knowledge of the Jinas,
When thou hast become a perfect Buddha,
Give to all flesh the baptism (river) of the Kingdom of Rightness.
Thou who once didst sacrifice thy feet, thy hands, thy precious body, and all thy riches for the world,
Thou whose life is pure, save flesh from its miseries !
In the presence of reviling be patient, O conqueror of self !
Lord of those who possess two feet, go forth on thy mission ?
Conquer the evil one and his army."

Thus run some more of these gâthâs :—

Light of the world ! *
In former kalpas this vow was made by thee ;
" For the worlds that are a prey to death and sickness I will be a refuge ! "
Lion of men, master of those that walk on two feet, the time for thy mission has come !
Under the sacred Bo-tree acquire immortal dignity, and give Amrita (immortality) to all !
When thou wert a king (in a former existence), and a subject insolently said to thee : " These lands and cities, give them to me ! "
Thou wert rejoiced and not troubled.
Once when thou wert a virtuous Rishi, and a cruel king in anger hacked off thy limbs, in thy death agony milk flowed from thy feet and thy hands.
When thou didst dwell on a mountain as the Rishi Syama, a king having transfixed thee with poisoned arrows, didst thou not forgive this king ?

* " Lampe du Monde," Foucaux's translation.

When thou wert the king of antelopes, didst thou not save thine enemy the hunter from a torrent ?
When thou wert an elephant and a hunter pierced thee, thou forgavest him, and didst reward him with thy beautiful tusks !
Once when thou wert a she-bear thou didst save a man from a torrent swollen with snow. Thou didst feed him on roots and fruit until he grew strong ;
And when he went away and brought back men to kill thee, thou forgavest him !
Once when thou wert the white horse,*
In pity for the suffering of man,
Thou didst fly across heaven to the region of the evil demons,
To secure the happiness of mankind,
Persecutions without end,
Revilings and many prisons
Death and murder,
These hast thou suffered with love and patience,
Forgiving thine executioners.
Kingless, men seek thee for a king !
Stablish them in the way of Brahma and of the ten virtues,
That when they pass away from amongst their fellow-men, they may all go to the abode of Brahma.

" By these gâthâs the prince is exhorted," says the narrative. And whilst the Jinas sing, beautiful women, with flowers and perfumes, and jewels and rich dresses, try to incite him to mortal love.

But to bring about their plans more quickly, the Spirits of the Pure Abode have conceived a new project. The beautiful women of the zenana are the main seductions of Mâra, the tempter, whom philologists prove to be closely connected with Kâma, the god of love. The Spirits of the Pure Abode determine that the prince shall see these women in a new light. By a subtle influence they induce him to visit the apartments of the women at the moment that they, the Jinas, have put all these women into a sound sleep.

* Yearly the sun-god as the zodiacal horse (Aries) was supposed by the Vedic Aryans to die to save all flesh. Hence the horse-sacrifice.

Everything is in disorder—the clothes of the women, their hair, their trinkets. Some are lolling ungracefully on couches, some have hideous faces, some cough, some laugh sillily in their dreams, some rave. Also deformities and blemishes that female art had been careful to conceal are now made prominent by the superior magic of the spirits. This one has a discoloured neck, this one an ill-formed leg, this one a clumsy fat arm. Smiles have become grins, and fascinations a naked hideousness. Sprawling on couches in ungainly attitudes, all lie amidst their tawdry finery, their silent tambourines and lutes.

"Of a verity I am in a graveyard!" said the prince, in great disgust.

And now comes an incident which is odd in the life of a professed atheist. Buddha has determined to leave the palace altogether. "Then he (Buddha) uncrossed his legs, and turning his eyes towards the eastern horizon, he put aside the precious trellis-work and repaired to the roof of the palace. Then joining the ten fingers of his hands, he thought of all the Buddhas and rendered homage to all the Buddhas, and, looking across the skies, he saw the god of the ten hundred eyes (Dasasata Nayana)."

This is S'iva as the thousand-headed serpent, Sesh. Of this more hereafter.

At the moment that Buddha joined his hands in homage towards the eastern horizon, the star Pushya, which had presided at his birth, was rising. The prince on seeing it said to Chandaka:—

"The benedication that is on me has attained its perfection this very night. Give me at once the king of horses covered with jewels!"

The highest spiritual philosophers in Buddhism, in Brahminism, in Christendom, in Islam, announce two kingdoms distinct from one another. They are called in India the Domain of Appetite (Kâmaloca) and the Domain of Spirit (Brahmaloca). The "Lalita Vistara" throughout describes a conflict between these two great camps. Buddha is offered a crown by his father. He has wives, palaces, jewels, but he leaves all for the thorny jungle where the Brahmacharin dreamt his dreams of God. This is called pessimism by some writers, who urge that we should enjoy life as we find it, but modern Europe having tried, denies that life is so enjoyable. Its motto is *Tout lasse, tout casse, tout passe.* Yes, say the optimists, but we need not all live a life like Jay Gould. A good son, a good father, a good husband, a good citizen, is happy enough. True, reply the pessimists, in so far as a mortal enters the domain of spirit he may be happy, for that is not a region but a state of the mind. But mundane accidents seem, almost by rule, to mar even that happiness. The husband loses his loved one, the artist his eyesight. Philosophers and statesmen find their great dreams and schemes baffled by the infirmities of age.

Age, disease, death! These are the evils for which the great Indian allegory proposes to find a remedy.

The Buddhas of the Past win the victory in spite of the fact that King Śuddhodana offers to resign the crown to his son if he will abandon the idea of a religious life. Buddha steals away one night on his horse Kantaka, and enlists as a disciple of a Brahmin named Arâta Kâlâma.

But, by-and-bye, becoming dissatisfied with his teacher, he retires to the silences of Buddha Gayâ and the famous Bo-tree. There occurs his celebrated conflict with Mâra, the Buddhist Satan, who comes in person to tempt him. Two of the temptations are precisely similar to those of Jesus. Buddha is said to have gone through a forty-nine days' fast, and the first temptation appeals to his hunger. For the second he is transported to the neighbourhood of the splendid city of Kapilavastu, which is made to revolve, like the " wheel of a potter," and display its magnificence. The third temptation introduces a prominent feature in a fasting ascetic's visions. Beautiful females, the daughters of Mârâ, come round him. But Buddha triumphs over them, and triumphs over their father, and by-and-bye baptises both.

It is announced that after the great battle with Mâra the *devatas* came from the sky and ministered to Buddha. But besides the " Fasting " and " Temptation " there is a third close resemblance to the story of Jesus, Buddha's Abhisheka or " Baptism." He plunges into the Nairanjana, the Jordan of India, and tries to get to the " other bank " (the Indian simile for Heaven). Mâra, the Spirit of Evil, prevents him for a time, and then the mystic Sophia, under the similitude of a tree, bends down her branches and helps him up.

This lady, the Divine Mother, figures constantly. She appears about the same time as a young peasant, and relieves the fasting Buddha by giving him in a gold pot the concentrated essence of the milk of one thousand cows, rice milk being at once by an obvious simile the food of the Buddhist monk and the immortal food. The Buddhists prettily call Buddha's advent the " Epoch when the Rice Milk came into the world."

And the work of Sophia or Dharma (whose symbol is the Tree as well as the Lotus) is not over. Buddha has reached the Tree of Knowledge, the great Bo-Tree, and a coruscation like that on the Jordan, as recorded in the " Gospel according to the Hebrews " when the heavenly dove reached Christ, took place, and the dazzling Heavens of the Buddhas were seen afar with their rim of matchless lapis lazuli. And from the sky came voices :—

He hath overthrown the Banner of Pride.
He hath won the Triple Knowledge.
The aggregations of the seen world give place to the aggregations of the unseen world.
The King of Physicians with his heavenly amrita will dull all human pain and lead all flesh to Nirvana.
Having entered the City of Omniscience and become one with all the Buddhas.
He is now indivisible.

Then Brahma in person appeared to the ascetic and commissioned him to preach the "glad tidings" (suba shita),* and to turn the wheel of the law.

* See Rajendra Lala Mitra, "Northern Buddhist Literature," p. 29.

PLATE 5.

BUDDHA PREACHING.

CHAPTER IV

"THE WISDOM OF THE OTHER BANK"

Fine mysticism of Buddhism—The man who was born blind—The Tevigga Sutta—The Sinner—The Penitent Thief—"God revealed in the form of mercy—Death of Buddha.

If the Roman Catholics were told that St. Francois de Salis, or St. Jerome, "altogether ignored in nature any spiritual aspirations,"* they would feel a little astonished. This is the view taken of Buddha by the Boden Professor of Sanskrit at Oxford. And yet the word "Buddha" means, he "who has attained the complete spiritual awakening." And Buddha's *Dharma* has for an alternative exponent the words *Prajñâ Pâramitâ* (the Wisdom of the Other Bank).

There are two states of the soul, say the Buddhists, call them ego and non-ego—the plane of matter and the plane of spirit,—what you will. As long as we live for the ego and its greedy joys, we are feverish, restless, miserable. Happiness consists in the destruction of the ego by the Bodhi, or Gnosis. This is that interior, that high state of the soul, attained by Fenelon and Wesley, by Mirza the Sufi, and Swedenborg, by Spinoza and Amiel.

"The kingdom of God is within you," says Christ.

"In whom are hid the treasures of *sophia* and *gnosis*," says St. Paul.

* Sir Monier Monier-Williams, "Buddhism," p. 149.

"The enlightened view both worlds," says Mirza, the Sufi, "but the bat flieth about in the darkness without seeing."

"Who speaks and acts with the inner quickening," says Buddha, "has joy for his accompanying shadow. Who speaks and acts without the inner quickening, him sorrow pursues as the chariot-wheel the horse."

Let us give here a pretty parable, and let Buddha speak for himself :—

"Once upon a time there was a man born blind, and he said, 'I cannot believe in a world of appearances. Colours bright or sombre exist not. There is no sun, no moon, no stars. None have witnessed such things.' His friends chid him ; but he still repeated the same words.

"In those days there was a Rishi, who had the inner vision ; and he detected on the steeps of the lofty Himalayas four simples that had the power to cure the man who was born blind. He culled them, and, mashing them with his teeth, applied them. Instantly the man born blind cried out, 'I see colours and appearances. I see beautiful trees and flowers. I see the bright sun. No one ever saw like this before.'

"Then certain holy men came to the man who was born blind and said to him, 'You are vain and arrogant and nearly as blind as you were before. You see the outside of things, not the inside. One whose supernatural senses are quickened sees the lapis-lazuli fields of the Buddhas of the Past, and hears heavenly conch shells sounded at a distance of five yoganas. Go off to a desert, a forest, a cavern in the mountains, and conquer this mean thirst of earthly things.'"

The man who was born blind obeyed ; and the parable ends with the obvious interpretation. Buddha is the old Rishi, and the four simples are the four great truths. He weans mankind from the lower life and opens the eyes of the blind.

I think that Sir Monier-Williams' fancy, that Buddha ignored the spiritual side of humanity, is due to the fact that by the word "knowledge" he conceives the Buddhists to mean knowledge of material facts. That Buddha's conceptions are nearer to the ideas of Swedenborg than of Mill is, I think, proved by the Cingalese book, the Samanna Phala Sutta. Buddha details, at considerable length, the practice of the ascetic, and then enlarges upon their exact object. Man has a body composed of the four elements. It is the fruit of the union of his father and mother.

It is nourished on rice and gruel, and may be truncated, crushed, destroyed. In this transitory body his intelligence is enchained. The ascetic, finding himself thus confined, directs his mind to the creation of a freer integument. He represents to himself in thought another body created from this material body—a body with a form, members, and organs. This body, in relation to the material body, is like the sword and the scabbard, or a serpent issuing from a basket in which it is confined. The ascetic, then, purified and perfected, commences to practise supernatural faculties. He find himself able to pass through material obstacles, walls, ramparts, etc.; he is able to throw his phantasmal appearance into many places at once; he is able to walk upon the surface of the water without immersing himself; he can fly through the air like a falcon furnished with large wings; he can leave this world and reach even the heaven of Brahma himself.

Another faculty is now conquered by his force of will, as the fashioner of ivory shapes the tusk of the elephant according to his fancy. He acquires the power of hearing the sounds of the unseen world as distinctly as those of the phenomenal world, more distinctly, in point of fact. Also by the power of Manas he is able to read the most secret thoughts of others, and to tell their characters. He is able to say, "There is a mind that is governed by passion." "There is a mind that is enfranchised. This man has noble ends in view. This man has no ends in view." As a child sees his earrings reflected in the water, and says, "Those are my earrings," so the purified ascetic recognises the truth. Then comes to him the faculty of "divine vision," and he sees all that men do on earth and after they die, and when they are again reborn. Then he detects the secrets of the universe, and why men are unhappy, and how they may cease to be so.

I will now quote a conversation between Buddha and some Brahmins, which, I think, throws much light on his teaching. It is given in the *Tevigga Sutta*.

When Buddha was dwelling at Manasâkata in the mango grove, certain Brahmins, learned in three Vedas, come to consult him on the question of union with the eternal Brahma. They ask if they are in the right pathway towards that union. Buddha replies at great length. He suggests an ideal case. He supposes that a man has fallen in love with the most beautiful woman in the land. Day and night he dreams of her, but has never seen her. He does not know whether she is tall or short, of Brahmin or Sûdra caste, of dark or fair complexion; he does not even know her name.

The Brahmins are asked if the talk of that man about that woman be wise or foolish. They confess that it is "foolish talk." Buddha then applies the same train of reasoning to them. The Brahmins versed in the three Vedas are made to confess that they have never seen Brahma, that they do not know whether he is tall or short, or anything about him, and that all their talk about union with him is also foolish talk. They are mounting a crooked staircase, and do not know whether it leads to a mansion or a precipice. They are standing on the bank of a river and calling to the other bank to come to them.

Now it seems to me that if Buddha were the uncompromising teacher of atheism that many folks picture him, he has at this point an admirable opportunity of urging his views. The Brahmins, he would of course contend, knew nothing about Brahma, for the simple reason that no such being as Brahma exists.

But this is exactly the line that Buddha does not take. His argument is that the Brahmins knew nothing about Brahma, because Brahma is purely spiritual, and they are purely materialistic.

Five "Veils," he shows, hide Brahma from mortal ken. These are :—

1. The Veil of Lustful Desire.
2. The Veil of Malice.
3. The Veil of Sloth and Idleness.
4. The Veil of Pride and Self-righteousness.
5. The Veil of Doubt.

Buddha then goes on with his questionings :—

" Is Brahma in possession of wives and wealth ? "

" He is not, Gautama ! " answers Vâsettha, the Brahmin.

" Is his mind full or anger, or free from anger ? "

" Free from anger, Gautama ! "

" Is his mind full of malice, or free from malice ? "

" Free from malice, Gautama. "

" Is his mind depraved or pure ? "

" It is pure, Gautama ! "

" Has he self-mastery, or has he not ? "

" He has, Gautama ! "

The Brahmins are then questioned about themselves.

" Are the Brahmins versed in the three Vedas in possession of wives and wealth, or are they not ? "

" They are, Gautama ! "

" Have they anger in their hearts, or have they not ? "

" They have, Gautama ! "

" Do they bear malice, or do they not ? "

"They do, Gautama."

"Are they pure in heart, or are they not?"

"They are not, Gautama!"

"Have they self-mastery, or have they not?"

"They have not, Gautama!"

These replies provoke, of course, the very obvious retort that no point of union can be found between such dissimilar entities. Brahma is free from malice, sinless, self-contained, so, of course, it is only the sinless that can hope to be in harmony with him.

Vâsettha then puts the question: "It has been told me, Gautama, that Śramaṇa Gautama knows the way to the state of union with Brahma?"

"Brahma I know, Vâsettha!" says Buddha in reply, "and the world of Brahma, and the path leading to it!"

The humbled Brahmins, learned in the three Vedas, then ask Buddha to "show them the way to a state of union with Brahma."

Buddha replies at considerable length, drawing a sharp contrast between the lower Brahminism and the higher Brahminism, the "householder," and the "houseless one." The householder Brahmins are gross, sensual, avaricious, insincere. They practise for lucre, black magic, fortune-telling, cozenage. They gain the ear of kings, breed wars, predict victories, sacrifice life, spoil the poor. As a foil to this he paints the recluse, who has renounced all worldly things and is pure, self-possessed and happy.

To teach this "higher life," a Tathâgatha, "from time to time is born into the world, blessed and worthy, abounding in wisdom, a guide to erring mortals." He sees the universe face to face, the spirit world of Brahma and that of Mâra, the tempter. He makes his knowledge known to others.

The houseless one, instructed by him, "lets his mind pervade one quarter of the world with thoughts of pity, sympathy, and equanimity; and so the second, and so the third, and so the fourth. And thus the whole wide world, above, below, around, and everywhere, does he continue to pervade with heart of pity, sympathy and equanimity, far-reaching, grown great, and beyond measure." *

"Verily this, Vâsettha, is the way to a state of union with Brahma," and he proceeds to announce that the Bhikshu, or Bhuddhist beggar, "who is free from anger, free from malice, pure in mind, master of himself, will after death, when the body is dissolved, become united with Brahma." The Brahmins at once see the full force of this teaching. It is as a conservative in their eyes that Buddha figures, and not an innovator. He takes the side of the ancient spiritual religion of the country against rapacious innovators.

"Thou hast set up what was thrown down," they say to him. In the Burmese life he is described more than once as one who has set the overturned chalice once more upon its base.

The word Dharma means much in Buddhism.

Obey the eternal law of the heavens. Who keeps this law lives happily in this world and in the next.

"For the enfranchised soul human suffering no longer exists." †

"In the darkness of this world few men see clearly. Very few soar heavenwards like a bird freed from a net." ‡

No doubt the discipline of extasia was expected to give vitality to this inner quickening. When actual visions of the Buddhas of the ten regions were before the eyes of the fasting visionary, it was judged that he would have a more practical belief in their lapis-lazuli domains. The heart of the eastern nations has

* Rhys Davids, "Buddhist Suttas," p. 201.

† "Dhammapada" v. 90.

‡ *Ibid*, v. 174.

been truer to its great teacher than their learned metaphysicians have been. The epoch of Buddha is called the "Era when the Milken Race (immortality) came into the world." * This certainty of a heavenly kingdom was not to be confined, as in the orthodox Brahminism, to a priestly caste. A king had become a beggar that he might preach to beggars. In the Chinese *Dhammapada* there is a pretty story of a very beautiful Magdalen, who heard of Buddha, and who started off to hear him preach. On the way, however, she saw her beautiful face in a fountain near which she stopped to drink, and she was unable to carry out her good resolution.

As she was returning she was overtaken by a courtesan still more beautiful than herself, and they journeyed together. Resting for a while at another fountain. the beautiful stranger was overcome with sleep, and placed her head on her fellow-traveller's lap. Suddenly the beautiful face became livid as a corpse, loathsome, a prey to hateful insects. The stranger was the great Buddha himself, who had put on this appearance to redeem poor Pundarî.† "There is a loveliness that is like a beautiful jar full of filth, a beauty that belongs to eyes, nose, mouth, body. It is this womanly beauty that causes sorrow, divides families, kills children."

The penitent thief, too, is to be heard of in Buddhism. Buddha confronts a cruel bandit in his mountain retreat and converts him.‡ All great movements, said St. Simon, must begin by working on the emotion of the masses.

Another originality of the teaching of Buddha was the necessity of individual effort.

Ceremonial, sacrifice, the exertions of others, could have no possible effect on any but themselves. Against

* Upham, "Hist. Buddhism," p. 48.

† "Chinese Dhammapada," p. 35.

‡ *Ibid*, p. 159.

the bloody sacrifice of the Brahmins he was specially remorseless.

"How can the system which requires the infliction of misery on others be called a religious system? . . . How having a body defiled with blood will the shedding of blood restore it to purity? To seek a good by doing an evil is surely no safe plan!" *

Even a Buddha could only show the sinner the right path. "Tathâgatas are only preachers. You yourself must make the effort." †

Buddha's theology made another great advance on other creeds, a step which our century is only now attempting to overtake. He strongly emphasised the remorseless logic of cause and effect in the deteriorating influences of evil actions on the individual character. The Judas of Buddhism, Devadetta, repents and is forgiven. But Buddha cannot annul the causation of his evil deeds. These will have to be dealt with by slow degrees in the purgatorial stages of the hereafter. He knows no theory of a dull bigot on his deathbed suddenly waking up with all the broad sympathies and large knowledge of the angel Gabriel. Unless in the next life a being takes up his intellectual and moral condition exactly at the stage he left it in this, it is plain that logically his individuality is lost. This teaching of Buddha has been whimsically enforced by some of his followers. His own words are trenchant and clear: "A fault once committed is like milk, which grows not sour all at once. Patiently and silently, like a smothered ember, shall it inch by inch devour the fool." ‡ "Both a good action and an evil action must ripen and bear their inevitable fruit." §

* "Romantic History," p. 159.

† *Ibid*, v. 71.

‡ "Dhammapada," v. 71.

§ Burnouf, Introd., p. 87.

This teaching has been powerfully inculcated in one or two fine parables in which the consequences of sin are imaged as an iron city of torment and the sins themselves figure as beautiful women luring man to his ruin. On the surface all is as bewitching as a scene of the "Arabian Nights." The palm trees of a soft island rustle gently and in a delicious palace the mean seeker of gold, the bad son, is fanned by women of a beauty unknown to earth. He has sought the unworthy prizes of the Kâmaloca, and he enjoys them for a time, because with Buddha the full basket and store of the Brahmin and the old Jew are not deemed the rewards of heaven, but of quite another region. From island to island the wanderer goes, each island being more delicious than the preceding one, but each being nearer to the iron-walled city of expiation. But the furies are cause and effect, and not an eternal Ahriman. There is no devil that Buddha cannot soften.*

This suggests another great advance made by Buddha. In his day the beneficent God was deemed the god of a nation, a tribe; and all the gods of other nations were deemed evil demons. This creed is the real "agnosticism" and "atheism," because its main postulate implies that the reason and conscience of humanity for thousands and thousands of years have been unable to discover God, and that if He has been found at all, it is to accident alone that the discovery is due; even if the discovered god should not upon examination be found to be composed of very poor clay. But the missionaries of Tathâgata were sent to every nation, and he proclaimed that even in the hell Avîchi was no recess sheltered from Tathâgata's all-pervading love.

But the crowning legacy to humanity of this priceless benefactor was his boundless compassion. "Buddha,"

* Beal, "Romantic History." Comp. "Story of the Five Hundred Merchants," p. 332, and "the Merchant," p. 342.

says his disciples, "was God revealed in the form of Mercy." The theory that Buddha was a myth seems to break down here, for some such character must have existed, that ideas so far in advance even of modern days could have been conceived. His majestic gentleness never varies. He converts the Very Wicked One. He speaks gently to the Daughters of Sin. He clears out even the lowest of hells when he visits earth, and makes devils as well as good men happy. A fool outrages and insults him. "My son," he replies, "outrage addressed to heaven is like spittle aimed into the skies: it returns upon the author of the outrage." * And he explained to his disciples that Tathâgata could never be made angry by foul actions and invectives. Such can only make him redouble his mercy and love.† When we reflect that the principle of retaliation was the rude policy of the day in which he lived, and that aggregations of men were obliged to foster a love of revenge, war, plunder, and bloodshed in their midst, prompted by the mere instinct of self-preservation, such great sentences as the following of Buddha are indeed noteworthy:—

"By love alone can we conquer wrath. By good alone can we conquer evil. The whole world dreads violence. All men tremble in the presence of death. Do to others that which ye would have them do to you. Kill not. Cause no death." ‡

"Say no harsh words to thy neighbour. He will reply to thee in the same tone." §

"I am injured and provoked, I have been beaten and plundered! They who speak thus will never cease to hate."

* "Sutra of Forty-two Sections," Sect. VIII.

† *Ibid*, sect. VII.

‡ Sutra of Forty-two Sections, Sect. VII., v. 129. M. Léon Feer gives here the very words of Luke vi. 31.

§ *Ibid*, v. 133.

"That which can cause hate to cease in the world is not hate, but the absence of hate." *

"If, like a trumpet trodden on in battle, thou complainest not, thou hast attained Nirvâna."

"Silently shall I endure abuse, as the war-elephant receives the shaft of the bowman."

"The awakened man goes not on revenge, but rewards with kindness the very being who has injured him, as the sandal-tree scents the axe of the woodman who fells it."†

I will now copy down a few miscellaneous sayings of Buddha:—

"The swans go on the path of the sun. They go through the air by means of their miraculous power. The wise are led out of this world when they have conquered Mâra and his train." ‡

"A man is not a Śramana by outward acts."

"Not by tonsure does an undisciplined man became a Śramana."

"There is no satisfying of lusts with a shower of gold pieces."

"A man is not a Bhikshu simply because he asks others for alms. A man is not a Muni because he observes silence. Not by discipline and vows, not by much spiritual knowledge, not by sleeping alone, not by the gift of holy inspiration, can I earn that release which no worldling can know. The real Śramana is he who has quieted all evil."

"If one man conquer in battle a thousand thousand men, and another conquer himself, the last is the greatest conqueror."

"Few are there amongst men who arrive at the other shore. Many run up and down the shore."

* Sutra of Forty-two Sections v. 4, 5.

† This is claimed by the Brahmins likewise, but it is quite foreign to their genius. *Vide* Hodgson, "Essays," p. 74.

‡ "Dhammapada."

"Let the fool wish for a false reputation, for precedence amongst the Bhikshus, for lordship in the convents, for worship amongst other people."

"A supernatural person is not easily found. He is not born everywhere. Wherever such a sage is born that race prospers."

"Call not out in this way as if I were the god Brahma" (Chinese parable).

"Religion is nothing but the faculty of love."

"The house of Brahma is that wherein children obey their parents."

"The elephant's cub, if he find not leafless and thorny creepers in the greenwood, becomes thin."

"Beauty and riches are like a knife smeared with honey. The child sucks and is wounded."

THE ONE THING NEEDFUL.

Certain subtle questions were proposed to Buddha, such as: What will best conquer the evil passions of man? What is the most savoury gift for the alms-bowl of the mendicant? Where is true happiness to be found? Buddha replied to them all with one word, *Dharma* (the heavenly life).

DEATH OF BUDDHA.

Some eighty miles due east of Buddha's birthplace, Kapilavastu, now stands a modest village called Mâthâ Küar (the "Dead Prince"). At the date of the pilgrimage of Hiouen Thsiang, there was a reason for this. Under a splendid temple-canopy reposed in marble a "Dead Prince," and this circumstance is still remembered by the natives. The ruins of this temple can still be traced. Exactly four hundred and seventy years before Christ the spot was a jangal of Sâla-trees, and beneath the shade of two of these lay calm and rigid the gentle teacher whom Indians call the "Best Friend of all the World." Buddha was journeying from Râjâgriha when he reached this resting place. Its name was Kuśinagara. At Beluva, near Vaiśâlî, he was attacked with a severe illness. Violent pains seized him. He was very nearly dying. Ânanda was disconsolate, but Buddha comforted him.

"What need hath the body of my followers of me now, Ânanda? I have declared the doctrine, and I have made no distinction between within and without. He who says, 'I will rule over the Sangha!' or 'Let the Sangha be subjected to me!' he, Ânanda, might declare his will in the church. The Tathâgata, however, does not say, 'I will rule over the church.' . . . I am now frail, Ânanda; I am aged, I am an old man who has finished his pilgrimage and reached old age. Eighty years old am I.

"Be to yourselves, Ânanda, your own light, your own refuge. Seek no other refuge. Let Dharma be your light and refuge. Seek no other refuge. . . . Whosoever now, Ânanda, or after my departure, shall be his own light, his own refuge, and seek no other refuge, will henceforth be my true disciple and walk in the right path."

Buddha journeyed on until he reached a place called Pâvâ. There he was attacked with a grievous sickness. Weary, the old pilgrim reached a stream, the Kakutthâ (the modern Badhi, according to General Cunningham). Buddha bathed and sipped some of the water; carts were passing and they thickened it with mud. A little farther on, by the side of the river Hâranyavatî (Chota Gandak), was a grove of Śâla trees. Between two of these blossoming trees was the Nirvâṇa that the sick and weary pilgrim was sighing for.

Under these two famous trees, with his head lying towards the north, the old man was laid. "Weep not, sorrow not, Ânanda," he said. "From all that man loves and enjoys he must tear himself.

"My existence is ripening to its close. The end of my life is near. I go hence. Ye remain behind.

"The place of refuge is ready for me."*

Before expiring, the teacher entered into the extasia of Samâdhi; and mighty thunders and earth-rockings announced the passing away of a great Chakravartin. Buddha's last words were:—

"Hearken, O disciples, I charge you. All that comes into being passes. Seek your salvation without weariness."

* Oldenburg, "Buddha," p. 199

CHAPTER V

KING ASOKA

King Asoka—Rock inscriptions—Only reliable records of early Buddhism—Not an atheism—Immortality—Dharma Râj—Kingdom of Justice—Helps to expose a portentous fraud—Buddhaghos'a and the Ceylon records—King Wijaya—Date altered by Buddhaghos'a one hundred years—Fictitious "Second Convocation"—Mahindo, Asoka's son, visits Ceylon—Vast literature of S'iva-Buddhism palmed upon him—Brief of modern English missonaries in their attack on Buddha.

In Buddha Gaya, in the year B.C. 520, Buddha sat under a pippala tree dreaming of a Dharma Râj. We have all our visions at times of this Dharma Râj, a bright kingdom of Dreamland where wrong is righted; but who, like Buddha, sees his dream made concrete?

Buddha sat under the renowned *Ficus religiosa*, B.C. 520. Two hundred and fifty years after this appeared King Asoka and the Dharma Râj.

Asoka, at the age of twenty-four, succeeded to the throne of Patna. His brothers raised troops, and sought to upset him. After a sharp struggle he overcame them, and treated them with the uusal mercy of Asiastics towards brothers near the throne. He was the grandson of Sandrocottus, who was placed on the throne by Brahmin intrigue. Asoka was at first a pious Brahmin, and 50,000 Brahmins were fed by him daily. Also he was a capable soldier, for he conquered more Indian territory than Clive, Lake, Wellington, and Napier, if they were to sum up the area of their united conquests.

But after his consecration he had several conversations with a Buddhist monk named Nigrauda. Much interested in Buddha, he received eagerly the details of his life and teaching. Soon the King was converted, and he made Buddhism the State religion.

Shortly before this, according to the calculations of Sir Alexander Cunningham and Professor Max Müller, India received the letters of the alphabet. The gift was happily timed, because the first use made of it was to scratch ideas on rocks and stones. In the year B.C. 251 King Asoka incised his earliest rock edict. He soon issued a great many more. Some idea of the extent of the rule and the spread of Buddhism may be gained from the fact that on the extreme west of India he cut a rock inscription at Girnar on the Gulf of Cutch. On the east coast, at Ganjam, were the Dhauli and Jaugada edicts; and Gandhara, or Peshawur, was reached in the north; and Chola and Pandiya, the extreme southern provinces of India, as I have said before.

It was a fortunate circumstance that the rude expedient was adopted of cutting the edicts on stone, because innovators cannot treat stone edicts like manuscripts on plantain leaves; and we get at once an opportunity of finding out at least what Buddha's disciples thought about God, spirit, and man's future.

KING ASOKA'S IDEAS ABOUT GOD.

"Much longing after the things (of this life) is a disobedience, I again declare; not less so is the laborious ambition of dominion by a prince who would be a propitiator of heaven. Confess and believe in God (Is'ana), who is the worthy object of obedience. For equal to this (belief), I declare unto you, ye shall not find such a means of propitiating heaven. Oh strive ye to obtain this inestimable treasure."*

* First Separate Edict. Dhauli, Prinsep.

"Thus spake King Devanampiya Piyadasi: The present moment and the past have departed under the same ardent hopes. How by the conversion of the Royal born may religion be increased? Through the conversion of the lowly born if religion thus increaseth, by how much (more) through the conviction of the high born and their conversion shall religion increase? Among whomsoever the name of God resteth, verily this is religion.

"Thus spake Devanampiya Piyadasi: Wherefore from this very hour I have caused religious discourses to be preached. I have appointed religious observances that mankind, having listened thereto, shall be brought to follow in the right path, and give glory to God."*

"It is well known, sirs, to what lengths have gone my respect for and faith in Buddha, Dharma, Sangha."†

"Whatever words have been spoken by the divine Buddha, they have all been well said."‡

"And he who acts in conformity with this edict shall be united with Sugato."§

"The white elephant whose name is The Bringer of Happiness to the Whole World."||

Is'ana is the name that has been selected by the Sanskrit scholars employed lately in translating "God save the Queen." Buddha, Dharma, and Sangha make up the Buddhist Trinity, which is precisely similar to that of Philo and the Gnostics. Buddha is spirit; Dharma, matter; Sangha, ideal humanity, the Christ. They figure together as three separate beings in the scuptulres of Buddha Gaya, one of Asoka's temples. Later on they got also to mean Buddha, his law and his monks.

* Edict No. VII., Prinsep.

† Second Bairat Rock, Burnouf.

‡ Second Bairat Rock, Wilson.

§ Delhi Pillar, Prinsep.

|| Final Sentence of the Rock Edicts, Kern.

ASOKA ON A FUTURE LIFE.

"On the many beings over whom I rule I confer happiness in this world; in the next they may obtain Swarga (paradise)."*

"This is good. With these means let a man seek Swarga. This is to be done. By these means it is to be done, as by them Swarga (paradise) is to be gained."†

"I pray with every variety of prayer for those who differ with me in creed, that they, following after my example, may with me attain unto eternal salvation."‡

"And whoso doeth this is blessed of the inhabitants of this world; and in the next world endless moral merit resulteth from such religious charity."§

"Unto no one can be repentance and peace of mind until he hath obtained supreme knowledge, perfect faith, which surmounteth all obstacles, and perpetual assent."||

"In the tenth year of his anointment, the beloved King Piyadasi obtained the Sambodhi, or complete knowledge." **

"All the heroism that Piyadasi, the beloved of the gods, has exhibited is in view of another life. Earthly glory brings little profit, but, on the contrary, produces a loss of virtue. To toil for heaven is difficult to peasant and to prince, unless by a supreme effort he gives up all."††

"May they (my loving subjects) obtain happiness in this world and in the next."‡‡

* Edict VI., Wilson.
† Edict IX., Wilson.
‡ Delhi Pillar, Edict VI., Prinsep.
§ Edict XI., Prinsep.
|| Rock Edict No. VII., Prinsep.
** Rock Edict No. VII., Burnouf.
†† Rock Edict No. X., Burnouf.
‡‡ Second Separate Edict, Burnouf.

"The beloved of the gods speaketh thus: It is more than thirty-two years and a half that I am a hearer of the law, and I did not exert myself strenuously; but it is a year or more that I have entered the community of ascetics, and that I have exerted myself strenuously. Those gods who during this time were considered to be true gods in Jambudvipa have now been abjured. . . . A small man who exerts himself somewhat can gain for himself great heavenly bliss, and for this purpose this sermon has been preached. Both great ones and small ones should exert themselves, and should in the end gain (true) knowledge. And this manner of acting should be what? Of long duration! For the spiritual good will grow the growth, and will grow exceedingly; at least it will grow one size and a half.

"This sermon has been preached by the departed.

"Two hundred and fifty years have elapsed since the departure of the teacher."*

MYSTICISM.

Did early Buddhism "relegate mysticism to the region of fairy-tales," as Professor Rhys Davids has asserted?

"There is no such charity as the charity which springeth from virtue (Dharma), which is the intimate knowledge of virtue (Dharma), the inheritance of virtue (Dharma), the close union with virtue (Dharma)."†

"The beloved of the gods, King Piyadasi, honours all forms of religious faith, whether professed by ascetics (pavajitani) or householders (gahthani).‡

"Whatever villages with their inhabitants may be given or maintained for the sake of the worship,

* Rupnâth Rock, Buhler.
† Edict XII., Prinsep.
‡ Rock Edict, No. XII., Wilson.

the devotees shall receive the same; and for an example unto my people, they shall exercise solitary austerities."*

"And he who acts in conformity with this edict shall be united with Sugato."†

"Dharma" has been translated "the Law," "Virtue," "Thought," "Righteousness," by various scholars. Let the Buddhists give their own translation in their ritual. "I salute that Dharma who is Prajna Paramita (the Wisdom of the Other Bank)."‡

Now, it seems easy for bishops and Boden Professors of Sanskrit to explain away Buddha. Says Sir Monier Williams, "He was an atheist." He "professed to know nothing of spirit as distinct from bodily organism." He had "no religion" (p. 28); "no prayers" (p. 28); no "Idea of original sin" (p. 114). He had no real morality, merely "monk morality" (p. 125). He "could not inculcate piety" (p. 124). All these statements may be and are accepted by many readers, but how are we to explain away Asoka, a king who professed to be specially Buddha's pupil; and who by the aid of a chisel and hard stone has placed beyond a doubt what he thought upon the subject of Buddha's religion. Could Cartouche build up a Fenelon? Could a Wilberforce develop himself prompted chiefly by a robust admiration of the president of the Hell-Fire Club?

It may be confidently affirmed that there is nothing in the world's history like the Dharma Râj of King Asoka. Imagine Napoleon and Fenelon rolled into one. He antedates Wilberforce in the matter of slavery. He antedates Howard in his humanity towards prisoners. He antedates Tolstoi in his desire to turn the sword into a pruning-hook. He antedates

* Delhi Pillar, Edict IV., Prinsep.

† Delhi Pillar, Prinsep.

‡ "Buddhism," p. 28.

Rousseau, St. Martin, Fichte, in their wish to make interior religion the all in all.

Here are two passages from his edicts that go beyond anything to be seen in any modern State :—

"Piyadasi, the friend of the Devas, attaches less importance to alms and outside rites than to his desire to witness the spread of interior religion."*

"Progress in Dharma may be obtained in two manners—by formal rules, and by the feelings that they help to arouse in the heart. In this double influence the first has a very inferior value, the inner quickening is what is really important."†

This is what he would have said at the Czar's Peace Congress :—

"Piyadasi, the friend of the Devas, values alone the harvest of the next woild. For this alone has this inscription been chiselled, that our sons and our grandsons should make no new conquests. Let them not think that conquests by the sword merit the name of conquests. Let them see there ruin, confusion, and violence. True conquests alone are the conquests of Dharma."‡

OTHER REFORMS.

"Formerly, in the great refectory and temple of King Piyadasi, the friend of the Devas, many hundred thousand animals were daily sacrificed for the sake of food meat, . . . but now the joyful chorus resounds again and again that henceforward not a single animal shall be put to death."§

"If a man is subject to slavery and ill-treatment, from this moment he shall be delivered by the King from this and other captivity. Many men in this

* Edict XIII., Senart.

† Delhi Pillar, Edict VIII., Senart, II. 96.

‡ Edict No. XIV., Senart, I. 322.

§ Rock Edict, No. I., Prinsep.

country suffer in captivity, therefore the Stûpa containing the commands of the King has been a great want."*

But King Asoka's Edicts throw a strong light upon one very important point indeed—the date of the rise of monks in the sense of housed sedentary idlers. This point I myself have overlooked in my early examination of these inscriptions.

Asoka's word for the Buddhist monks is Pavajitani. This means houseless ascetics. The Sanskrit word for a monastery is Sangharâma, the Garden of the Monks. In point of fact, in the earliest days the monastery was a forest.

"Everywhere the heaven-beloved Râja Piyadasi's double system of medical aid is established, both medical aid for men and medical aid for animals. . . . And wherever there is not such provision, in all such places it is to be prepared and planted, both root drugs and herbs. Wheresoever there is not a provision of them, in all such places shall they be deposited and planted. And in the public highways wells are to be dug and trees to be planted for the accommodation of men and animals."

Here is another inscription:—

"Whenever devotees shall abide around (or circumambulate) the holy fig-tree for the performance of pious acts, the benefit and pleasure of the country and its inhabitants shall be in making offerings, and according to their generosity or otherwise they shall enjoy prosperity or adversity; and they shall give thanks for the coming of the faith. Whatever villages with their inhabitants may be given or maintained for the sake of the worship, the devotees shall receive the same, and for the example of my people they shall exercise solitary austerities. And likewise whatever blessings they shall pronounce, by these shall my devotees accumulate for the worship. Furthermore,

* Dhauli Edict, No I., Prinsep.

the people in the night shall attend the great myrobalan-tree and the holy fig-tree. My people shall accumulate the great myrobalan-tree."

But as regards our present inquiry the King's Rock Edicts are quite priceless. They enable us to expose one of the most shameless frauds in all religious history.

About the beginning of the fourth century A.D., there came to Magadha a young Brahmin who excelled in religious disputation. Near the bo-tree there was a convent where the youth obtained shelter. And thanks to the good-natured toleration of the Buddhists, he was allowed day after day to rehearse his fiery speeches, "clasp his hands," and otherwise get up his logic and gestures. He attracted the attention of the Mahâthêrô, who by-and-by converted him.

The eloquence of the new convert soon became more renowned than ever. He was called "Buddhaghosa," the "Voice of Buddha," because he was as "eloquent as Buddha himself." These details are from the Mahâwanso, and so are the significant passages that follow.

One day the head of the Buddhist Church, one Rewato, came to the young man, and said:—

"In the island of Ceylon is a commentary on the Buddhist holy books. It is called the Aṭṭhakathâ, and was written in the Cingalese language by Mahindo, the son of Asoka. Outside Ceylon this commentary does not exist. Go thither and translate this commentary into Pâli."

Buddhaghosa repaired to Ceylon, to the convent at Anuradhapura, and commenced his task. A miracle authenticated his qualifications. The Aṭṭhakathâ in its present form contains more than one life of Buddha, lives of the six previous Buddhas, and long-winded commentaries on all the Cingalese Scriptures. These in turn were "recompiled" by the young convert. The Buddhist Scriptures of

Ceylon, "if translated into English," says Dr. Rhys Davids, "would be about four times as long as our Bible."* Yet when this colossal task was completed, the spirits (devas) conjured away the manuscript, and the painstaking convert went to work a second time. Again his completed work was spirited away, and again he finished it. The mischievous spirits then restored the two previous translations, and lo and behold, in the three great compilations, not a "verse," a "meaning of a word," a "letter," or a transposition differed. By this miracle Buddhaghosa proved his powers. "Of a truth," said the monks of Ceylon, "this is the coming Buddha Maitreyo!"

In the long and elaborate article in the "Journal of the Asiatic Society of Bengal," from which I have been quoting,† Turnour makes patent a wholesale falsification of the ancient Cingalese chronicles by Buddhaghosa.

The main objects of this, in his view, were:—

(1) To show that Wijayo, who figures in these chronicles as the first King of Ceylon, was a disciple of Buddha; that he was sent by Buddha to Ceylon; that he arrived there at Buddha's death (B.C. 593 in the annals of Ceylon). As the historical Wijayo, according to Turnour, did not appear on the page of history until about one hundred years later, the lives of some of the kings who ruled in Ceylon prior to Asoka have to be spread out like niggard butter on abundant bread to make up these one hundred years. One dies over a hundred years of age. Another "commences a turbulent reign" at ninety. A third seems to have been 147 years of age.‡ The two dates that can be checked by Western chronology, the date of Alexander's expedition and that of Megasthenes to

* "Buddhism," p. 20.

† "Journ. Beng. As. Soc.," Vol. VI., p. 725.

‡ "Journ. Beng. As. Soc.," Vol. VI., p. 721.

King Chandragupta at Patna, are both dislodged by these changed dates. Alexander, according to the Ceylon chronology, must have visited India in the days of Asoka, and not "during the commotions which preceded the usurpation of the Indian empire by his grandfather, Sandrocottus."* And the embassy of Megasthenes to Patna would have to be set down in Asòka's reign likewise.

(2) To fill up the same gap, preposterous ages have to be given also to the monks, who take part in the three convocations that Buddhaghosa describes.

We must examine more closely these changes of date, but as a preliminary I must point out that both Rewato, the head of the monastery at Magadha, and Buddhaghosa were strong partisans of the Mahâyâna teaching. The Chinese traveller, Fa Hian, visited this monastery fourteen years before Buddhaghosa came on the scene and he calls the monastery "the very lofty and very beautiful Great Vehicle Monastery."†

Another point is this, the India Office employed recently the eminent Chinese scholar, Bunyiu Nanjio, a Japanese, to officially classify the Buddhist literature from the ancient Chinese lists. He marks down the Brahmajâla Sûtra, and many other works that are prominent in Buddhaghosa's Aṭṭhakathâ as Mahâyâna treatises.

Bearing this in mind one fact certainly emerges. Buddhaghosa had a strong interest to represent the literature of his day as dating from the earliest times. He records that a Convocation was held at Rajagriha by King Ajatàsatto, of Magadha, at the date of Buddha's death, namely B.C. 543.

"At this Convocation," says Mr. Turnour, "the orthodox version of the Pitakattayan ('Baskets' of

* "Journ. Beng. As. Soc.," Vol. VI., p. 716.

† Fa Hian, "Pilgrimage," p. 254. (Stanislaus Julien's Trans.).

Buddhist teaching) was defined and authenticated with a degree of precision which fixed even the number of syllables of which it should consist. The 'Commentaries' made or delivered on that occasion acquired the designation of Aṭṭhakathâ."*

But Buddhaghosa plainly attached more significance to another point, hence his frantic falsification of the date of King Wijayo. He wanted to show that that monarch was an envoy sent specially by the kingdom of heaven to fuse together the civil and religious government of Ceylon, for he announces that Wijayo was sent there as monarch by Buddha himself, as we have shown. Inferentially the king would thus also be held to have brought with him the earliest Buddhist teaching.

All this is intelligible, but now come the difficulties. Asoka comes upon the scene B.C. 260, and converts India. He holds a Convocation, the Council of Patna, which "reaffirmed" the "Baskets" and Commentaries, a literature that according to Professor Rhys Davids is in bulk four times as voluminous as the Christian's Bible.†

A son of Asoka, Mahindo, was to have started for Ceylon carrying this great mass of Buddhist teachings immediately after the Convocation. He was delayed a year. Then he reached Ceylon in safety, and had the "Baskets" and Commentary translated into the language of the country, the Singhalese Prâkrit. It is to this translation that the Mahâthêrô Rewato alluded when speaking to Buddhaghosa. He talks as if it were only a Commentary, but the important point was the "Baskets," which he was about to fill with treatises of Mahâyânâ teaching.

The reader may have observed that I have avoided such words as "Scriptures," "Literature," "Docu-

* Turnour "Journ. As. Soc. Bengal," Vol. VI., p. 505.

† Rhys Davids "Buddhism," p. 20.

ments," in speaking of these baskets. In point of fact Buddhist teaching was retained exclusively by the memory of the monks and nuns until the date of King Wittaganini (B.C. 104 to 76).

From this it will be judged that the feat of Mahindo was rather a noteworthy one. Imagine twenty Oxford Professors getting by heart the Bible, the Apocrypha, and the Library of Antenicene Fathers, and proceeding to Ceylon and helping twenty natives of the Island to translate all this, and become letter perfect with the translation, without the least aid of any writing or printing. Taking Buddhaghosa's story as he gives it, is it a plausible one? His main idea escapes. If he intended to saturate the old scriptures with the strong curry powder of the Mahâyâna, his adversaries would at once detect the addition, but he could plead that he was falling back on the real teaching of Mahindo, which fortunately was still extant, if dormant, in the Cingalese tongue.

But this suggests two awkward questions. Was this Ceylon version an official Buddhist Scripture, acknowledged by the Buddhists of Ceylon, and as a corollary by the Buddhists of the Monastery of Magadha, which was presided over by the Buddhist Pope. If the answer to this be in the negative there comes up another question, namely—Who took the immense trouble to get by heart Mahindo's enormous "Baskets" and Commentaries, and to persuade other Non-Buddhists to learn them up and pass them on after their death? Certainly for one hundred and fifty years after the advent of Mahindo, the orthodox Buddhist scriptures in the Pâli language were passed on *viva voce*. No documents existed until the date of King Wittaganini (B.C. 146 to 76).

On the other hand, if there was no secret at all about Mahindo's translation, what was the rationale of

Buddhaghosa's astounding feat of penmanship? If the "Baskets" and Commentary were four times as big as our Bible, his MS. must have been twelve times as big. And in the presence of the official Pâli version, it would have had no authority, for the Pâli version claimed to have been ticked off to the very syllable by the Convocation of Râjagriha, and carefully "re-affirmed" by the Convocations of Vaisali and Patna. With one sweep of his chisel Asoka disperses all these air bubbles.

The old history of Ceylon, the Mahâwanso, announces that the King was puzzled with the question: "Of what religion was Sugato?" which word Mr. Turnour renders "the Deity of Happy Advent." In consequence he determined to summon a council of all the monks of Jambudwipa, to be presided over by Moggaliputra. The Ninth Edict talks of "consultations upon matters of religion" (Senart's translation). The Third Edict talks of an Anusaṁyâna (general assembly). The convocation is dated by scholars, B.C. 244. Certainly the following inscription seems to give us its results:—

"It is well-known, sirs, to what lengths have gone my respect for and faith in Buddha, Dharma, Saṅgha. All that our Lord Buddha has spoken is well spoken. Wherefore, sirs, it must indeed be regarded as having indisputable authority. So the true faith shall last long. Thus, my lords, I honour with the highest honour those religious works, Vinayasamaka ('Lessons in Discipline'), Aryavasas ('the Supernatural Powers of the Aryas') Anâgatabhayas, ('the Terrors of the Future'), Munigâtha ('the Metrical Life of Buddha'), Upatisapasina ('the Question of Upatishya'), Moneyasûta ('the Sûtra on the Inner Life'), and the Admonition to Râhula concerning falsehood uttered by our Lord Buddha. These religious works, sir, I would that the Bhikshus and Bhikshunis, for the advancement of their good name, shall uninterruptedly study and remember." *

This is the inscription, and it is difficult to see how any Orientalist, or any non-Orientalist, can undervalue its importance. Would Asoka have had "doubts" and "consultations" as to what Buddha had taught, if a literature four times as copious as the Christian's Bible was already received as canonical? And supposing that the canon was fixed before his time, why should he reject the greater part of it, and only require about one per cent. of the whole to be learnt and chanted out by his monks and nuns? The "Question of Upatishya" has come down to us, and also the "Admonition to Rahûla regarding Falsehood." The two together would be about as long as the Epistle to Philemon in the Bible, and the Life of Buddha was also probably very short.

Dr. Oldenburg holds that the seven tractates mentioned on the Second Bairât Rock are only a portion of the vast literature that Mahinda carried to Ceylon: but as the memory of the monks was the sole vehicle by which Buddhist teaching in those days could be handed down, who committed to memory the remaining literature?—about ninety-nine per cent. of the whole. Aśoka's monks and nuns were ordered all of them to learn up and chant the seven Aśoka tractates only.

I have said that we have two of the seven tractates mentioned on the Second Bairât Rock, the Admonition to Râhula regarding falsehood and the "Question of Upatishya." I will return to this latter by-and-by.

Munigâtha, a third one, means the metrical life of the Muni (Buddha); and very ancient metrical scraps, whether genuine or not, are sprinkled about in the "Lalita Vistara," and in the translation of the Chinese biography by the Rev. Samuel Beal. From the Chinese

* Second Bairât Rock.

records he pronounces that the earliest biography was called " Leaving the Palace for a Religious Life." Here is a verse where the Prince sees one of the Four Presaging Tokens, the sick man :—

> "The Prince asked the Coachman and said
> What man is this enduring such pain ?
> The Coachman replied to the Prince
> The four elements ill-adjusted—therefore sickness is produced."

The Sûtra on Vinaya or Discipline, was probably even shorter than the Metrical life.

The early disciples were Bhikshus, or beggars. Their monasteries were trees ; their temples were forests ; their monks' cowls, tree bark ; their gospel, the human mind.

This comes out in an important set of Buddhist rules—the " Twelve Observances." The " mob of beggars," as Buddha called his followers, are expressly forbidden to have any covering over them except a tree. Their " one seat " is to be mother earth. Their clothes are to be rags from the dustheap, the dung-heap, the graveyard. The tree that covers the beggar must be, if possible, in a graveyard. He is to be called Durkhrodpa (" He who lives in a graveyard "). He is not allowed to sleep twice under the same tree.

Apropos of the early Buddhist ascetic, Dr. Oldenburg cites this from the Cûla Hatthi padopama sûtta :—

" He dwells in a lonely spot, in a grove, at the foot of a tree, on a mountain in a cave, in a mountain grotto, in a burial-place in the wilderness, under an open sky, on a heap of straw."

The sculptures of the early Topes represent marble worshippers crouching before a small throne or table placed before a marble tree. On the altar are often two footprints. The recent exhumation of the remains of the Stûpa of Bharhut (B.C. 250) has placed the meaning of these emblems beyond the region of controversy. Such designs have been there discovered, and they are furnished with explanations incised in the Pâli character. One, it is said, is the throne and tree of Kaśyapa, another the throne and tree of Kanaka Muni, and so on through the list of the Seven Great Buddhas.

Every great Buddha has his tree and his worship. And here I must mention a curious piece of Chinese puzzle adjustment, which shows how closely the ritual fits the ancient temple, and the temple the ritual. In Vol. XVI. of the Asiatic Researches, Professor Wilson gives a ritual from Nepal, called the Praise of the Seven Buddhas (p. 453). Each Buddha is "adored" in a separate paragraph, and it is announced that he found emancipation under a special tree. Comparing a list of these trees with that of the Bharhut Stûpa, as given by General Cunningham,* we find that five of the trees exactly correspond. The sixth, that of Visvabhu, is obliterated. Sakya Muni's tree in one list is the asvattha, and in the other the pippala—synonyms for the *Ficus religiosa*. This seems to give great antiquity to the litany.

I will copy down one or two of these addresses :—

"I adore Jinendra, the consuming fire of sorrow, the treasure of holy knowledge, whom all revere, who bore the name of Vipasvi, who was born in the race of mighty monarchs in the city of Bandumati, who was, for eighty thousand years the preceptor of gods and men ; and by whom, endowed with ten kinds of power, the degree of Jinendra was obtained at the foot of a patala-tree."

This is the praise of Śâkya Muni :—

"I adore Śâkya Simha the Buddha, the kinsman of the sun, worshipped by men and gods, who was born at the splendid city Kapilapura, of the family of the

* "Stûpa of Bharhut," p. 46.

chief of the Sâkya kings, the life of which best friend to all the world lasted one hundred years.

" Having speedily subdued desire, undoubted wisdom was acquired by him at the foot of the asvatha tree."

Is it making a great jump to suggest that the little work, the " Praise of the Seven Buddhas," represents the Aryavasas (the Supernatural powers of the Aryas) mentioned on the Bairât Rock and that the Vinayasamaka (Lessons in Discipline) was practically the same as the Twelve Observances. The discipline of Wanderers not allowed to stay more than a day in one place, could not have been very elaborate.

An analysis of Buddha's story tells much.

The torso has been hacked about, but it has proved too stout for the pious Harlequins of the second school of Buddhism. Summed up in a word its main thesis is man's terror of Death and of its two grim attendants, Sickness and Old Age. Buddha, like Christ, proposes to find a remedy. What is that remedy? The Amrita.

Professor Rhys Davids declares that this word does not mean Immortality, but its reverse.* It seems to me that he might as well say that the French word " immortalité," also differs completely in meaning from our word " immortality."

" Amrita," " Immortalitas," " Immortalité," " Immortality," are at once four words and one word —the Sanskrit " Mrita," with a privative, changed in Italy into " Mors," with a privative. Asoka's Council has given us a genuine Buddhist parable. Does it teach that annihilation is the supreme desideratum of humanity? It is very short. I will give it.

THE QUESTION OF UPATISHYA.

Upatishya had one supreme fear, the fear of death. One day, in company with Maudgalyayana (they were

* " Hibbert Lectures," pp. 109 and 137.

both seekers of truth), they witnessed a festival from a hilltop. "See," said Upatishya, "in two hundred years all these living beings will be the prey of death. If there is a principle of destruction, can there not also be a principle of life?"

This was the "Question of Upatishya," and he propounded it to many teachers, but none solved it satisfactorily, until he came across Athadzi, a disciple who expounded to him Buddha's Dharma.

We now come to a valuable piece of testimony, that of a Greek visiting India. Seleucus Nicator sent an ambassador, named Megasthenes, to King Chandragupta (B.C. 302-298). He visited that monarch at his capital, Palibothra, or Patna. His account of the India of that day is unfortunately lost; but through Diodorus Siculus, Strabo, Arrian, and Clement of Alexandria, some valuable fragments have come down to us. Patna, it must be remembered, was in the very heart of the Buddhist Holy Land. Clement of Alexandria cites a passage from Megasthenes, on Indian Affairs. On the same page he thus describes the Indian "philosophers":—

"Of these there are two classes, some of them called Sarmanae, and others Brahmins. And those of the Sarmanae who are called Hylobii neither inhabit cities nor have roofs over them, but are clothed in the bark of trees, feed on nuts, and drink water in their hands. Like those called Encratites in the present day, they know not marriage nor begetting of children. Some, too, of the Indians obey the precepts of Buddha, whom, on account of his extraordinary sanctity, they have raised to divine honours."

The importance of this passage is this, that from Strabo we get the description given by Megasthenes of the Indian philosophers, and it is made certain that the earlier part of this passage is from the same source.

Strabo describes the Brahmins and the "Germanes," also called, he says, "Hylobii." He gives the same details as Clement of Alexandria about their feeding on wild fruits and wearing the bark of trees. He, too, draws a distinction between the Germanes and the Brahmins on the subject of continency, the Brahmins being polygamists.

From this it seems certain that Clement of Alexandria was writing the original work of Megasthenes before him. We may therefore, conclude that this passage about Buddha, sandwiched as it is between two genuine citations, was also in Megasthenes. Strabo had handed down to us another statement of Megasthenes about the Hylobii :—

"By their means the kings serve and worship the Deity."

There can be no doubt that the Sarmanes (Sramanae) and Brahmins of Megasthenes were the Brahmins and the Buddhists. To the first, according to Megasthenes, were confided sacrifices and ceremonies, for the dead as well as for the living. They were a caste apart, and none outside this caste could perform their duties. The gods would not accept the sacrifice of such an interloper. Their ideas on life and death were very similar to those of Plato and the Greeks. The Brahmins ate flesh and had many wives. Every new year there was a great synod of them.

The theories about early Buddhism held by many moderns—sceptical philosophers, like Ludwig Büchner as well as the Bishop of Colombo and the Society for Promoting Christian Knowledge—fade completely away in the presence of these rock chisellings of Asoka. Early Buddhism was "atheism, pessimism, cosmism," says Büchner. Asoka says "Confess and believe in God," and he urged that man's supreme duty was to obtain "union with Sugato." Turnour translates this "the Deity of Happy Advent." And Buddha certainly sought to relieve the Indian mind of the cruel yoke of the Metemphychosis, an idea which plunged him back a thousand times into all the sufferings of old age, disease and death. All who joined his spiritual Sañgha were at once liberated from its woeful entanglements.

Buddhism when it first emerges in the light is Saint-worship. The seven great Buddhas, the seven mortal teachers, instead of residing after death in a Nirvâṇa of Nothingness, were believed still to be interested in human affairs. His houseless monks (Pavajitani) were certainly not the monks of the modern Buddhist convents, contemplative monks are not allowed to speak at all. "The increase of converts is the lustre of religion," says the king in the Twelfth Edict.

"For a very long time there have been no ministers of religion who, intermingling among all unbelievers, may overwhelm them with the inundation of religion, and with the abundance of the sacred doctrines. Through Kamboja, Gândhâra, Surashtra, and Petenica, and elsewhere, finding their way unto the uttermost limits of the barbarian countries, for the benefit and pleasure of all mankind . . . are they appointed. Intermingling equally among the dreaded and among the respected, both in Pataliputra and in foreign places, teaching better things shall they everywhere penetrate." * Edict XII. enjoins that these teachers are to be very gentle and conciliatory with the "unconverted heretics."

"By such and such conciliatory demeanours shall even the unconverted heretics be propitiated, and such conduct increaseth the number of converted heretics."

"Moreover, hear ye the religion of the faithful, and attend thereto, even such as desire the act, the

* Edict IV., Senart.

hope of the beloved of the gods, that all unbelievers may be speedily purified and brought into contentment speedily."*

The imaginary descriptions of Buddhaghosa have the local colour of his day; he could not get beyond that. His account of the Convocation at Buddha's death bristles with splendid monasteries—"eighteen great viharas filled with rubbish" furbished up for the occasion with "flowers," "halls," "preaching desks," "ivory fans." He talks of the "enormous wealth" bestowed by the faithful for religious purposes. And in the account of the Second Convocation he describes lazy monks, fat and idle, living in sumptuous monasteries and disputing whether or not they might have fringes to their couches and drink whey. Professor Oldenburgh pronounces this Convocation a fictitious one, as it is not mentioned in the Sanskrit records. Turnour demolishes it by giving an alleged fact which borders on the farcical. It is said that "eight pious priests" attended it who had beheld Buddha. As the Convocation was held exactly one hundred years after Buddha's death, each of these, as Mr. Turnour shows, must have been at least one hundred and seven years old.†

One hundred and fifty years after the alleged Convocation there came a Greek into the same part of the country, namely Megasthenes. Did he discover these splendid monasteries with "preaching halls" and "ivory fans?"‡ On the contrary he describes certain Wanderers, Sarmanæ, Germanes (the Buddhist Sramanas), water-drinking Wanderers, sleeping under

* Edict V., Prinsep.

† Turnour, *Journ. Bengal As. Soc.*, Vol. VI., p. 723.

‡ The Atthakathâ is the brief used by the missionaries against Buddha.

trees, clad in bark, feeding on wild fruits and vowed to absolute continence.

We have now to consider what I call the religion of S'iva-Buddhism. Summed up in a word, it was the intrusion of S'iva as Bhairava into the early religion, with his "left-handed" Tântrika rites,—sacrifices to demons as well as to new gods and Buddhas. These could not have taken place in Asoka's day, because, as he tells us he forbade animal sacrifice altogether.

Let us begin with the new gods.

CHAPTER VI

THE MAHÂYÂNA

New gods—All of them S'iva—A Mask of Buddhism on some of them—Dhyâni or Heavenly Buddhas—Dhyâni Bodhisatwas—Conversion of the Relic Cairn of Early Buddhism into S'iva's Lingam Disguised as a Chaitya—Chaitya Worship at Mathura—S'iva Buddhism a Worship of S'iva with "Left-handed" Tântrika Rites—It is to be found in all Buddhist Kingdoms—Rapid survey.

THE Mahâyâna movement introduced many new gods.

As a test question let us inquire who, according to the Mahâyâna made the world?

The first answer is—"Îshwara or Âdi Buddha," —the "Cause of all existence." "From his Dhyâna the universe was produced by him!"*

I copy this from Mr. Hodgson's extracts of the old Sanskrit literature rescued in Nepal when Buddhism was driven from India.

Another name is mentioned by him—"Tathâgata." He also made the world, for he is the same being as Âdi Buddha.*

But the matter does not stop here:—

Îshwara being the Absolute, and being imaged as residing in Nirvritti, the awful and untravelled haunts of divine repose, deputed five Dhyâni or heavenly Buddhas to make the World.

* Hodgson, "Religion of Nepal," p. 77.

Their names are :—

(1) Vairochana.

(2) Akshobhya.

(3) Ratna Sambhava.

(4) Amitâbha.

(5) Amoghasiddha.

But these seem to have passed on the work to five "Heavenly Bodhisatwas."*

(1) Samantabhadra.

(2) Vajra Pâni.

(3) Ratna Pâni.

(4) Padma Pâni.

(5) Viswa Pâni.

Still, the number of divine beings credited with making the earth is by no means exhausted :—

"I salute that Dharma (Durgâ) who is Prajnâ Pâramitâ (the Wisdom of the Other Bank), pointing out the way of perfect tranquility to all mortals, and leading them in the paths of perfect Wisdom; who by the testimony of all the sages produced and created all things."†

But even that does not exhaust the whole list.

"For the sake of obtaining Nirvritti I devote myself to the feet of 'Sañgha,' who having assumed the three gunas created the three worlds."‡

But again the list is still unexhausted, for it appears that Sangha in the work of creation is mixed up with Amitâbha.

But the creation of the world even after all this elucidation is still a puzzle, for we learn that Sangha is another name for Padmapâni, one of the "Bodhisatwas," and that Padmapâni is "Avalokitishwara," and "Maitreya," the coming Buddha.§

* Hodgson, "Religion of Nepal."

† *Ibid*, p. 142.

‡ *Ibid*, p. 88.

§ Hodgson, p. 142.

PLATE 6.

THE CHAITYA LINGAM.

S'iva has got a thousand names, and if we concede that the Mahâyâna was his Pantheism we might pass over this absurd and contradictory catalogue of mythological phantoms without much comment. But literal minds, when they discourse about Buddhism, treat all these phantoms as real beings, and make the contradictions doubly contradictory. Resolved into their ultimate these gods are two—Sîva, and Maitreya Buddha or Sîva wearing the mask of Ŝâkya Muni.

What was S'ivism viewed from the outside? "His worshippers," says Professor Hayman Wilson, "contented themselves with flinging 'water, oil and faded flowers' on his emblem the Lingam."

What was early Buddhism viewed from the outside? Offerings to the relics of Ŝâkya Muni, placed under a Tope or Stûpa? (heap).

Now S'iva Buddhism to harmonise these two ideas converted the relic-mound or Chaitya from the curve taken by a heap of stones thrown at random one upon the other to a dome like the lingam.

A rough sketch (Pl. 6) shows how this was done. Above (Fig. 1) is an early cairn, like the Sanchi Tope. Then (Fig. 2) I give the early Lingam, which was a large block of bed-rock, left when excavating a cave-temple. Fig. 3 is a miniature dome-chaitya, the old relic-mound made into S'iva's emblem. In Fig. 4 we get the "Jew's harp," as it is called, the Lingam to be seen in every bazaar.

When Mr. Brian Hodgson went as British Minister to Nepal he was astonished to find an abundance of these lingams. The Chaitya, or relic-mound, had been "metamorphosed into a lingam"; and, as he tells us "its worship may now be seen in numerous instances in Nepal, *e.g.*, at Kâlî's temple, on the road-side near Tundi Khel."* He applied to his teacher, Amirta Nanda Bandhya, who assured him that the

* Hodgson, "Religion of Nepal," p. 137.

borrowing had been on the other way, the Hindus had taken the Buddhist Chaitya and broken off the Chûla mani, or spire, from each, and called it a S'iva lingam, but that is a gloss that we cannot accept.

To build a sepulchral cairn to a dead saint or Buddha, and to honour his relics with offerings and rotatory peregrinations is a conceivable act, especially if, as with the Abbé Paris, strange cures can be effected at his tomb. But to build a sepulchral Tope to a saint who is not yet dead, nor even yet born, is a wild idea. Its object was to banish Sâkya Muni to a Nirvâna of Nothingness, and to change the worship of him and his relic-mounds to a worship of relic-domes despoiled of relics but tenanted by Maitreya, and other Bodhisatwas (monks of high spiritual progress that will one day be Buddhas).

The invaluable Chinese traveller, Hiouen Thsiang, describes in his "history"* the relic-mound worship at Mathurâ when he visited the city. The early Buddhists, the disciples of the Little Vehicle, paid homage to the relics of Sâriputra, Maudgalyâyana, Ânanda, and other great Buddhist saints, who had each one a handsome stûpa in that city, but the disciples of the Great Vehicle "worshipped the Bodhisattwas" in their topes. Fa Hian bears a similar testimony.†

That traveller was nearly lost at sea, but he prayed to "Bodhisatwa Avalokitiswara," and the storm abated. Hiouen Thsiang, on the other hand, was caught by pirates on the Ganges, who proposed to sacrifice him to Durgâ. He prayed to Maitreya Bodhisatwa, the coming Buddha, and likewise escaped.

Now, the forcible intrusion of S'iva and his lingam —and also his left-handed or Tântrika rites is what I call S'iva-Buddhism. Let us make a hasty examina-

* Hiouen Thsiang, "Histoire," p. 104.

† Fa Hian, "Pilgrimage," p. 101.

tion of the chief Buddhist kingdoms, one by one, to see if the change was at all general.

TIBET.

The Tibetans have Tantric rites and human sacrifices, and many writers maintain that these are only outside relics of the earlier, or Bon, religion; but that is against all evidence. The Dalai Lâma claims to be the head of the Buddhist movement. Avalokitishwara (S'iva in person) is said to have brought Buddhism to Tibet.* He is incarnate always in the Dalai Lâma. He is represented like S'iva, with four arms. His wife Avalokitî, as the "White Târâ," is compared by Surgeon-Major Waddell to the Madonna, as regards her benign influence in the community; but she transcends all that has been hitherto imagined of cruel malignity and devilry as "Lha-mo," the "great Mahâranî." "She is credited with letting loose the demons of disease, and her name is scarcely ever mentioned, and only then with bated breath."†

Tibet is also furnished with an army of fiends, the demons of the terrible Kâla-Chakra, as soberly organised as the army of gods and Buddhas. Indeed, they may be described as that army daubed over with Indian ink. Every god of the Brahmans has his counterpart presentment in hell.

These are clothed for the most part in the richest China silks and crapes, and wear pantomine masks, and upon their stomachs human skulls, skulls richly embroidered. And the celestial Buddhas figure as "demoniacal Buddhas," Kâla-Chakra, Heruka, Achala, Vajra-vairabha, etc. The "celestial Bodhisatwas" are also "ferocious and bloodthirsty, and only to be conciliated by constant worship of themselves and their female energies, with offerings and sacrifices,

* Schlagintweit, "Buddhism in Tibet," p. 63.

† Waddell, "Buddhism of Tibet," p. 364.

magic circles, special mantras, charms."* The "energies" of these demoniacal Bodhisatwas are the "Dakkini fiendesses." All the Buddhist Lâmas crowd to the festival of the "She-devil Devî," who is worshipped for seven days like Devî, in India, to gain security from disease for the coming year.†

Of the vast literature of orthodox Buddhist sorcery I will speak in the next section.

NEPAL.

I have already dealt with S'iva worship in Nepal in treating of the Chaitya. Mr. Hodgson found this worship of the Chaitya, or lingam as he supposed it, everywhere. He also was astonished to find the statue of S'iva in every temple, "even in the penetralia."

The Buddhist Dharma, the Sophia of the Gnostics, has for one name "S'iva Sakti," the wife or female energy of S'iva. One of the holy books is called Trikand Sesh (the three-throated Serpent—Sesh, S'iva's emblem). The initiation, or baptism, is given by Mr. Hodgson :—

Several names of S'iva are used in this ritual, Avalokitisvara, Visva Karma, Vajra Pâni, and the postulant vows to devote himself to the worship of the Chaitya. "When the purely Buddhist ritual is exhausted," says Mr. Hodgson, "the Tantric esoteric comes on,—which consists of the worship of the Balis. Flesh, blood and spirits are put into a conch shell. The celebrant wears a mask of Bhairava, and holds his terrible pasá or noose. Nâgas, Yakshas, Râkhsasas, devatas, have all their Balis. Many names are given including the Bali of Mahâ Kâla himself—(S'iva as "great Time").

If the foulest Tantrik rites form the chief part of the initiation of a Buddhist postulant, it seems quite

* Waddell, "Buddhism of Tibet," p. 131.

† *Ibid.* p, 365.

PLATE 7.

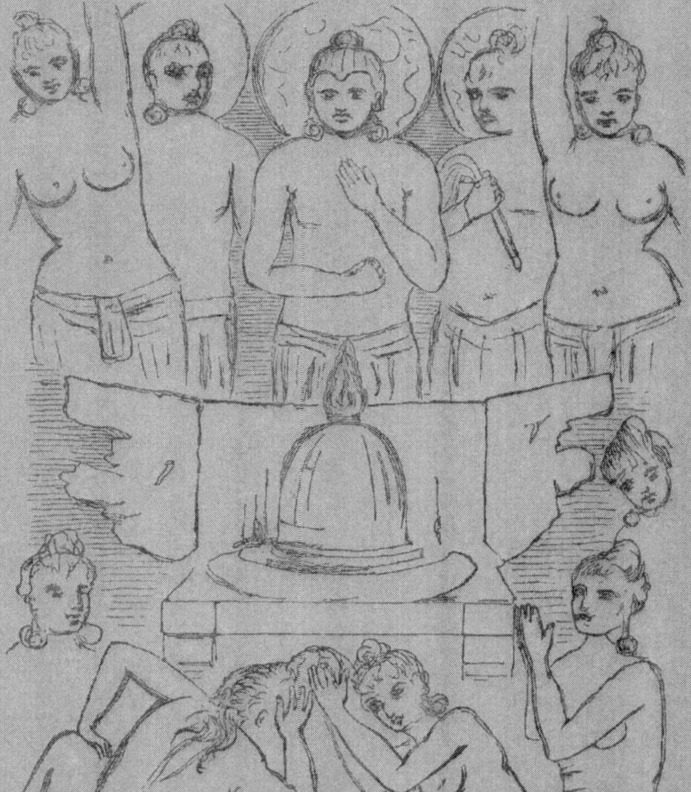

From Amarâvati.

CHAITYA-LINGAM WORSHIP.

PLATE 8.

SAMANA DEVA RÂJAH.

plain that they cannot be called mere barnacles on the outside of the ship.

When the Buddhist hierarchy was driven northward from their monastery at Nalanda near Buddha Gaya, Nepal received for safety a large portion of the esoteric Sanskrit literature. A great number of these rituals are called Tântras, or treatises setting forth the worship of the "left-handed" gods. No less than seventy-four of these Tântras are catalogued by Brian Hodgson, including the terrible Kâla Chakra. Great secrecy is maintained concerning these books.

CHINA.

The Rev. Samuel Beal has told us that the divine being "Quan Yin," was there sometimes worshipped as a female and sometimes worshipped as a male. He has told us, too, that Quan Yin in Chinese is the same as the Sanskrit word Avalokitisvara, or "S'iva looking down." Quan Yin dominates the rituals.

And China, too, has the Kâla Chakra and all the Tântras or esoteric works; and practises all the sorceries. These superstitions are put down to local "Dragon worship" and "Taoism"; but a great religion like Buddhism of old, which has an imposing ecclesiastical centre, and many branch churches which have each in its most secret penetralia some seventy-four cherished spell books and grimoires, expounding secret esoteric rites to, let us say, seventy-four different yakshas—such a church cannot be called a mere prey to paltry local superstitions.

CEYLON.

A god with a white elephant at his feet is a popular print in Ceylon. There are several in Mr. Upham's book. He tells us that this god is Samana Deva Râjah, so called from Samane Galle (Adam's Peak), "where he is now living with his deities with power over Ceylon." The white elephant is Buddha in a Nirvâṇa of uselessness. I give a rough sketch of one of these from my sketch book. A strange, spoon-shaped aureole or cadre surmounts all the principal gods and demons in Ceylon prints, and each stands on a stone,—aureole, god and stone making up the outline of a columnar Lingam. Buddha is reported to have handed over this stone, the Minne Phalange, or Stone of Supremacy, at the date of his death to Samane Deva Râjah.

Sagittarius in the Indian Zodiac is called the Bow of S'iva.

Ceylon took a very prominent part in the present strange revival of interest in the West of the Buddhist movement. Great credit is due to the missionaries, who studied the language for their own purposes. And in the records of the island they found it asserted that the Buddhism of Ceylon was the earliest and genuine Buddhism. But since the travels of the Chinese pilgrim Hiouen Tsiang have been disinterred, that idea is no longer tenable.* The great revolution called the Mahâyâna (Great Vehicle) included Ceylon in its vortex. Indeed, one prominent Oriental scholar, Horace Hayman Wilson, thought that the fusion of strict Buddhism with the Indian religions came from Ceylon.†

Samana Deva Râjah, as his name implies, is Deva or S'iva, and the Kappooism, or devil-dancing in Ceylon, is pretty well known. The amount of devils to be conciliated is large, if according to Mr. Moncure Conway, eighty-four thousand charms are required for the purpose. It is urged that this sorcery is a reminiscence of the Nâga worship that prevailed

* See Monier Williams, "Buddhism," p. 162. Major Waddell, "Buddhism in Tibet," p. 123. See also my "Buddha and Early Buddhism" which deals with the dishonesty of the Cingalese records.

† See Emerson Tennant, "Ceylon," Vol. I., p. 379.

in the island before it was converted to Buddhism. Again we have the defence set up that these devils are mere barnacles on the outside of the ship.

Much has been made of the fact that the names of some of the Mahâyâna gods mentioned at the beginning of this chapter are not known in Ceylon. From this it is argued that Ceylon knows nothing of the Mahâyâna movement, but the names Tathâgatha, Sañgha as a god, Puruså, Maitreya, are in all the rituals and holy books, and these are Mahâyâna gods. The test name is "Maitreya," who according to Professor Rhys Davids under the name of Nâth has his statue in almost all the Wiharas.* In the Mahâwanso it is announced that the Cingalese King Dhatuseno, built a fine temple to Bodhisatto Mettêyyo and "invested his image with every regal ornament."† Guards to the distance of one yogana specially protected this temple. Was this Mettêyyo an ordinary Bodhisattwa, *i.e.*, a yokel ignorant as yet of all spiritual illumination? If so, how did Dhatuseno know that he was to be the next Buddha, and that his name was "Nâth." If, on the other hand, this Maitreya was the clumsy subterfuge by the aid of which the Mahâyâna sought to depose the worship of Sâkya Muni, it is plain that King Dhatuseno was not altogether ignorant of Mahâyâna teachings.

BURMAH.

If a Burmese is knocked down suddenly in the street, he cries out, "Phra Kaiba" ("God help me"), but he does not believe in any God at all. This is what we learn from Bishop Bigandet,‡ who goes on to say that the "God" thus involuntarily invoked cannot be Buddha, for folks there openly maintain

* Rhys Davids, "Buddhism," p. 201.

† Turnour, "The Mahâwanso," p. 258.

‡ "Bigandet," 183.

that Buddha never interferes in human affairs. For Tantrik rites, the Burmese are well furnished with spirits called "Nats." Major Waddell believes that this word is the Sanskrit "Nâth" (Lord), also applied to the Spirits of the left-handed Tântrika. Major Phaire combats this, and says it is an old local word for local demons. The Burmese priests advise the laity to have recourse to the devil dancers when they get ill. A wigwam is built up for the offerings, then the dancer commences to dance softly, working up bit by bit to corybantic frenzy. When she (for a woman is preferred) falls down exhausted and half dead, she is consulted by the sorcerer about the malady, and the Nat that is causing it.

This theory of a Buddha still intelligent, but no longer interested in the cares of humanity, is plainly a version of the teaching of the Seśvara Sankhya, which says the same thing of S'iva.

JAPAN.

I had many opportunities of conversing with Captain Pfoundes, a gentleman who spent more than eight years of his life in a Japanese temple. He tells me that the statue of Amitâbha is everywhere in Japan, under the title of Amida Butz, and that this is quite distinct from Shaky Muni, and much more reverenced by them. Under the title Niorai, a loftier and more abstract divinity, still is known to the Japanese. Here we get Ishwara, also his five activities for Amitâbha is one of the five Dhyâni Buddhas. And the Tantrik rites can, of course, be credited to the Shinto exorcists.

Professor Knox tells us that Shaka Muny is completely obliterated by Amitâbha ; also that the demons of the Islands fought a great battle with the demons of Buddhism on its arrival, but the magical powers of the latter were deemed superior. Then Shinto was pacified on being told that their demons were incarnations of Buddha.*

SIAM.

The Siamese believe that there is no God, only causation (Karma), which word perhaps ought to be rendered "Destiny."

An old scripture, the "Traiphoom" describes the making, and also the periodical destruction of worlds, and the conversion through long stretches of time of devils into angels, and of angels back again into devils.†

In Crawford's "Embassy to Siam" is an account of a funeral procession in honour of a dead king. Sixty or seventy giants and masked figures, gods, Balis, and Yakshas followed the corpse. The left-handed gods of Buddhism are said to be gigantic.

JAVA.

Mr. Crawford, treating of Java, declares that the fact most worthy of attention in respect to the images of Buddha is that they never appear in any of the great central temples as the primary object of worship, but in the smaller surrounding ones.

He instances the fact that the lingam is everywhere and also palpable images of S'iva as the Yogi, or with Ganga in his topknot. His view is that "genuine Buddhism was S'ivism;" and that in Java Buddha is not worshipped at all. It is through him that I can shortly give some valuable information about a head without a jaw, which betrays all the attempts of the Buddhists to appropriate S'ivan temples. Mr. Crawford was before his time.

And what was the philosophy of these Buddhist organisations?

* Knox, "Religion of Japan," p. 88.

† Alabaster, "The Modern Buddhist," p. 17.

The Buddhists of the S'iva Buddha movement were divided broadly into two great schools,—the Swabhavikas and the Aishwarikas.

Mr. Brian Hodgson thus speaks of these two sects :—

"The Swabhavikas deny the existence of immateriality. They assert that matter is the sole substance, and they give it two modes called Pravritti and Nirvritti, or action and rest, concretion and abstraction. Matter itself, they say, is eternal (however infinitesimally attenuated in Nirvritti) ; and so are the powers of matter, which powers possess not only activity, but intelligence."*

On the other hand, as Hodgson tells us, the Aishwarika sect "admits of immaterial essence, and of a supreme, infinite, self-existent Deity, Âdi Buddha (or, as their name suggests, Īshwara S'iva), but they deny that he interferes with the affairs of men."†

These schools are plainly echoes of the two ancient Yoga treatises of S'iva's ascetics, the Karika of Kapila, and the Yoga Ŝâstra of Patanjali.

Launched in the West by the Buddhist missionaries, these two tractates have strongly affected the Gnostics, the Christians, the Moslem, the secret societies of the Middle Ages. And now, thanks to Spinoza, it is their quaint destiny to be the Bibles of the great modern controversy.

Büchner, the High Priest of the Scientists, has declared that the Sankhya's inert, unknowable Ishwara is the God of modern science, whereas, thanks to Spiritualists like Bœhme, and to the Kabbala, S'ivism has had immense influence with the secret mystical societies.

* Hodgson, "Religion of Tibet," p. 23.

† Hodgson, "Religion of Nepal," p. 25.

CHAPTER VII

AVALOKITISHWARA

The great Monastery of Nalanda—The "High Priest of all the World"—Is he the modern Pontiff of Tibet?—S'iva supposed to be incarnate in each successor—S'iva and Durgâ worshipped in all Buddhist rituals.—Great revolution effected by King Kaniska—Strong remonstrance on the part of the "High Priest of all the World"—He declares that the encroaching cultus is pure S'ivism and Nihilism.

SCHLAGINTWEIT tells us that Avalokitishwara brought Buddhism to Tibet in the seventh century A.D.*

We have seen that the Dalai Lâma claims to be the head of the Buddhist Church with Avalokitishwara for divine guide. Was this a more ancient claim?

Certainly, there was a "High Priest of all the world" as early as the second convocation, according to the Mahâwanso,† and this Achârya, as he was also called, was always the pupil of his predecessor, as General Cunningham has pointed out.‡

Hiouen Thsiang throws some light on the status of the Âchârya in his day. He gives him the same title as is given to him in the Mahâwanso. It must be mentioned that India at this time was governed by a powerful monarch, Sîlâditya, whose dominions, according to Dr. Hunter, extended from the Punjab to North-East Bengal—from the Himalayas to the Narbadda River.

* Schlagintweit, "Buddhism in Tibet," p. 63.

† "Mahâwanso," p. 21.

‡ "Bhilsa Topes," p. 72.

But the centre of the Buddhist spiritual power and the centre of the imperial power were many miles apart. The emperor's capital was Kanouj. The Rome of the Buddhists was still in Magadha, and their largest ecclesiastical centre on a mountain at Nalanda (Baragaon). It would seem as if this spot was not in the actual territory ruled by Sîlâditya, for a king named Kumâra, in Eastern India, sent a message to the Mahâthêrô that if he did not send Hiouen Thsiang to him, he would come to Nalanda and make it a heap of ruins. As a nod from King Sîlâditya brought this king fawning along the Ganges in a superb travelling palace to pay his homage, we may presume that Sîlâditya's soldiers were not actually posted at Nalanda. If they had been, King Kumâra would no more have thought of threatening to lay it in ruins than the King of the Belgians would propose to go and burn the palace of the Archbishop of Paris.

Hiouen Thsiang's visit to Nalanda and its convents throws some light on the sunny days of Buddhism. These convents were built by King Śakrâditya and his five successors. There were eight courts surrounded by a long brick wall. Lines of tall towers pierced the sky. Pavilions adorned with coral were surmounted, some with domes, and some with graceful pinnacles, amongst which floated the mountain mists. The houses of the "Men of Pure Life" were four storeyed. The temples had pillars, ornamented with dragons, and rafters shining with rainbow tints. Precious jade adorned the red columns and the richly-carved roof. The pilgrim tells us that Indian architecture was exactly like the Chinese. "Carved balustrades allowed the light to shine through them," says the worthy pilgrim. We can easily conjure up the scene.

Vast tanks outside the convents were spread with the blue lotus. The spot had once been a mango garden, and as such, was given to Buddha by a rich merchant. The fine mango plantations still gave shade to the "Men of Pure Life." Inside, or attached to the convent, when Hiouen Thsiang visited it, were no less than ten thousand monks. Amongst the many convents in India, he adds, were none as rich and as grand as this.*

The Achârya was so respected that "nobody dared even mention his name."† He was alluded to as the "Treasury of Dharma (Saddharmakośa)."

Hitherto, in India, kings and monks had always paid their reverence to the Chinese pilgrim. As his adventures are given to us by two of his disciples, this may be a little exaggeration to gratify Chinese susceptibilities. But when Hiouen Thisang was presented to the Achârya in the Nalanda convent, there can be no mistake as to who paid the homage on that occasion. Twenty old monks introduced the pilgrim to Dharmakośa :—

"When he was in the presence of the superior he paid him all the duties of a disciple, and exhausted every token of homage. In obedience to the sacred regulations and the official etiquette, he (the Chinese pilgrim) moved forwards on his knees, supporting himself on his elbows. He struck the ground with his forehead, and made it resound with the tappings of his feet."‡

The Convocation of Kanouj took place shortly after this, and its details were fixed by the High Priest of all the World.

The Grand Lâma of Tibet seems to me to be the representative of the Âchârya of Magadha, who, on the sacking of the great vihâra of Nalanda, took refuge first of all in North India, and on the expulsion

* "Hiouen Thsiang," Vol. I., pp. 150, 151.

† See p. 144.

‡ "Hiouen Thsang," Vol. I., p. 144.

of the Buddhists from that quarter, escaped to Tibet. The traditions that we possess, though scanty, seem to point to this conclusion. In 1417, there was already a Grand Lâma in Tibet, one Tsonkhapa, a Buddhist from India. Like the earliest Âchâryas, he appointed his successor to the office, one Dharma Rancha.* It is worthy of remark that the Lâma is recognised as the head of the Buddhist Church by the Chinese and Japanese. M. Abel de Rémusat, in his "Origines de l'Hiérarchie Lamaïque," cites the literature of the latter to show that it was conceived that at the death of Buddha he at once reappeared on earth in Bengal as a "teacher" of kings. That seems to be as the Âchârya; and it is stated that Buddha as the Grand Lâma is always on earth.† Gengis Khan patronised the Buddhists; and his grandson officially designated the "Master of Doctrine" in Tibet, the "Living God," the "Self-existent Buddha," etc.‡ Intolerant Mussulmans could only have proceeded to such extremities on the supposition that a vast body of Buddhists in their dominions believed that the Grand Lâma was the Âchârya, and that it was politic to conciliate them.

The Roman Catholic bishop Bigandet, was much astonished to find amongst "the Burmans, Siamese, Cingalese and Tibetans" a distinct "hierarchy, well-defined, with constitutions and laws," with "postulants," "catechumens," "heads of houses and communities," with a "Provincial" whose jurisdiction extends over the Communities of his district, and with a "Supérieur Général." In fact, he found in Buddhism a hierarchical system very like that of the Roman Catholics, with even a Pontifical Court and a College of Cardinals. He makes a special note of

* Schlagintweit, "Buddhism in Tibet," p. 153.

† See pp. 24, 25.

‡ See pp. 27, 28, 29.

the fact that these hierarchies are so solidly organised that they have everywhere lasted through centuries of change.*

Let us now consider the ritual of the Buddhist Churches to see if there is any trace of S'iva worship there.

This is part of the litany in China :—

" And thou ever-present Kwan-shi-Yin Bodhisatwa who hast perfected wondrous merit, and art posessed of great mercy, who in virtue of thine infinite power and wisdom art manifested throughout the universe for the defence and procection of all creatures, and who leadest all to the attainment of boundless wisdom."

Professor Beal gives us this as part of a Chinese ritual. He has explained to us before that Kwan-sh-i yin is Avalokitishwara, that is, " S'iva looking down."

Let us now turn to Nepal.

"I salute that ' Sangha,' who is Avalokitishwara."

This is part of the solemn consecration of the novice.†

Let us now turn to Tibet.

" We implore thee, Oh, Revered Victorious Bhâgavatî (Durgâ) and Merciful one, to purify us and all other beings of the universe thoroughly from the two evil thoughts, and make us quickly obtain the perfection of Buddhahood. If we cannot obtain this perfection within a few life cycles, then grant us the highest heavenly and earthly happiness and all knowledge, and preserve us from evil spirits, plague, disease, untimely death, etc.‡

Here is portion of a hymn addressed to Durgâ as the " White Târâ (Star)."

> All hail Târâ, hail to thee!
> Deliveress sublime,
> Avalokita's messenger
> Rich in power and thought.

* Bigandet " Legende de Gaudama," p. 477.
† Hodgson " Buddhism in Nepal," p. 142.
‡ Waddell, " Buddhism of Tibet," p. 438.

Hail to thee whose hand is decked
With the lotus gold and blue,
Eager soother of our woe
Ever tireless worker thou."

Surgeon-Major Waddell is here reminded of the Litanies to the Virgin Mary. who is "Stella Maris," like Târâ, also "Rosa mystica," the rose doing duty for the lotus in the west.

The word "Durgâ" also means "Tower," and the Virgin Mary is the "Tower of Ivory." Why Ivory? A curious Indian detail.

Other prayers are not so innocent.

"O Ghosts of heroes! Witches! Demoniacal Defenders of the Faith! The holy guardians of the Commandments! and all those that we invited to this place, I beg you all now to depart!

"O most powerful King of the Angry Deities, Strong Iśwara, and the host of Country Guardian Gods and the others that we invited to this place with all their retinues. I beg you all now to depart." *

It is here confessed that the Yakshas and female demons were "invited to the place;" does that mean summoned by black magic?

Now, if we view these separate Buddhist organisations as a whole what do we find?

(1) That the recognised head of the Buddhist hierarchies chased from India, has taken refuge in Tibet, and that this Pontiff now is believed to be S'iva in person.

(2) Everywhere S'iva, and the worship of the Lingam, has displaced the harmless rites of early Buddhism.

(3) Everywhere the Left-handed Tântrikas, the cultus of S'iva as Bhairava, and Durgâ as the terrible corpse-eating Kâlî, is adopted by each Buddhist hierarchy in cases of sickness and worldly trouble.

* Waddell, "Buddhism in Tibet," p. 443.

(4) Hodgson, giving the ritual of initiation, not of Nepal alone, but of Nalanda, the Buddhist Rome, shows that the postulant is given a little model Lingam with his rosaries and begging bowl and other monkish necessaries, and is thus solemnly conjured :—

" First of all devote yourself to the Worship of the Chaitya," * the miniature Lingam.

(5) The worship of S'iva has invaded every ritual. " I salute that 'Sangha,' who is Avalokitishwara, etc."

(6) The popular chapel, if we may so call it, of the Buddhist Cathedral, is a chapel for cultus of S'iva.

(7) All the Lâmas take part in the great Festival of the New Year in honour of " She Devil Devî." And I will show by and by that the Cingalese honoured Pattinee and her son with a similar festival, the Perahar. Each lasted seven days, and was in fact the Durgâ Pûjah.

(8) The Bible of S'iva Buddhism is the Yoga S'âstra, the Bible of the deistic followers of S'iva.

(9) The pihlosophy of S'iva Buddhism goes completely on the lines of the controversy between the two forms of the Sankhya philosophy—that which proclaims and that which denies a God.

Now this is no case of mere barnacles outside a ship. The barnacles have boarded the vessel and a " barnacle" commands.

Many Orientalists have almost confessed this, but they will not consider each Buddhist organisation as a portion of a harmonious and carefully organised whole. Professor Rhys Davids believes the Âdi Buddha came into existence in the tenth century, A.D. ; and Hindus only half converted, " whose minds were still steeped in Brahmin mythology and philosophy," craved after

* Major Waddell cites the ritual at length and bears witness to its general application.

their old gods and restored the ancient rites.* Surgeon-Major Waddell believes that "Tantrism" came into Buddhism in the seventh century A.D., and that the Buddhists of India brought in the worship of Durgâ in order to secure the support of the semi-origines,† but, if so, why did they wait twelve hundred years for this desired assistance. In point of fact, the Buddhists had that support all along, for Buddhism was practically the religion of the yellow races and Pariahs, who were forbidden by the white-faced Aryas to cultivate the spiritual life, or even to look into the holy books under penalty of death.

And there is a crucial reason why S'iva-Buddhism cannot be attributed to piecemeal and independent influences acting from time to time from the outside. The change must have been from the centre outwards, for a hierarchy in each Buddhist kingdom had to be moved, and a hierarchy is established to suffocate novel ideas, not to propagate them. Bishop Bigandet, as we have seen, informs us that the Buddhist hierarchies mock time and its changes They calmly watch the rise and fall of creeds and monarchies, and governments from beyond the seas. In their presence even the Vatican is a mushroom.

Now it seems to me that unusually strong leverage must have been put in motion to simultaneously push all the hierarchies then in existence to radical change. And since the days of Asoka no other monarch had appeared in history who seemed as well qualified as Kaniška for the gigantic task. With threats and wiles, Nalanda and the Buddhist pope would have to be converted. The hierarchies must have worked from the centre outwards.

Of course, the great change was almost unthinkable. It was a Makara swallowing an elephant like the

* "Buddhism," p. 206.

† Waddell, "Buddhism in Tibet," p. 27-129.

Capricorn of the Indian Zodiac. I was at first as sceptical as the rest of the world; although, knowing nothing of the theories of Mr. Beal, I myself had already accepted about half of it, and put it forward in my "Popular Life of Buddha" in the year 1883. I believed that the worshippers of S'iva had changed the philosophy of early Buddhism, but I never guessed that they had forced on the rising creed a new God, new rites, new architecture, new biography.

I will quote a passage :—

"We see from the writings of Hiouen Thsiang that from its political side the movement was aimed against the authority of the Âchârya of Magadha, the Rome of the Buddhists. Kaniśka, a powerful Kashmîri, had conquered vast territories that included Hindû Kush, Kabul, Yarkand, Khokan, Kashmir, and Ladâk,—the plains of the Upper Ganges as far as Agra,—the Punjâb, Râjputâna, Guzerat, Scinde. Such a large Buddhist empire would require a strengthened discipline amongst the great army of monks. Magadha was not included in this empire, and the two leading monks of Kaniśka, Pârśvika, and Vasubandhu may have wished to etsablish an ecclesiastical authority independent of the 'High Priest of all the World,' as the Âchârya of Magadha is called in the Mahâwanso. Perhaps the authority of the latter was ill-defined, and perhaps it had become weakened, now that Magadha was no longer the head quarters of a large empire. The leader of the religious movement was a monk of the convent of Ayodhyâ—a visionary, one Asangha, who was transported one night to the heaven Tuśita, and received the Yoga S'âstra, the principal scripture from Maitreya himself. He indited many of the chief S'âstras of the innovating Buddhism. He presided at the Convocation summoned by King Kaniśka to introduce it. The King wanted to hold the Convocation at Magadha.

"He wished to repair to Râjagriha," says Hiouen Thsiang, the Chinese pilgrim, "to the stone palace where Kaśyapa had formed the collection of sacred books. But the Honourable Pârśvika (his senior monk) said to him:—'Take care, in that city are many heretics. Many conflicting opinions will be expressed, and we shall not have time to answer and refute them. Why compose S'âstras? The whole convocation is attached to this kingdom. Your realms are defended on all sides by high mountains under the guardianship of Yakshas.'*

"It is plain from this that the new creed was established in the teeth of the High Priest of Magadha in his head-quarters at Nalanda, but Magadha afterwards took it up."†

But the garrulous Chinese pilgrim lets in a great deal more light. He tells us what the early Buddhists said of the change:—

"They said that the doctrine of the Great Vehicle did not come from Buddha at all." It "differed in nothing from the teachings of the Kâpâlikas." It was the "Carriage that drives to Nothingness" (Śunyapushpa).

It is difficult to condense the controversy more lucidly than this. The word Śunyapushpa describes the great Bible of the new creed, the Rakshâ Bhâgavatî, a philosophy called justly by Brian Hodgson blank "Pyrrhonism." It was urged that man was nothing, the outside world was nothing, he came from nothingness, and to nothingness would return. Rajendra Lala Mitra, the great native Orientalist, said that this school, the Śunya Vâdis, was a well-known school of Hindu philosophers—plainly S'iva worshippers. The Kâpâlika is the naked S'iva mendicant, who,

* Hiouen Thsiang "Memoirs" (Vol. I., p. 174), translated by Stanislaus Julien.

† Lillie's "Popular Life of Buddha," pp. 175, 176.

PLATE 9.

THE HEAD WITHOUT A JAW.

smeared with cow dung and ashes, haunts tombs and eats offal.

The pilgrim announces that the leader of the great change was a Buddhist monk of the monastery of Ayodhyâ, a visionary named Asangha, who was miraculously transported one night to the Heaven Tuśita to the presence of Maitreya, the coming Buddha. From his sacred hand he received the Bible of the new creed, the Yoga S'âstra.* Now this volume, of course, had been the Bible of the followers of S'iva for hundreds of years, a fact that Asangha did not seem to know. Its alternative title is "Sesvara Sankyha" (The Treatise of S'iva, the Serpent Sesh), and one of the two chief schools of the innovating Buddhism that of the Aiśwarikas, or followers of Ishwara (S'iva) plainly modelled all their ideas on this volume. Of them more hereafter.

In a chapter about Avalokitishwara, there is one other point of great importance. A stray passage in Crawfurd's "History of the Indian Archipelago" seems to me to throw much light upon him. Mr. Crawfurd says that S'iva worship in these regions has quite displaced the worship of Śâkya Muni, and he mentions a very curious fact. In the temples he saw often a monstrous head without a lower jaw. He asked the Munis what this meant, and he was told that it represented S'îva. Now the word "Avalokitiswara" means "S'iva looking down." At once I jumped to the conclusion that the single head without the jaw was a simple expedient to accentuate his all-seeing eyes. I was soon able to collect ample evidence that this surmise was correct. I made some sketches, which I reproduce. (Plate 9).

No. 1 and No. 2 I drew from idols in the India Museum, South Kensington. No. 3 comes from Tibet.

* Hiouen Thsiang, "Histoire," translated by Stanislaus Julien, p. 114 *et seq.*

I took it from Major Waddell's book. No. 4 shows the goggle eyes in profile.

The central design on the same page is from the "Essay on the Architecture of the Hindus" by Râm Râz, a native gentleman, published in the year 1834. He calls this design a specimen of the "Ornaments at the top of a Vimâna." His work gives numerous drawings of temples and gateways (gopuras), and this strange head with the black goggle eyes, and I may add, this strange arch, dominates almost every one. It is plain that it means S'iva in his character of Avalokitiswara, S'iva who looks down on all things; and the absence of the lower jaw is a homely way of accentuating the importance of this special divine function. It is to be observed that this head of Down-looking S'iva is not always without a lower jaw. Major Moor's Hindu Pantheon has many specimens of this divinity, some with lower jaws, some without. It came to Greece as the head of Pan. It was also the Gorgon, as S'iva and Durgâ are one.

Another thing it certainly does, it gives us a touchstone which enables us to detach the symbolism of S'iva-Buddhism from the symbolism of the earlier cultus.

CHAPTER VIII

THE CAVE TEMPLE AND ITS MYSTERIES

Maurice on Temple Worship—Description of Cave Temples—Worship the same in Egypt and Persia—Immense labour employed in constructing them. Cave Mysteries everywhere an object of dread—Cicero on them—Elusis—Lucian on Tree Festival at Hieropolis—Bacchantic Festivals derived from S'iva as Somnâth (Lord of Soma, the first intoxicant)—These Festivals still secretly celebrated in India.

A BOOK was published in 1806 entitled "Indian Antiquities." Its author was named Maurice. On some points no doubt its knowledge is behind our present knowledge, but we get a learned and intelligent writer dealing freely with the matter that was available. The question of the Cave temple and its mysteries specially attracted him.

Mr. Maurice holds that the old Cave temple was an apparatus so accurately fitted in all its parts to certain special requirements, that the Cave temples of India, Egypt, and Eleusis, exhibiting as they do the same means to the same end, must have had the same origin. In the case of Eleusis we know that the idea was brought from Egypt by Melampus.

From Mr. Maurice we can get a fairly good idea of one of these Indian Cave temples. They are said by the natives to be "the work of giants and genii in the earliest ages of the world." They are "admitted to be of the most profound autiquity, of such profound antiquity, indeed, that we are unable to obtain any light concerning the particluar era of their fabrication." Of the excavations in the Island of Salsette he writes that Grose in his "Voyage to the East Indies" declares that "their formation would have required a labour equal to that of erecting the pyramids of Egypt." In the same caves are "above six hundred idols, ninety of them in and about the great pagoda." An artist who made sketches there for Governor Boon was so struck with the magnitude of the colossal work that he declared the labour must have occupied forty thousand men for forty years together.

Maurice tells us that the mighty stone giants in these caves were carefully painted, a fact which made them more awful and imposing in the dim light. Two figures at Salsette were twenty-seven feet in height. The great triple bust at Elephanta is "fifteen feet from the base to the top of the cap," whilst the face of another statue, measured by Mr. Grose, is five feet in length.

We must now turn to Maurice's description of an Indian Cave temple. He starts with Elephanta:—

"This astonishing Pantheon of the gods presents itself about half-way up the steep ascent of the mountain, from whose strong bosom it is excavated. Ovington states the dimensions of this temple at about one hundred and twenty feet, and the height at eighteen feet. The enormous mass of solid rock above is supported by four rows of pillars of beautiful proportion, but of an order of architecture totally different from that of Greece. The Capital is also fluted, and is described by Mr. Hunter as having the appearance of a cushion pressed flat by the superincumbent mountain. Along the sides of the cavern are ranged those mighty colossal statues before alluded to, to the number of forty or fifty, each of them twelve or fifteen feet in height. Some of them have aspects that inspire the beholder with terror, and in the words of

PLATE 10.

A CAVE TEMPLE.

Linschoten are distorted into 'such horrible and fearfull formes that they make a man's hayre stand upright.'"

The temple was an observatory, a model of the Kosmos, the figures sculptured on the walls were in their ultimate the heavenly bodies.

"At the west end of the grand pagoda is a dark recess, or Sacellum, twenty feet square, totally destitute of any external ornament except the altar in the centre, and the gigantic figures which guard the four several doors that lead into it. These figures, according to Niebuhr, are naked; are eight in number, two to each door. They are of the enormous height of thirteen feet and a half, and appear starting from the wall to which they are attached. These formidable guardians of this sacred recess point out the use to which it was applied. It was devoted to the most sacred mysteries of their religion."*

This, by the worshippers of S'iva, is deemed the Holy of Holies in their temples. It is called the "Sanctuary of the S'iva Lingam," the Lingam that is specially holy. "The Catechism of the Shaiva Religion," by a Hindu writer, Sabhapati Maudalyar, may be here consulted. He announces that none but Ati Shaiva Brahmins may enter this recess (p. 53).

Additional details are furnished by a German Orientalist.

Lassen, in his "Indische Alterthumskunde," has furnished us with an account of the Greater Mysteries in an Indian Cave temple. Mr. Mackenzie, an English Freemason, gives a capital digest of this, he considering that these rites are very like the secret rites of Masonry. At eight years of age the child girded on the sacred Cord. For the "Fellow Craft degree of the Mason," as Mr. Mackenzie, calls it, the disciple was "led into a gloomy cavern in which the apporheta

* Crawfurd, "Hist. Indian Archipelago," p. 226.

were to be displayed to him. Here a striking similarity to the Masonic system may be found." Three chief officers or hierophants are seated in the east, west, and south, attended by their subordinates. After an invocation to the sun, an oath was demanded of the aspirant of implicit obedience to his superiors, purity of body, and inviolable secrecy. Water was then sprinkled over him. He was deprived of his sandals and shoes, and was made to circumambulate the cavern (query the Mahâdeo in the middle of it) thrice. Suitable addresses were then made to him, after which he was conducted through seven ranges of caverns in utter darkness. The piercing shrieks of Mahâdevî rent the air, she like Mylitta and Isis bewailing the fact that S'iva, or Time, had grown impotent in the winter, and that earth without him would lack food and perish.

The ancient mysteries depicted the passage of a soul through hell to heaven, and in the scenes described by Lassen, the initiate in the midst of his trepidations was suddenly confronted with the φωτισμος. A brilliant light flashed into the darkness and disclosed Kailâs, the heaven of S'iva, "redolent with perfume and radiant with all the gorgeous beauty of an Indian clime, the Gandharves sounded their vînas and sang their sublime songs. Beautiful Apsaras danced around to give a representation of Heaven. This they certainly got in the Cave temple of Elora. The patient Indians, provided only with a small steel chisel and an iron mallet, had converted a mountain into a paradise, into one of the wonders of the world."

Cicero declared that the word "mysteries" was in his day almost synonymous with "abominations," because it was generally believed that human flesh was eaten in them. Human sacrifices were offered at Saturn's festivals. Plutarch, in Themistocles, mentions three beautiful women who were at the same time offered to Bacchus. Clement, of Alexandria, states that Erectheus, King of Athens, and Marius, a Roman general, both sacrificed their daughters. Livy describes the bloody rites of the worship of Bacchus.

These mysterious rites at first were imparted only to few, but afterwards communicated to a great number of both men and women. To the religious ceremonies of these were added the pleasures of wine and feasting in order to allure a greater number of proselytes. Livy goes on to declare that horrible scenes of debauchery were witnessed, as well as secret murders. There was loud shouting, and the noise of drums and cymbals so that none of the cries of persons suffering violation or murder could be heard abroad. One, Rutilus, had a step-son named Aebutius whom he wanted to get rid of. He persuaded the young man's mother to get him initiated into the mysteries of Bacchus. Aebutius had a female friend named Hispalia. He told her of his resolve.

"May the gods forbid," she cried. "Better for both of us to die." Asked for the meaning of these words she confessed that she had accompanied her mistress once to Bacchanalian celebrations, and that the orgies she witnessed there were too awful for words. To think nothing unlawful was the grand maxim of this religion, and that all who showed any disinclination in submitting to dishonour, or the commission of vice, were sacrificed at once as sacred victims.

It is to be observed that the food offered to the gods was considered the food of the gods, and as such immortal food. What wonder that in the Greek rites of Bacchus folk battled for the wine and the warm blood.

But in dealing with ancient mysteries if we treat the question from the point of view of naturalism, we are liable to go wrong. The excitement produced by the new intoxicants was viewed at first like the frenzy of the prophet, an influence beyond the earth, and supremely holy. This mistake could by-and-bye give birth to many excesses, but there is no doubt that an intoxicant soon became the chief ingredient in all temple worship. Even in our own days the "Cup" is forbidden to the laity in the Roman Church because originally the laity represented the non-initiates.

Turning to Eleusis, a suburb of Athens, we find a Cave temple, and similar ceremonies. All the city in solemn procession marches to the "Holy Fig Tree" along the "Sacred Way," the Mustai proud of their garlands, the Epoptai or complete initiates in their white garments bear proud myrtle on their brows. A monotonous low chant such as we hear at Indian festivals goes up into the balmy air, recounting the woes of the mighty mother, the wife of Kronos.

That lady, who gave Agriculture to Greece, comes flaunting along in her car drawn by dragons.

The procession now reaches the great Temple, and all who are not initiates are warned away, for the penalty is death to all who reveal the mysteries and all who discover them. There are seven dark caverns and seven light ones. Ceres, and Bacchus, with his torch, are supposed to be seeking Porsepine in hell. Earth abandoned by the goddess no longer bears fruits, like the Indian soil deprived of S'iva's creative force. Hence the wailings and lamentations that occur. The initiate goes through the dark caverns, and the light ones. Thrice blessed is the postulant who is able at last to repeat the culminating formula :—

"I have fasted. I have drunk the Cyceon. I have taken out of the Cista and placed that which I took into the Kalatheon. I have taken out of the

Kalatheon and placed that which I took into the Cista."*

Lucian gives an account of the Tree festival at Hieropolis which reads very like the Durgâ-Pûjah in India. The sacrifices and processions are described as being of the splendid and extravagant description. Multitudes flocked there from all countries, including Brahmins from India. And it is said that the visitors brought their gods with them, a detail that throws light on the similarities that we find everywhere. The two mighty Mahâdeo Columns in front had an inscription that unblushingly stated what these columns symbolised. Maurice draws a parallel between the Kusbis of the Indian temples and the Syrian matrons, who as Bunsen puts it "could only escape being sacrificed to the gods by prostitution." The main thesis of Lucian is that the Dea Syria was taken from the Greek Rhea, the wife of Kronos; and that the noise of the drums and the clashing of cymbals denoted the warring winds and boiling waters, and the roar and crackle of the subterranean fires, to show the grief of earth that her womb was still uncultivated. Especially noisy were the rattling sistra and the clashing of the various implements of husbandry, which in the first instance were of brass. The priests were said to be eunuchs, and many young men dismembered themselves during the frenzies of the rites.

Of the actual tree worship, Lucian gives an interesting picture. "They cut down," he says, "a number of large trees and set them upright in the fore court of the temple. Then bringing together goats, sheep, and other victims proper for their purpose, they hang them up alive on these trees. To these are added birds, articles of apparel, and various sorts of furniture, jewels, in short, whatever the devout in their benevolence pleased to contribute to so solemn

* "Eleusinian and Bacchic Mysteries," T. Taylor, p. 16.

a sacrifice." Then the trees are set on fire, and the poor animals burnt alive.

But Mylitta had rites more sinister still. Near the temple was a mighty chasm made by the gods in order to drain off the water of Deucalion's Deluge, so ran the legends. Into this chasm animals are flung, and babies in sacks. The tree goddess, Mylitta, was fond of babies. Had this rift and its sinister rites any connection with S'iva and his subterranean home? The two great columns were said to be very much older than the rest of the temple, and to represent some earlier worship. The place was then called "Mahog," which name Colonel Wilford connects with the Mahâbhâga of the Purânas?

Love, lust, wine, gluttony, cruelty, mixed with religious fervour, have they not had their orgies in all lands? The carnival was always the carnival, and the Feast of Fools in the Middle Ages with its "Boy Bishop," and his rollicking companions burlesquing for three days all the holy rites in the cathedral, —that, with much else, was Bacchantic enough.

Mr. Mackenzie, a Freemason, in the passage he cites from Lassen, says that the initiation of the Freemasons is very like the initiation in the Indian temple. One or two of these details can easily be learned by a non-initiate, from Masonic tractates. Over the "Grand-master's" head is a canopy marked with the equilateral triangle which is the special emblem of S'iva. It symbolises also the God worshipped by the Masons, and is called "Le Delta sacré," in France. The triangle is somewhat lamely repeated in the Masonic trowel. Then when the frightened postulant with a "cable tow" (Durgâ's pasha) round his neck is introduced to the conclave, he finds each initiate clutching his neck in a throttling manner to emphasise the absolute necessity of secrecy. The crowning ceremony of all the circling round the "Copestone" need not be dwelt on in these pages. Plainly the "Copestone" is the Mahâdeo. One thing is certain. The terrible secret society of the Thugs or Bhurtotes in India is very ancient. Colonel Meadows Taylor found evidence of these stranglers in the bas reliefs of Elora. They most probably date from a day when the religion of S'iva was furiously persecuted by the Brahmans, and terrorism had to oppose terrorism.

An article in the Asiatic Researches, Vol. VIII., seems to furnish the backbone of the Mystery of S'iva. It gives from the Mahâkâla Sanhita, the death of the Year-god. S'iva dies at Easter and rises up almost immediately as Bâlishwara the Baby-S'iva, the New year. This death in all the old religions took place March 24th, and the resurrection on March 25th. A human victim personified the god.

The "abominations" that shocked Cicero have been going on in India from the earliest days. The Bacchantic festivals seem, even in name, to have been derived from India, for the word Bacchus with some Orientalists is a form of the Sanscrit word Bhâga, the special emblem of maternity. S'iva as Somnâth, is Lord of the Soma, the earliest intoxicant; and he figures as in Greece as a drunken Silenus at the festivals.* Intoxicating liquors, blood (sometimes human), flesh, and fish, are ingredients of the banquet. A woman, stark naked, personifies the Goddess. "These votaries of Sakti assemble at midnight in retired places," says the Reverend W. Simpson, the editor of "Moor's Pantheon," "every stage of the proceedings is invested with a mystical meaning, and the whole terminates in licentious sensual indulgence." This author declares that he had good authority for the statement that they still existed in Madras in his day.† It must, however, be mentioned that the rites of the followers of S'iva are

* "Jacobs's Mythological Dictionary, Article "S'iva."

† Moor, "Hindu Pantheon," Madras edition, p. 365.

divided into two sections, the Right-handed Tantrik rites, the Dakshinas, and the Left-handed Tantrik rites, the Vâmâcharîs. This means practically Black and White magic. The early gods were ranged at different sides of the Zodaic, and the Tantrikas were the worship of the wicked gods, the worship of S'iva as Bhairava and Durgâ as Kâlî. At the beginning, all were no doubt wicked, and much like the gods of Dahomey. And perhaps the rudest excesses of the festivals were deemed logical in some rude days of polyandry. The Sakti sect represents only a small portion of S'iva's followers.

CHAPTER IX

ARCHITECTURE

Mr. James Fergusson—The " Sangharâma of Kasyapa "—Was it Elora ?—Points of contact—Kailâs—Importance of the head of Avalokitishwara—Found on all S'ivan buildings ancient and modern—Buddhist arch, the head of the Cobra—Serpent not worshipped in Buddhism until union with S'ivism—Fergusson on the Lingam—Calls it a " Dagoba "—Believes the Kailâs temples at Elora, and the Mahabalipur Rathas, to have been intended for dormitories of Buddhist monks—Proposition contested—Strange discovery that Avalokitishwara's head is very plentiful on both these old groups of rock-detached temples.

VICTOR HUGO affirms that art throws more light on an early creed than literature, for literature, unfortunately, can be much falsified by mistaken religious zeal. Can art help our present inquiry ?

A puerile story in the sacred books of the natives of India sometimes means much, as we have seen. I commence with a legend from the Purânas.

One Andheke, a Daitya, that is, one of a non-Aryan race, conquered the Dikpalas in fight, and obliged them to take refuge in the " Immoveable Mountain " (Mandara Achala), the lofty home of the Brahman gods. But the Dikpalas, assisted by their gods, returned in great force, and put Andheke and his army to flight ; and the Daitya had to take refuge in a cave, twelve Kos (twenty-four miles) deep. In these straits he sacrificed to S'iva, who came to help him, and after the victory the god remained with him in the cave under the title of Andhekisvara.

The legend was, of course, written to account for the Cave-worship of the followers of S'iva. They seemed to have used caves as early certainly as the date of the Rig Veda, when Bala detained the cows there until struck with the bolt of Indra. A distinguished French Orientalist tells us that Bala was the father of the Asuras (demons) and the cave that he frequented was the mighty darkness of night, and the cows the morning rays. This may be the case, but the poet in his boldest flights has probably something concrete to go upon. Might he not have known of a real Bala, in a real cave, with real cows? At a place called Bolor, the Chinese Pilgrim, Hiouen Thsiang, saw folks who, to escape the cold, occupied the caverns around in company with their beasts.

We must now consider S'iva from the point of view of Architecture.

And the subject is beset with difficulty. If we can produce evidence that the worship of large fragments of bed-rock in a cave as a symbol of life, and its giver, has been utilitarian, open, and long anterior to the Sex worship in Egypt and Assyria, we strengthen our case that the religion of Bal, Bel, Ba'al, Belenus, takes its origin in India; but to establish this in at all a satisfactory manner will require a separate chapter, for a celebrated authority on Indian architecture has got half India to believe that the cave temples of S'iva are very modern, in fact that they are mere copies of the cave temples of the Buddhists.

Mr. James Fergusson came out to India as a merchant about the year 1826; and having amassed, fortunately for himself (and still more fortunately for the world), an Indian fortune, he went home and became an architect with a view to a profound study of the architecture of India, which from the first seems to have interested him very much. He was gifted with a quick intelligence and great industry; and he brought out many valuable works, revealing to the English public the wealth of topes and caves and Dravidian Gopuras and Salukian shrines, which in those days were crumbling away unheeded and misvalued.

But Mr. Fergusson, as all who knew him can testify, was very decided in his opinions and very masterful—witness the fact that he persuaded the Home Government to place him on a Committee with half-a-dozen military experts, to settle what heavy guns, and what casemates, should be set up to make the south coast of England secure against hostile battleships, although there is no evidence that Mr. Fergusson had ever been in a casemate in his life.

I do not, of course, propose to write a treatise on Indian architecture. It will be enough for my special study if I examine four statements of Mr. Fergusson, which contain the pith of the matter.

(1) He held that the Cave temple of Elora was a Buddhist Cave temple dating some time between 750 and 950 A.D.*

(2) He believed that the large lump of bedrock that figures in most of the caves, and which the natives of India call a "lingam," was a Buddhist "Dagoba." This word is written "Dhatugarbha" in the Mahâwânso (womb or enclosure of a portion of the human body).

(3) He held that the Cave temples of the followers of S'iva came into existence after the Cave temples of the Buddhists.

(4) He asserts that the five Raths or detached, rock-cut edifices of Mahavalipur were executed in the fifth or sixth century A.D.†

Early Buddhism had for its temples large numbers of funereal cairns spread over India, each containing, or said to contain, the ashes of Buddha or other saintly

* Fergusson, "Hist. Ind. Architecture," p. 337.

† Fergusson, "Hist. Ind. Architecture," p. 326.

human ashes. The worship, in a word, was the worship of Buddha by peregrination round a cairn.

Kaniśka changed all this. A theory was started that Buddha was non-existent; that great Buddhas on obtaining the Buddha-hood were absorbed into the divinity. The Cave temple was introduced and cairn worship discouraged.

In the year 400 A.D. a Buddhist pilgrim from China named Fa Hian visited the Dekhan. He describes a great "Sangharâma of a former Buddha, Kasyapa." Until Mr. Fergusson's day most Orientalists declared that this must be Elora. "It was constructed out of a great mountain of rock," says the Chinese traveller, "hewn to the proper shape." This seems to point to a detached rock-cut temple like Kailâs in Elora, or the Raths of Mahâbalipur. Fa Hian describes many cave temples, but never uses such language about them. The Chinese traveller did not see the temple. The country around was uninhabited and dangerous to the traveller, ; indeed, the pilgrim was advised to fly. "The law of Buddha was unknown."

Now the first question to ask is, Where is this great temple? If it was in the Dekhan at the date of Fa Hian it must be there still. A large rock-cut temple is one of the few things that cannot be conjured away. Was it Elora?

In 1825, Captain Seely, an Indian officer, published a work, "The Wonders of Elora," which gives a careful and very minute description of the rock excavations. Let us compare this and the Chinese account of Kasyapa's "Sangharâma."

To begin with, there is a statue of Kasyapa at Elora. He was one of the Seven Great Saints of the Brahmans (the Seven Rishis), but also one of the Seven Mânushi, or Mortal Buddhas. We can understand that the Chinese pilgrim, when hearing from outsiders a number of unfamiliar names, Brahman gods and saints, warriors, giants, demons,—would have fastened on that most familiar with a Buddhist. Fa Hian was told the temple had five storeys, " the lowest is made with elephant shapes, and has five hundred stone cells."

" On entering," says Captain Seely, " various figures are represented, especially Bhavânî (Durgâ) sitting on a lotus, and two elephants with their trunks entwined by her. On either side under a ledge of rock, which serves as a bridge for communicating with the great temple, and the rooms over the entrance, are two elephants in a mutilated state."*

" The second (storey)," says Fa Hian, " is made with lion shapes and has four hundred chambers. The third is made with horse shapes and has three hundred chambers."

" On the eastern and southern sides of the great temple," says Seely, " are two flights of stairs winding inwards half way up, thirty-six in number. These bring you to a portico.

" On the top of this portico are the remains of a lion, and on the inside two figures of Sphinxes " ; but our author tells us that numbers of elephants, lions, and other animals abound, sculptured in part, but with much of their bodies buried away as if they were in the act of supporting the vast mass of rock above. Amongst these the informants consulted by Fa Hian might easily have found their " horse."

Says Fa Hian, " The fourth is made with ox shapes and has two hundred chambers ; the fifth is made with dove shapes and has one hundred chambers."

At this point Professor Beal, the acute Chinese scholar, intervenes, and convicts Fa Hian of misreading the word " Po lo yu," which he renders " Pârâvita," (a pigeon), whereas it should have been " Pârvatî " (Durgâ). Now above the portico already described there is a separate room built, with a fine

* Seely, " Elora " p. 101.

"figure of Nandi," the bull of S'iva, with the god and Durgâ riding upon it, bulls being plentiful at Elora. Turning to Captain Seely's frontispiece, a view of the Cave of Indra, we see that above the excavations was a patch of bare hill, but across this higher up was a wall or entablature with sculptured figures. This might be called an additional storey, Pârvatî's storey. Pârvatî means "mountain" as well as the goddess. Hiouen Thsiang, another Buddhist traveller, describes a fine five-storeyed Sangharâma with large halls, and Buddhas cast in gold. This spot he calls Brahmaragiri (the mountain of Brahmara, or Durgâ). Professor Beal suggests that these two mountains, Pârvatî mountain, and Brahmaragiri mountain, and the two temples, are probably one and the same.

Neither of these Chinese travellers saw this temple, we must recollect, and each calls it a Sangharâma. But all the old travellers call Elora a Hindu temple. Captain Seely, who made the closest study of all, calls it a temple of S'iva and Durgâ, and says that the lingam is everywhere.

At the great entrance of Kailâs are two enormous statues of S'iva and Durgâ, one on each side. The Holy of Holies, says Captain Seely, is a bare cave with a lingam in the middle. Two mighty giants with clubs guard the Sacullum, and a great statue of Nandi, the bull, also stands sentry by it.

Heeren, the learned German, makes a strong point in favour of the antiquity of these temples. He says that the inscriptions are in Sanskrit, which points to a date when Sanskrit was a spoken language in India. A pious donor erecting, say a fine hospital in Manchester, would not record the fact in the language of the Ancient Britons. Sanskrit was no longer a spoken language about 300 B.C.

Professor Beal mentions that the rock temple described by Hiouen Tsiang was according to that

Plate 11.

After Daniell.]

KAILÂS, SEEN FROM THE TOP.

authority erected by King Sadvaha at the instance of Nâgârjuna,* who for the mighty outlay necessary for the purpose changed all the "great stones" to gold. It is possible that Nâgârjuna influenced the King, and it is possible that this monk, as Beal thinks, was the chief agent in effecting the great Buddhist change of front. But if he was mixed up in any way with Elora it must have been only in burnishing it up with a little Buddhist polish. Recollect that according to Fa Hian there were fifteen hundred cells for the monks in his temple, according to Hiouen Tsiang one thousand. Elora, according to Seely and Heeren, has many "dormitories," but not so many as this. What an enormous rock temple it must have been that the Chinese describe. If it was not Elora, where is it? Says Heeren, "The completion of these surprising works must, according to our calculations, have required some hundreds of years.

"Let the reader imagine to himself a chain of rocky mountains consisting principally of very hard granite, and in a semi-circular or rather horse-shoe form, with a distance of nearly five miles between the extreme points. In this range is found a series of grotto temples, some of two and even three storeys in height, partly in juxtaposition with each other and partly separated by intervals, which in their turn are filled with a number of smaller temples, and the whole ornamented with innumerable reliefs. All that is great, splendid, and ornamental in architecture above ground, is here seen—also, beneath the earth—peristyles, staircases, bridges, chapels, columns, porticos, obelisks, colossal statues."

Seely follows suit and says that although Kailâs, being rock detached, is one of the wonders of the world, the Tin Tal (three storeyed) cave at Elora is

* "Buddhist Records," II., 217.

really finer as a cave, and the Viśvakarma, and a number of the other caves are very grand.

"What must have been the labour and zeal of the workmen in thus attacking a mountain formed of the firm, primeval rock, and cutting hundreds of thousands of feet of that hard material by the aid of an iron instrument* (a chisel four inches long)."

All this about the immense labour expended upon Elora is important, because, if Sadvaha constructed it at all, he must have finished it in a lifetime; for at his death, says Hiouen Tsiang, the Brahmans seized the cave temple and "strongly barricaded the place" to keep the Buddhists out.† The same difficulty surges up if we suppose that Elora was begun and finished in the lifetime of Kanis'ka. Says the Chinese traveller: "After Kanis'ka's death the Kritiya race again assumed the government, banished the priesthood, and overthrew religion."‡

Another difficulty is this: Why should the Buddhists in constructing a matchless temple make it what we might call an Encyclopædia of the Brahman religion, a Pantheon of the gods that Buddhism came into the world to specially attack? a Kylâs where every saint and hero of India finds his dwelling-place?

Elora is the most eclectic of fanes. Indra is there, and Brahma with his four heads, and Lakshmî, but the latter, says Heeren, figures as a menial attendant at the great marriage of S'iva and Durgâ; and the statues and bas reliefs of the Brahmin gods are insignificant§ compared with those of S'iva and Durgâ.

At Elora is one portentous cavern, a grotto driven into the hard rock one hundred and thirteen feet, so

* "Elora," 175.

† Beal, "Buddhist Records," Vol. II., 217.

‡ *Ibid*, Vol. I., p. 156.

§ Heeren, "Historical Researches," Vol. II., p. 60.

Captain Seely assures us*. Unlike the rest of the profusely sculptured caves, it is very dark, very solemn, quite bare of decoration. Here we have plainly the "Sanctuary of the S'iva-linga," the most exalted Mahâdeo of S'iva worship. And on this stone Mahâdeo, a Buddha has been cut. He sits on the lotus throne of Padmapani. Does not this seem to have been intended to accentuate the fact that Âdi Buddha and S'iva are one? The cave is named after Ṿisvakarma, which is a name for S'iva, as well as for a Brahman god.

I now propose to show the immense importance of the head without a jaw which the Hindu in Java assured Mr. Crawfurd always meant S'iva. If this detached head really means S'iva, it is evident that it pulverises Mr. Fergusson's theory that Elora, Karle, etc., are purely Buddhist excavations. Captain Seely gives as his frontispiece a fine engraving of the façade of the cavern of Indra at Elora, and there are two heads of Avalokitishwara plainly visible. In the Buddhist temple of Boro Bador in Java, we are assured by Crawfurd there are four hundred of these heads in one colonnade. Mr. Fergusson himself almost caps this, for he gives us a drawing of a portion of the railing at Kinheri, which is quite plentifully furnished with Avalokitishwaras. Plainly, Mr. Fergusson attached little importance to the symbol, for sometimes, whether by accident or design, he omits it even in the designs that he copies. Thus Râm Râz and Mr. Fergusson both give the Vimâna of S'rî Rangam. That of Râm Râz is capped with an arch of the S'ivan horse-shoe pattern, and a very prominent Avalokitishwara. Mr. Fergusson omits it in his copy. He omits, too, the two down-looking heads that Captain Seely gives in the façade of the Indra Cave at Elora. Râm Râz was a Hindu gentleman in government employ-

* Seely, "Elora," page 203.

ment. He wrote an able work on Hindu architecture. Avalokitishwara grins on all the Vimânas and Gopuras of his copious illustrations.

Another discovery that came to me at this time was that the serpent symbolism dates in Buddhism from its great change of front. In earlier Buddhism there was no serpent worship. This also is important. I will take it up completely later on.

That a huge dome-shaped lump of bedrock like the Lingam of Karle should be deemed a relic casket (Dhâtu garbha) by any native of India seems impossible. What receptacle for relics has ever been discovered in any one of them? And if any folks were specially opposed to such an idea it would be the ministers of King Kanis'ka who were doing their utmost to eliminate relic worship from Buddhism altogether. I have been carefully through the narratives of the Buddhist travellers in India from China, and I can nowhere find any hint of relic worship inside a cave. The large halls of cave temples are always called "preaching halls," and the Dâgoba, when it is mentioned, is plainly with them, as with all Buddhists, a cairn out in the open. Thus Fa Hian, describing Anuradapura, talks of the Sangharâma with a hall containing a figure of Buddha in the middle. But the "stûpa," or cairn outside, seems specially to attract his attention, "adorned with gold and silver, and every precious substance." Dâgoba worship was necessarily out in the open, as the early Buddhists were forbidden the shelter of a house.

Mr. Athol Forbes, in an article in the "Pall Mall Magazine," a short time ago, assured us that there are over a thousand cave temples in India, and almost all of them are crowded with lingams. Little Lingam temples are built in groups, eight, sixteen, thirty-six, etc. The Buddhist travellers speak of "tens of Deva temples."

Heeren believes that the evolution of Indian temples proceeded something after this fashion:—First, cave excavations and work chiefly inside; next, work outside as well, culminating in the attempt to detach the 'fane from the mountain, as at Kailâs in Elora, and the Raths of Mahâbalipur; this suggested the art of building in the open.

Mr. Gwilt in his "Cyclopœdia of Architecture," has much the same idea. Humanity had three stages of progress. First the hunter, who had no protection from the elements except his cave; secondly, the shepherd, who had invented the tent; and thirdly the agriculturist, who had learned to build in the open.

Mr. Gwilt quotes Pliny as asserting that the Egyptians from time immemorial dwelt in caves. He holds that Egyptian architecture sprang from cave temples.

"Everything points to its origin; its simplicity, not to say monotony; its solidity, almost heaviness, form its principal characteristics. Then the want of profile and the paucity of members, the small projection of its mouldings, the absence of apertures, the enormous diameter of the columns employed, much resembling the pillars left in quarrying for supports, the pyramidal form of the doors, the omission of roofs and pediments, the ignorance of the arch, all enable us to recur to the type from which we have set out." He adds that "all the upper parts are constructed without reference to anything but stone work."

It seems to me that from these two writers we get a right idea of the rise of Indian architecture. Bala or S'iva at the date of the Rig Veda lived in his cave, like the modern Aghora. By-and-by he made it into a temple by judicious enlargement and decoration. Then he began to ornament and shape the mountain outside. Finally, he detached it and formed the large pyramidal Ratha of Mahâbalipur.

Has not early Indian architecture all the characteristics detailed by Mr. Gwilt, simplicity, monotony, heaviness, want of profile, small projection of mouldings? From base to the very summit it is decorated with stone carvings of the pattern that we might call Chinese card-case ornamentation, a speciality learned probably in a cave temple, where from want of height the ornament was never very far from the observer's eye. And we all know that early Indian columns are usually enormous at top and slender below, a topsy-turvy feature also learned in a cave temple.

Râm Râz shows that when the Hindus began to build temples out in the open, each temple consisted of two parts:—

(1) Of a magnificent pyramidal structure which seemed on the surface to have no religious functions at all. It was called a "Gopura." Râm Râz calls these gopuras "towers over the gateways of temples." He does not seem to know of any uses which we would call distinctly religious.

(2) A very much smaller and very much less pretentious building was erected for sacrifices, rites, etc., in old as well as modern times. This was called the "Vimâna."

Do the titles of these structures throw any light on their origin?

Gopura, the "City of the Bull." S'iva is the great Bull—and his "City" would be the same as the "Kailâs" of Elora. It would be the Paradise of his followers. The pyramid is one of his special symbols.

Vimâna. This word is applied to the moveable pavilion of drapery and boards and tinsel which bears a special god in the processions. The god of a Vimâna would plainly be much lower in rank and importance than the Supreme God of the Gopura.

MADRAS GOPURA.

Can we draw up the evolution of the Gopura ?

The Aghora dwelt in a natural cavern. But this by-and-by changed into a temple, and when a rude observatory was required, to regulate agriculture by the stars, the outside would be roughly raised up by piling up stones ; and a rude pyramid would be the convenient form. Numbers of little yogi-cells are to be seen all over India of this fashion ; and the Egyptian pyramid was evolved somewhat in the same way.

But as time advanced, and rock chiselling had became an important operation inside the temple, a bold thought came to the temple producer. Instead of piling up a few rough stones to make a rude pyramid, why not remove with a chisel the stone masses from the top ? Why not change a mountain into a Gopura ?

But a second peculiarity, difficult at first to understand, is that this Gopura is often found without any subordinate buildings near it ; the ornamental and apparently useless part of the Temple alone is set up.

We must remember that in the old days in India the favourite form of religious expression was the pilgrimage. In the great epic, the Mahâbhârata, there is no mention of temples. A sage says to Arjuna : " It is the greatest mystery of the Rishis, O excellent son of Bharata. The holy pilgrimage to the Tîrthas is more important than sacrifices to the gods." The Tîrtha was the sacred* tank so necessary in pilgrimages.

Now this passage explains the solitary rock-detached pyramid, which viewed by Mr. Fergusson's theories is quite inexplicable. Pilgrimages meant money, and it came into the head of one set of priests to produce an unexampled " Home of S'iva." They executed a pyramid of solid stone, ornamented as richly as the temple interiors ; and produced it practically in the open. Round this could be set a tank,

* " Mahab. Vanaparva," v. 4059.

and the ordinary fripperies of the pilgrimages and processions. A pilgrimage to such a building would eclipse all rivals, like the Kaâba in the religion of Mahomet, which is also called the "Home of God."

Thus with a chisel was evolved the Gopura; and stone Vimânas were by and by added.

In the year 1772, a gentleman named Chambers went from Madras to examine some ruins at no great distance off; "ruins," he says, "hitherto little observed." They were on the sea; and as he approached a fine pyramid broke the sky line, a lofty pile used as "a guide to mariners." * By the pyramid were four other temples, all rock detached and ornamented with sculptures, but the pyramid was much higher than these. The place was called Mahvellipuram, the Tamulian for Mahâbalipur, its old Sanskrit name, the second language having no *h* in it and using *v* for *b*. Now the word Mahâbalipur is practically the same word as describes the Gopura, S'iva's pyramid, the "City of S'iva," the "City of the Bull." And the stone temples were called "Rathas," which is a synonym for the word "Vimâna." Each describes the carriage made of drapery and wood of a god at the festivals.

The City of Mahâbalipur was an amazing sight. The waves were gradually eating it up. Mr. Chambers saw a fine temple half demolished by the sea; and other buildings that no traveller now can see. The natives told him that not long before the glitter of the metal on the spires of temples could be seen a long way from the shore. They told him also that this city was once the most famous city of the East, that some strange cataclysm had visited it. He was also told that it had had from the most ancient days another name, the "Seven Pagodas," which fact induced Mr. Chambers to come to the conclusion that the Rathas had once been

* (See Pl. 13.) From a photograph given by Mr. Fergusson.

PLATE 13.

From a photograph.

THE PYRAMID, MAHÂBÂLIPUR.

seven, and that two of them had been demolished by the advancing tide.

Mahâbalipur is the famous Maliarpha of Ptolemy. Whether it had anything to do with the "Sheba," or "Tarshish," or "Pout," of the Egyptians and Jews we have not space to inquire.

And now what is the date of this Gopura pyramid? Perhaps Mr. Fergusson is right when he tells us confidently that it came into being 500 A.D. On the other hand there are potentialities of distant ages that make us tremble. With a chisel of four inches how long would it take to change a range of rocky hills into a range of temples? Then, how long would it take for a mighty city to rise up step by step, and to powerfully influence the civilised world, under the wing of the God of the Gopura? Then again, how long would it take the sea to destroy a large city? And a more crucial question, how long would it take for the soft lapping waves to reduce to sand and hide quite away two Rathas of solid rock?

I give a drawing of the Rathas done on the spot by that excellent artist Daniell a hundred years ago. (See Frontispiece). The taller pyramid from its position does not quite show how much taller it is than its neighbours.

I also give by the same excellent artist a view of the Kailâs rock-detached temples of Elora as seen from the top. (Pl. 11, page 147). The two viewed together bring out some striking facts.

1. Each is a group of minor buildings dominated by a great pyramid.

2. These pyramids have practically the same name, the City of S'iva (Mahâbalipur, Kailâs, Gopura).

3. The minor buildings have the same name Vimânas at Elora, Rathas at Mahâbalipur, synonyms for processional god-carriages.

4. In both cases we have a mountain changed into a group of temples by the aid of a small chisel.

5. The tall pyramid had steps cut out that it might be used as an observatory.

6. It is plainly the parent, first of solid pyramids built up of small stones; and when the arch had been discovered, of doorway pyramids pierced with a small passage, like the huge traditional "Gopuras" of Southern India.

But a more startling discovery is in reserve. It quite blows to the winds Mr. Fergusson's theories.

Daniell's drawing of Kailâs is folio size; and from it I discovered a strange fact not to be detected in any of Mr. Fergusson's drawings of the same piles. The Kailâs piles are crowded with heads of Avalokitishwara in little windows or archways. And if the photo of the Mahâbalipur pyramid is viewed with a powerful magnifying glass, the same fact emerges there. I enlarge

one of these heads from Daniell's drawing. Above is a second head, Ganga, pouring down the Ganges on S'iva.

And on the point of history Mr. Fergusson breaks down. Râm Râz cites the great poem of the Râmâyana to show that Ayodhyâ was "adorned with arched gateways," and was "full of buildings erected close to one another," and palaces with gardens "like the celestial mansions which the Siddhas obtain through the virtues of their austerity." *

Then the S'iva-Buddha alliance did not last. By and by it changed from admiration to fierce war, and S'ivan persecution. Huguenots flying from a Dragonnade are not the sort of people who build a Nôtre Dame Cathedral or an Egyptian pyramid. Van Heeren thinks that Elora must have taken several centuries to complete, and Mr. Fergusson seems to have chosen for its construction the very centuries when the fierce followers of S'iva, Kumârilla Bhatta (A.D. 700), and Sankara Âchârya (750), were spreading Hindustan with Buddhist blood.

Fa Hian, who visited the Dekhan about A.D. 400, found that the Buddhists had long been chased away from those regions. Let us suppose that they came back again A.D. 750, Fergusson's date, and commenced the mighty works of Elora. Kumârilla Bhatta and Sankara Âchârya would have soon made the operations impossible. Supposing, on the other hand, that they delayed the commencement until Mr. Fergusson's other date, A.D. 950. How could the few sparse Buddhists left in India find the money for such a gigantic enterprise. Also, why did they build a temple with all the distinctive features of the temples of their sanguinary persecutors? "Sankara" is one of the names of S'iva. "Achârya" means "Teacher."

A practical question! If the structures of Mahâbalipur and Elora were intended for the dormitories of monks, traces of this would be found in them. Mr. Fergusson admits that this is not the case, but he says, that they are all unfinished, except the "little Ratha" at Mahâbalipur. He makes a further confession that

* Râm Râz, "Architecture of the Hindus," p. 48.

this has also no dormitories, but he says that in form it is a "mere pansil" (hut of leaves and boughs of an ascetic in a jungle*). May not this be a solution of the puzzle? The earliest stone structure in the open was suggested to the Indians by pansils and tents.

The dormitory theory is the most weak part of Mr. Fergusson's case. Fa Hian tells us that there were fifteen hundred dormitories in the Sangharâma that he talks of. Now we learn from Heeren that at Elora there is "a vast number of smaller grottoes," where priests can rest and where, what seems most important, many thousands of pilgrims and penitents can be put up. Remember that this Sangharâma was in the Dekhan. Remember also that it was not a mere rock temple, but was "constructed out of a great mountain of rock, hewn to the proper shape." Where else in the Dekhan is a hint of these dormitories?

Sir Alexander Cunningham in his work the "Stûpa of Bharhut," gives a bas relief representing some buildings of the period (B.C. 270). I reproduce it here.

* Fergusson, "Indian Architecture," p. 230.

Mr. Fergusson calls it a round temple and part of a palace." Compare this with the small Ratha of Mahâbalipur, as drawn by Daniell. Can we really believe with Mr. Fergusson that a race which B.C. 270 could build thus in the open would six hundred years after this waste half a century or so to produce with a small chisel an edifice like the Mahâbalipur Pansil.

To sum up, in ancient India there were three main religions.

(1) The religion of S'iva, which dates from the Caveman, Mr. Gwilt's first stage. The Aryans found this god flourishing in India as Ahi the Serpent, Bala, the Lingam, etc. The Zend Avestha also takes note of him as Shouru, who seduced some of the Eranians to heresies performed in his cave. That cave was supplied with a number of dark recesses for the impressive horrors of the S'ivan mystery, and vast halls for the Kailâs illuminations; the temple being made apparently to suit the worship and the worship to suit the temple.

(2) The pastoral period of Mr. Gwilt. The Aryan shepherds crossed the Hindu Kush and invaded India with their flocks and many gods. At the date of Megasthenes their priests lived in the open. In the early epics there are no temples.

(3) The early Buddhists—forbidden by the "Twelve Observances" to sleep more than one night in one place, and forbidden the protection of a roof. What good would a vast pile like Elora be to them? The monks could not enter it. The same remark applies to the rock-detached Rathas of Mahâbalipur. Whatever their design it could not have been dormitories for folks who used no dormitories at all. Indeed, the great topes like the Sanchi seem to accentuate the fact that the worship for which they were designed was entirely open-air worship,—circumambulation round a pathway between the great hemisphere of

earth and the richly carved stone railings. This purely open-air worship was carried on even when kings, converted to S'iva-Buddhism, had seized the S'iva rock temples.

Thus we find two distinct religions and two distinct architectural modes of giving effect to them.

(1) The worship of a man (deified) by perambulation round his relics in a cairn in the open.

(2) The worship of the Supreme God by an ancient and elaborate mystery which required large halls, dark grottoes, deep gloom, flashes of light, and Lingams composed of large lumps of bed-rock. There are more than a thousand rock temples in India all plentifully furnished with Lingams. Can we believe with Mr. Fergusson that these are all due to the Buddhists, who in his view originated the pattern.

CHAPTER X

THE ESSENES

Was Essenism due to Buddhist missionaries?—Testimony of Asoka—The μοναστήριον compared with the Sangharâma—"Apostles of the Bloodless Oblation"—Tertullian on the similarity between the rites of the Christians and the Mithraists—Testimony of Philo—Thirty thousand monks go from Alexandria to Ruanwelli in Ceylon, and are hospitably received on the occasion of the consecration of the great temple there, B.C. 170.

We have now reached the critical chapters of the work. Its main contention is that it was through the Jewish sect of the Essenes that Buddhist influences reached Palestine, and were passed on to Christianity. We have therefore to consider:

(1) Was Essenism due to Buddhism?

(2) Did Christianity emerge from Essenism.

The first question will form the subject of this chapter, and the second will be treated afterwards. In my first edition of this work I attached great importance to the evidence of King Asoka. That monarch, as we have seen in Chapter V., has given to Buddhism a record which no other religion can boast of, simply because in lieu of a reed and leaves of plantain trees or other ephemeral methods he has used a chisel and hard stone. By this means he has baffled the pious improver of sacred records, but the King's system was necessarily a little crude. On one pillar he tells us about his "double system of medical aid," on another of the "villages set apart for the monks," on a third, the accommodation of men and animals, on others we read of "the planting of trees and digging of wells," and then of monks "exercising solitary austerities."

Thus when I read in the inscription of the Girnar Rock in Guzerat the king's statement that he had sent into the domains of King Antiochus his "medicaments," and his "double system of medical aid," I thought that the king's statement about his medicaments was important as proving an early connection between India and Egypt, but I did not see how far reaching and overwhelming that evidence was.

A recent and more careful study of the king's inscriptions has proved to me that his Sangharâmas, the establishments that he set up upon roads and in jungles, were all of a pattern and all complete. They were for utilitarian as well as religious purposes. The problem before the king was to send abroad his laws, his religion, his commerce, his officials wherever he could, and especially to reclaim and pierce the vast jungles of his dominions. These had potent sentries, the tiger and the fever. The Indian epics tell us how these were dreaded. Thus roads, wells, herbs for medicines, grain for food, and trees for shade, would be required everywhere, for each Sangharâma was a rude caravanserai, hospital, college, monastery, church, burying-ground, as well as a collection of little leafy pansils where the ascetic could dream his dreams of God.

This gives the Girnar rock-inscription an importance that it is impossible to estimate. If Asoka spread through the dominions of Antiochus his "root drugs and herbs," and his "medical aid for men and animals," the remainder of the Sangharâma, the religion and the fasting monks, must have been present likewise, a pregnant fact.

Let us read the passage carefully. "And moreover within the dominions of Antiochus, the Greek king, of which the generals of Antiochus are the rulers, everywhere the double system of medical aid of the Beloved of the Angels (Asoka) is established, both medical aid for men and medical aid for animals."*

Indeed, these conclusions are completely confirmed by a second passage on the Girnar Rock.

"And the Greek king besides, by whom the four Greek kings (Chapta Yona râjah) Ptolemaios, and Gengakenos and Magas . . . have been induced to permit . . . both here and in foreign countries everywhere (the people) follow the doctrine of the religion of Devanampiya (the friend of the Angels) wherever it reacheth."†

The king's name is never actually mentioned on the inscriptions. He is called the "Friend of the Angels" or Devas. According to Polybius, Antiochus the Great led his army into India and renewed his alliance with Sophagasenes, king of that country. As the Asoka edicts were incised on rocks some six years after Antiochus came to the throne, Prinsep and Wilford believe that this was King Asoka. Meanwhile the building of Alexandria had given a powerful fillip to the intercourse with India by sea. Alexander had designed it to be the capital of his vast empire, and the bridge between India and the West. This project was ably carried out after his death by his lieutenant, the first Ptolemy. Under his wise government and that of his successors, Alexandria soon became the first commercial city in the world. Of more importance was his large tolerance of creeds, whether Egyptian, Grecian, or Jewish. In the year 209 B.C. Ptolemy Evergetes was on the throne. He conquered Abyssinia and the greater part of Asia, including Syria, Phœnicia, Babylonia, Persia, Media.

* Translation by Prinsep, "Journ. Beng. As. Soc.," Vol. VII., p. 159.

† *Ibid*, p. 261.

His conquests extended to Bactria, and he had a large fleet on the Red Sea. This placed him in contact with India from two different directions. He married the daughter of the "Magas" of the inscriptions, the king of Cyrene.

We have now to consider whether there is any evidence corroborating the testimony of Asoka. Jumping over some two hundred years we reach Philo (25 B.C. to 45 A.D.), Josephus (born 37 A.D.) and Pliny (23 to 79 A.D.). These witnesses describe an institution pin for pin like the Sangharâma, namely the μοναστήριον, and we get from them a knowledge of two remarkable sects of the Jews, the Essenes and the Therapeuts.

When did these sects arise? On that point evidence is scanty. Eusebius declared that they were Christian monks brought there by St. Mark, but Philo, Josephus, and Pliny, if they know nothing very definite, disprove this. Philo declares that their laws, which differ radically from the Jewish laws, date from Moses. "Our law giver trained into fellowship great numbers of pupils whom he calls Essenes."* He repeats this statement in the same work. He says likewise that they possess commentaries of ancient men who were founders of the school. This throws the Therapeuts back a long way. Josephus also gives to the Essenes Moses as a law giver, and states that anyone who blasphemed him was to be punished with death. He says, too, that the Essenes are as old as the Pharisees and Sadducees.† And Pliny the elder, who witnessed the Essene gatherings on the shores of the Dead Sea, their central haunt, affirms that they had existed there "through thousands of ages."

It is to be observed too, that these Therapeuts were spread widely about, especially in Egypt, to which as we have seen, Asoka sent his Sangharâmas. Says

* Fragment of "Apology for the Jews."

† "Antiquities," Book XVIII., C.1.

Philo: "There are many parts of the world in which these folks are found, for both Greece and the Barbarian lands must needs have their share in what is good and perfect. They are, however, in greatest abundance in Egypt, in every one of the so-called departments, and especially round about Alexandria. The principal persons draw up their colony from all quarters as to a fatherland of Therapeuts, unto a well-regarded spot which lies on Lake Marea, on a somewhat low hill, very well situated both with regard to security and the mildness of the air."* In fact Egypt swarmed with monks, for many centuries after Christ as well as before, and it was difficult to distinguish the sect of Christians from the worshippers of Serapis, whom we shall by-and-by show to have been S'iva a little disguised. From Rufinus and St. Gerome, three centuries after Christ's death, we get pictures of them.

The theatre of the Eremites was chiefly the valley of the Nile. The huge deserts on each side of the river were peopled with Eremites and monasteries, that of Oxyrinque harboured ten thousand monks and two thousand nuns. Another near Nechia, forty miles from Alexandria, had five thousand monks. To get the dates of the rise of these is now impossible.

Philo, as we have seen, announced that in his day the forty-two districts of Egypt were full of them.

But a question arises: Were the Essenes and the Therapeuts the same, or closely like each other? Some Christian apologists deny this, and they cite Josephus to show that the Essenes dwelt in cities and "employed themselves solely to the labour of agriculture."†

I think a description of a Buddhist monastery may throw a light on these and similar contradictions.

* Vita Contemp.

† "Antiq.," XVIII., 1, par. 5.

A modern Buddhist monastery consists of a quadrangle with a line of separate huts along each side just like the "huts lightly built" of Philo. Each hut is tenanted by a monk and his two servant pupils. Each hut has guest chambers, for two or more guests. The huts in Asoka's time, and also in modern times when the community migrates to the jungle for the Varsha or Lent, were called pansils, and have simply a covering of boughs and leaves, and perhaps mud walls, that as in the days of Job, thieves can "dig into." In the centre of the quadrangle is the sanctuary, a larger building whither the monks resort for worship. Nocturnal worship was a prominent feature with Asoka's monks, and with the Therapeuts and Christians.

A Buddhist Sangharâma consists of :—

(1) Contemplative ascetics trying to develop "visions," and what St. Paul calls "spiritual gifts." Josephus tells us that the Essenes had "knowledge of divine things." Philo calls the Therapeuts "Citizens of Heaven," and says they seek a "divine illumination," an "alliance with the upper world."

(2) Their pupil servants—who in return for spiritual initiation attend to their material wants, like Josephus with Banus.

(3) Inferior monks who have small vocation for the spiritual life. These till the ground in countries like Tibet, and work the convent farms.

(4) Brothers who have found that they have no vocation at all. These may return to civil life, and marry and trade. But the Essenes in cities were bound by "oaths that make one shudder," as Josephus puts it, "never to betray the brethren, and to such of their persuasion as are come from any other place, whatever they have is thrown open as freely as if it were their own, and they go to visit those they have never seen before, as if they were most intimate." This reminds us of the disciples of Christ, and explains

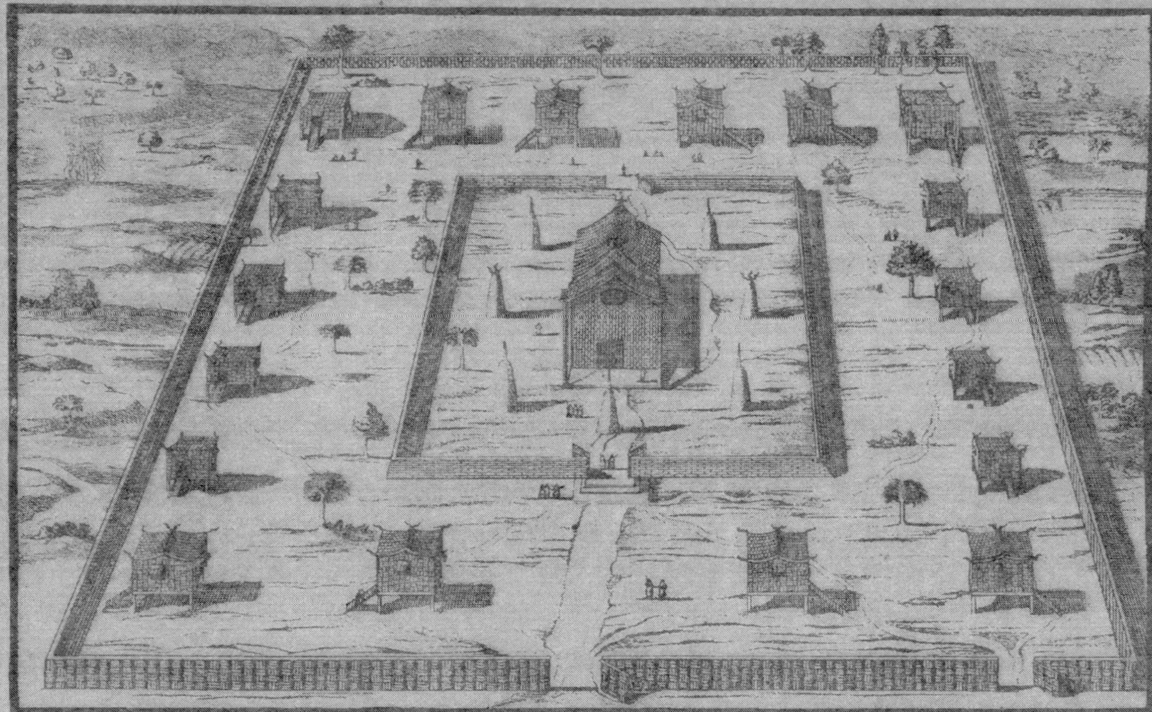

BUDDHIST MONASTERY, SIAM.

the anathemas they were called upon to pronounce "if any receive you not."

(5) Prophets dreaming in solitude and prophets who had failed in life were both part of the same mechanism; for the prophet when he had obtained the inner light was turned into an itinerant missionary. In a work recently recovered, the "Teaching of the Apostles," the Christian missionaries are called "Prophets," and they were only allowed to remain three nights in one place. The Parivrâjikas, or wandering missionaries of Buddhism, could only sleep one night in the same place, and that not in a house. These wandering missionaries, although their work is finished, still exist in Tibet. In that cold climate they say their home is "the starry tent of Buddha," and as often as not sleep in the open on the snow.

It is evident that in countries like Palestine where any doctrines that in the least swerved from Mosaism were promptly punished, the city monks would be a necessary complement to the missionaries.

The analogies between the Essenes and Therapeuts are close enough. Both believed in the immortality of the soul. Both explained the sacred scriptures allegorically. Both lived in monasteries and had goods in common, despised wealth, and before entering the community they parted with all their property. Both considered marriage and sexual intercourse inimical to the higher life. Both abstained from flesh meat and wine, and refused to take part in the animal sacrifices in the Temple. For each was an active cohort in the Great Army which, led as it were by Buddha, assailed sacrificial religion everywhere, and sought to substitute the religion of conscience for religion by body-corporate.

In point of fact, Buddha's missionaries were preaching in Persia long before the days of King Asoka. The Mithraists, the Neo Pythagoreans, the Hermitists were similar secret societies, grouped together as the "Apostles of the Bloodless Altar."

There are two Zoroasters. One of these Zoroasters lived 6,000 years B.C. according to Darmesteter, and the other about 500 years B.C.

The earlier Zoroaster swathed Persia in a network of silly rites and regulations. A culprit who "threw away a dead dog" was to receive a thousand blows with the horse-goad, and one thousand with the Craosha charana. A culprit who slew a dog with a "prickly back" and a "woolly muzzle" was to receive a similar punishment.* This Zoroaster was particular about the number of gnats, ants, lizards that the devout were enjoined to kill.† This Zoroaster proclaimed a god who loved to see on his altar a "hundred horses, a thousand cows, ten thousand small cattle," and so on.‡ But the second Zoroaster proclaimed a bloodless altar, and sought to tear the network of the first Zoroaster to shreds. What was the meaning of this? Simply that the Buddhist Wanderers had by this time invaded Persia, and had fastened their doctrines upon the chief local prophet. This was their habit. A study of this second religion, the religion of Mithras, will help us to some of the secrets of Buddhist propagandism.

Mr. Felix Oswald cites Wassiljew as announcing that the Buddhist missionaries had reached Western Persia B.C. 450. This date would, of course, depend on the date of Buddha's life and Buddha's death. The latter is now definitely fixed by Buhler's translation of Asoka Rupnath rock-inscription, B.C. 470. Wassiljew, citing Daranatha, announces that Madeantica, a convert of Ananda, Buddha's leading disciple, reached Ouchira in Kashmir. From Kashmir Budd-

* "Zendavesta," Fargard, XXX.

† *Ibid*, XIV.

‡ "Khordah Avesta," XII.

hism passed promptly to Kandahar and Kabul (p. 40). Thence it penetrated quickly to Bactria, and soon invaded "all the country embraced by the word Turkistan, where it flourished until disturbed by Mahomet."

Tertullian has two passages which describe the religion of Mithras.

He says that the devil, to "pervert the truth," by "the mystic rites of his idols, vies even with the essential portions of the sacraments of God. He, too, baptises some—that is, his own believers and faithful followers. He promises the putting away of sins by a laver (of his own), and, if my memory still serves me, Mithras there (in the kingdom of Satan) sets his mark on the foreheads of his soldiers, celebrates also the oblation of bread, and introduces an image of the resurrection, and before a sword wreathes a crown."*

Here is another passage:—

"Some soldier of Mithras, who at his initiation in the gloomy cavern,—in the camp, it may well be said, of darkness,—when at the sword's point a sword is presented to him as though in mimicry of martyrdom, and thereupon a crown is put upon his head, is admonished to resist and cast it off, and, if he likes, transfer it to his shoulders, saying that Mithras is his crown. He even has his virgins and his ascetics (continentes). Let us take note of the devices of the devil, who is wont to ape some of God's things."†

From this it is plain that the worshippers of Mithras had the simple rites of Buddhist and Christian, baptism and the bloodless altar; also an early Freemasonry, which some detect veiled in the Indian life of Buddha. Thus the incident of the sword and crown in the Mithraic initiation is plainly based on the menacing sword of Mara in the "Lalita Vistara,"

* Pres., V., Hoer, Chap. XI.

† "De Corona," XV.

and the crown that he offered Buddha. In modern Masonry it is feigned that Hiram Abiff, the architect of Solomon's temple, made three efforts to escape from three assassins. These are plainly Old Age, Disease and Death. He sought to evade the first at the east of the temple, in the same way that Buddha tried to escape by the eastern gate. The second and third flights of Hiram and Buddha were to the same points of the compass. Then Buddha escaped the lower life through the Gate of Benediction, and Hiram was killed. The disciples of Mithras had, in the comedy of their initiation, "seven tortures,"—heat, cold, hunger, thirst, fire, water, etc.—experiences by no means confined to histrionics in the experience of Buddha's Wanderers. A modern mason goes through the comedy of giving up his gold and silver, and baring his breast and feet, a form that once had a meaning. Mithras was born in a cave; and at Easter there was the ceremony called by Tertullian the "image of the resurrection." The worshippers, Fermicus tells us,* placed by night a stone image on a bier in a cave and went through the forms of mourning. The dead god was then placed in a tomb, and after a time withdrawn from it. Then lights were lit, and poems of rejoicing sounded out: and the priest comforted the devotees. "You shall have salvation from your sorrows!" Dupuis naturally compares all this to the cierge pascal and Catholic rites. In Jerusalem the Greek pontiff goes into the cave called Christ's sepulchre and brings out miraculous fire to the worshippers, who are fighting and biting each other outside, imaging unconsciously Buddha's great battle with Mara and the legions of hell, its thunder and lightning and turmoil, followed by a bright coruscation, and by the angels who greeted his victory. This sudden illumination, which is the chief rite of

* "De Errore," XXIII.

Freemasonry, of Mithraism, and of Christianity, has oddly enough been thrown overboard by the English Church.

That Mithraism was at once Freemasonry and Buddhism is proved by its great spread. Judaism and the other old priestcrafts were for a "chosen people." At the epoch of Christ, Mithraism had already honeycombed the Roman paganism. Experts have discovered its records in Arthur's Oon and other British caves.

A similar Freemasonry was Pythagoreanism in Greece. Colebrooke, the prince of Orientalists, saw at once that its philosophy was purely Buddhist. Its rites were identical with those of the Mithraists and Essenes. Alexandria was built by the great invader of India, to bridge the East and the West. And an exceptional toleration of creeds was the result.

On the subject of the Essenes Philo wrote a most interesting letter to a man named Hephæstion, of which the following is a portion :—

"I am sorry to find you saying that you are not likely to visit Alexandria again. This restless, wicked city can present but few attractions, I grant, to a lover of philosophic quiet. But I cannot commend the extreme to which I see so many hastening. A passion for ascetic seclusion is becoming daily more prevalent among the devout and the thoughtful, whether Jew or Gentile. Yet surely the attempt to combine contemplation and action should not be so soon abandoned. A man ought at least to have evinced some competency for the discharge of the social duties before he abandons them for the divine. First the less, then the greater.

"I have tried the life of the recluse. Solitude brings no escape from spiritual danger. If it closes some avenues of temptation, there are few in whose case it does not open more. Yet the Terapeutæ, a sect similar to the Essenes, with whom you are acquainted, number many among them whose lives are truly exemplary. Their cells are scattered about the region bordering on the farther shore of the Lake Mareotis. The members of either sex live a single and ascetic life, spending their time in fasting and contemplation, in prayer or reading. They believe themselves favoured with divine illumination—an inner light. They assemble on the Sabbath for worship, and listen to mystical discourses on the traditionary lore which they say has been handed down in secret among themselves. They also celebrate solemn dances and processions of a mystic significance by moonlight on the shore of the great mere. Sometimes, on an occasion of public rejoicing, the margin of the lake on our side will be lit with a fiery chain of illuminations, and galleys, hung with lights, row to and fro with strains of music sounding over the broad water. Then the Therapeutæ are all hidden in their little hermitages, and these sights and sounds of the world they have abandoned make them withdraw into themselves and pray.

" Their principle at least is true. The soul which is occupied with things above, and is initiated into the mysteries of the Lord, cannot but account the body evil, and even hostile. The soul of man is divine, and his highest wisdom is to become as much as possible a stranger to the body with its embarrassing appetites. God has breathed into man from heaven a portion of His own divinity. That which is divine is indivisible. It may be extended, but it is incapable of separation. Consider how vast is the range of our thought over the past and the future, the heavens and the earth. This alliance with an upper world, of which we are conscious, would be impossible were not the soul of man an indivisible portion of that divine and blessed spirit. Contemplation of the divine essence is the noblest exercise of man; it is the only means of attaining to the highest truth and virtue, and therein to behold God is the consummation of our happiness here."

Here we have the higher Buddhism, which seeks to reach the plane of spirit, an "alliance with the upper world," by the aid of solitary reverie. That Philo knew where this religion had come from is, I think, proved by another passage.

"Among the Persians there is the order of Magi who deeply investigate the works of nature for the discovery of truth, and in leisure's quiet are initiated into, and expound in clearest significance, the divine virtues.

"In India, too, there is the sect of the Gymnosophists, who, in addition to speculative philosophy, diligently cultivate the ethical also, and have made their life an absolute ensample of virtue.

"Palestine, moreover, and Syria are not without their harvest of virtuous excellence, which region is inhabited by no small portion of the very populous nation of the Jews. There are counted amongst them certain ones, by name Essenes, in number about four thousand, who derive their name in my opinion by an inaccurate trace from the term in the Greek language for holiness (Essen or Essaios—Hosios, holy), inasmuch as they have shown themselves pre-eminent by devotion to the service of God; not in the sacrifice of living animals, but rather in the determination to make their own minds fit for a holy offering."*

Plainly here the Essenes are pronounced of the same faith as the Gymnosophists of India, who abstain from the bloody sacrifice, that is the Buddhists.

I think I have now proved that Essenism was due to a Buddhism influence. Few deny this now, and

* Philo, "Every virtuous man is free."

fewer would support that energetic but rather wild apologist, Dr. Lightfoot, in his assertion that "there is no notice in either heathen or Christian writers, which points to the presence of a Buddhist within the limits of the Roman Empire till long after the Essenes ceased to exist."

But supposing this to be true, we have at any rate an historical statement that 30,000 Buddhist monks went back to India if they did not come from it. In the Mahâwanso, or ancient Buddhist history of Ceylon, it is announced that on the occasion of the consecration of the famous Buddhist tope at Ruanwelli (160 to 137 B.C.), Buddhist monks came from all parts, including "30,000 from the vicinity of A'lasadda, the capital of the Yona country." (Alexandria, the capital of Greece).*

Dr. Lightfoot, the champion controversialist of his day, springs up at this and maintains that the Yona country is Bactria alone, and that the Alexandria here mentioned is a small town fifteen miles from Caubul. The first assertion disappears in the presence of Asoka's Girnar inscription. The "dominions of Ptolemaios" must certainly have included Egypt; and no town in Afghanistan could possibly be called "The capital of the Greek dominions."

The second suggestion of this distinguished controversialist, brings with it developments that its author could never have anticipated, for the Cingalese historian announces that the invited monks arrived at Ruanwelli and were properly fêted.

Let us suppose for a moment that Dr. Lightfoot's *ipse dixit* is correct, and that 30,000 monks were at Alexandria in Afghanistan. This Alexandria must have been a small village. It is not now discoverable on any map. Imagine 30,000 monks living by daily begging in such a thrifty place. It took the English

* "Mahâwanso" (Turnour's translation), p. 171.

government three and a half months to prepare supplies for the Tirah campaign. Imagine 30,000 monks marching from Caubul to Peshawur. Did they lay in a vast store of food with camels, mules, etc., for carriage? If so, had they armed men with them to protect this food from the starving robbers of the passes? And how did they traverse the fifteen or sixteen hundred miles that separate Peshawur from Adam's bridge? How were they fed in the numerous dense jungles and wastes that crossed their path? Also, could 30,000 Buddhists march safely across the kingdoms in India that had never been converted to Buddhism, and who viewed the followers of Buddha as graceless heretics, and burnt them on red hot iron beds?

CHAPTER XI

THE ESSENE JESUS

Was Jesus an Essene?—Nazarites or Nazareens—Baptised by the Nazarite John—A Secret Society—"Inquire who is worthy!"—Essene Bread Oblation—Miracle of the Loaves—Probably an Essene Passover gathering—The Codex Nazaraeus—The earliest gathering of Christians at Rome—Essene water drinkers and vegetarians—The Gospel according to the Hebrews—Gospel of the Infancy.

WAS Jesus an Essene?

Historical questions are sometimes made more clear by being treated broadly. Let us first deal with this from the impersonal side, leaving out altogether the alleged words and deeds of Christ, Paul, etc. Fifty years before Christ's birth there was a sect dwelling in the stony waste where John prepared a people for the Lord. Fifty years after Christ's death there was a sect in the same part of Palestine. The sect that existed fifty years before Christ was called Essenes or Nazarites, or Nazareens. The sect that existed fifty years after Christ's death were called Nazarines or Nazarites, Therapeuts, Gnostics, Continentes, and according to Epiphanius "Essenes or Jesseans." They were not called Christians in the first century at all.

Each had two prominent rites: baptism, and what Tertullian calls the "oblation of bread." Each had for officers, deacons, presbyters, ephemereuts. Each sect had monks, nuns, celibacy, community of goods.

Each interpreted the Old Testament in a mystical way,—so mystical, in fact, that it enabled each to discover that the bloody sacrifice of Mosaism was forbidden, not enjoined. The most minute likenesses have been pointed out between these two sects by all Catholic writers from Eusebius and Origen to the poet Racine, who translated Philo's Contemplative Life for the benefit of pious court ladies. Was there any connection between these two sects? It is difficult to conceive that there can be two answers to such a question.

And if it can be proved, as Bishop Lightfoot affirms, that Christ was an anti-Essene, who announced that His mission was to preserve intact every jot and tittle of Mosaism as interpreted by the recognised interpreters, this would simply show that He had nothing to do with the movement to which His name has been given.

The first prominent fact of His life is His baptism by John. If John was an Essene, the full meaning of this may be learnt from Josephus:

"To one that aims at entering their sect, admission is not immediate: but he remains a whole year outside it, and is subjected to their rule of life, being invested with an axe, the girdle aforesaid, and a white garment. Provided that over this space of time he has given proof of his perseverance, he approaches nearer to this course of life, and partakes of the holier water of cleansing; but he is not admitted to their community of life. Following the proof of his strength of control, his moral conduct is tested for two years more; and when he has made clear his worthiness, he is then adjudged to be one of their number. But before he touches the common meal, he pledges to them in oaths to make one shudder, first, that he will reverence the Divine Being; and secondly, that he will abide in justice unto men, and will injure no one, either of his own accord or by command, but will always detest the iniquitous and strive on the side of the righteous; that he will ever show fidelity to all, and most of all to those who are in power, for to no one comes rule without God; and that, if he becomes a ruler himself, he will never carry insolence into his authority, or outshine those placed under him by dress or any superior adornment; that he will always love truth, and press forward to convict those that tell lies. That he will keep his hands from peculation, and his soul pure from unholy gain; that he will neither conceal anything from the brethren of this order, nor babble to others any of their secrets, even though in the presence of force and at the hazard of his life. In addition to all this, they take oath not to communicate the doctrines to any one in any other way than as imparted to themselves; to abstain from robbery, and to keep close, with equal care, the books of their sect and the names of the angels. Such are the oaths by which they receive those that join them." *

As a pendant to this, I will give the early Christian initiation from the Clementine Homilies.

"If any one having been tested is found worthy, then they hand over to him according to the initiation of Moses, by which he delivered his books to the Seventy who succeeded to his chair."

These books are only to be delivered to "one who is good and religious, and who wishes to teach, and who is circumcised and faithful."

"Wherefore let him be proved not less than six years, and then, according to the initiation of Moses, he (the initiator) should bring him to a river or fountain, which is living water, where the regeneration of the righteous takes place." The novice then calls to witness heaven, earth, water, and air, that he will keep secret the teachings of these holy books, and guard them from

* Josephus, De B. J., II., 8, 2, 13.

falling into profane hands, under the penalty of becoming " accursed, living and dying, and being punished with everlasting punishment."

" After this let him partake of bread and salt with him who commits them unto him."

Now, if, as believed by Dr. Lightfoot, the chief object of Christ's mission was to establish for ever the Mosaism of the bloody altar, and combat the main teaching of the " Ascetic " as he was called, which " postulates the false principle of the malignity of matter," why did He go to a Mystic to be baptised? Whether or not Christ belonged to mystical Israel, there can be no discussion about the Baptist. He was a Nazarite " separated from his mother's womb," who had induced a whole " people " to come out to the desert and adopt the Essene rites and their community of goods. And we see, from a comparison of the Essene and early Christian initiations, what such baptism carried with it. It implied preliminary instruction and vows of implicit obedience to the instructor.

It is plain, too, that the Essene Christ knows at first nothing of any antagonism to His teacher.

" The law and the prophets were until John. Since that time the kingdom of God is preached, and every man presseth into it " (Luke xvi. 16).

This shows that far from believing that He had come to preserve the Mosaism of the bloody altar, He considered that John and the Essenes had power to abrogate it.

Listen, too, to Christ's instructions to His twelve disciples :—

" As ye go, preach, saying the kingdom of heaven is at hand."

This is the simple gospel of John.

" Provide neither gold nor silver nor brass in your purses, nor scrip for your journey, neither two coats, neither shoes."

Here again we have the barefooted Essenes without silver or gold. "He that hath two coats let him impart to him that hath none," said the Baptist.

"And into whatsoever city or town ye shall enter, inquire who in it is worthy; and there abide till ye go thence. And when ye come into an house, salute it. And if the house be worthy, let your peace come upon it; but if it be not worthy, let your peace return to you. And whosoever shall not receive you, nor hear your words, when ye depart out of that house or city, shake off the dust of your feet. Verily I say unto you, it shall be more tolerable for the land of Sodom and Gomorrha in the day of judgment, than for that city. Behold I send you forth, as sheep in the midst of wolves: be ye therefore wise as serpents, and harmless as doves. But beware of men; for they will deliver you up to the councils, and they will scourge you in their synagogues; and ye shall be brought before governors and kings for my sake, for a testimony against them and the Gentiles. But when they deliver you up, take no thought how or what ye shall speak; for it shall be given you in that same hour what ye shall speak. For it is not ye that speak, but the Spirit of your Father which speaketh in you. And the brother shall deliver up the brother to death, and the father the child: and the children shall rise up against their parents, and cause them to be put to death. And ye shall be hated of all men for my name's sake: but he that endureth to the end shall be saved."

This passage is remarkable. No Christian disciple had yet begun to preach, and yet what do we find? A vast secret organisation in every city. It is composed of those who are "worthy" (the word used by Josephus for Essene initiates); and they are plainly bound to succour the brethren at the risk of their lives. This shows that Christ's movement was affiliated with an earlier propagandism.

There is another question. On the hypothesis that Christ was an orthodox Jew, why should He, plainly knowing beforehand what mistakes and bloodshed it would cause, make His disciples mimic the Essenes in externals? The Essenes had two main rites, baptism and the bloodless oblation. Christ adopted them. The Essenes had a new name on conversion.

"Thou shalt be called Cephas, which is, by interpretation, a stone" (John i. 42).

The Essenes had community of goods:—

"And all that believed were together, and had all things common" (Acts ii. 44).

"If thou wilt be perfect, go and sell that thou hast, and give to the poor, and thou shalt have treasure in heaven; and come and follow me" (Matt. xix. 21).

A rigid continence was exacted:—

"All men cannot receive this saying, save they to whom it is given. . . . There be eunuchs which have made themselves eunuchs for the kingdom of heaven's sake. He that is able to receive it, let him receive it" (Matt. xix. 11, 12).

"And I looked, and, lo! a Lamb stood on Mount Zion, and with Him an hundred and forty-four thousand, having His Father's name written on their foreheads. . . . These are they which were not defiled with women, for they are virgins" (Rev. xiv. 1, 4).

Divines tell us that this first passage is to have only a "spiritual" interpretation. It forbids not marriage, but excess. We might listen to this if we had not historical cognisance of a sect in Palestine at this date which enforced celibacy in its monasteries. The second passage shows that the disciples understand Him literally.

The bloody sacrifice forbidden:—

"I will have mercy and not sacrifice" (Matt. ix. 13).

"Unless ye cease from sacrificing, the wrath shall not cease from you."*

"To love his neighbour as himself is more than whole burnt offerings and sacrifices" (Mark xii. 33).

Bishop Lightfoot, as I have mentioned, considers that Jesus was an orthodox Jew, whose mission was to perpetuate every jot and tittle of Mosaism; and that "emancipation" from the "swathing-bands" of the law came from the apostles.† It might be thought that this was a quaint undertaking, for the Maker of the million million starry systems, to come to this insignificant planet in bodily form to "perpetuate" institutions that Titus in thirty years was to end for ever; even if we could forget that human sacrifices, concubinage, polygamy, slavery, and border raids were amongst these institutions. But if this is the historical Christ, it appears to me that we must eliminate the Christ of the Gospels almost entirely. For capital offences against the Mosaic Law, the recognised authorities three times sought the life of Jesus, twice after formal condemnation by the Sanhedrim. These offences were Sabbath-breaking, witchcraft, and speaking against Mosaic institutions. According to the Synoptics, He never went to Jerusalem during His ministry until just the end of it; although the three visits for the yearly festivals were rigidly exacted.

And the miracle of the loaves was apparently performed during a passover festival in Galilee, a passover that infringed all the rites of the dominant party (John vi. 1-13).

Bishop Lightfoot makes much of the fact that John's Gospel makes Christ go up once for the Feast of Tabernacles. But did He go as an orthodox wor-

* Cited from "Gospel of the Hebrews," by Epiphanius, Hoer, XXX. 16.

† "Com. on Galatians," pp. 286, 287.

shipper, to present his offerings for the bloody sacrifice? On the contrary, on this very occasion He was accused of Sabbath-breaking and demoniac possession; and the rulers of the people sent officers to arrest Him.

I must say a few words here about the Codex Nazaræus, the Bible of the disciples of John the Baptist. It is sometimes called the "Book of Adam," and it contains views about the Logos analogous to those of Plato; and is, the great French authority Adolf Franck thinks, earlier by centuries than Christianity. John's disciples are called "Nazarines" in the book; and it bristles with Essene sayings, many of which were afterwards placed in Christ's lips in His "Sermon on the Mount."

"Blessed are the peaceful."

"Blessed are the just, the peacemakers, and the believers."

"Blessed are the peacemakers who abstain from evil."

"Desire not gold nor silver nor the riches of the world, for the world will perish and all its riches."

"Feed the hungry, give drink to the thirsty, clothe the naked, for he who gives will receive abundantly."

"Put on your stoles and white garments, O Peacemakers, symbols of the Water of Life. Put on your heads white crowns like the crowns of glory of heaven's angels. Take up arms not of steel but of more worthy metal, the weapons of faith and justice, the weapons of the Nazarine."

One point is its strong hostility to the Mosaism of the bloody altar.

"Then shall appear that ignoble nation which will kill fat offerings, and make God's sanctuary swim in blood. It will commit wicked acts, and call itself the People of the House of Israel. It will circumcise with a bloody sword, and smear its face and lips with gore. Its sons will burn with infamous lusts, perverting the faith. . . . A generation of slaves and adulterers, instead of honouring the Most High, they will discard Moses the Prophet of the Holy Ghost who gave them the law, and dishonour Abraham, that other Prophet of God."

This shows that the breach between the Nazarines and dominant Mosaism was no half-quarrel. Philo, Josephus, Christ, and the author of the "Clementine Homilies," all hold that the bloody sacrifice did not come from God.

"Say not that to the Most High alone is known the mysteries. He has revealed them to you."

"When thou eatest, drinkest, or sleepest or restest, in all things strive to exalt the Name of the great King of Light, and hasten to the Jordan to receive His baptism."

"Give bread and water, and a home to him who is tormented by the tyranny of persecution."

"When thou makest a gift, O chosen one, seek no witness thereof to mar thy bounty."

"The mercy, goodness and majesty of the King of Light cannot be fathomed."

"None can know these things save the life that is within thee, and the spirits and messengers that gird thee around."

"Thy creatures they know not even thy name."

"The Kings of Light ask one another, What is the name of the Great Light?

"They answer, He has no name!

"No poor sculptor of earth has fashioned his throne.

"The palace of the King was not built up by earthly masons.

"Immoveable he dwells in a city of Adamant, a city without discord or broils.

"In that city are no butchers, or gluttons surcharged with animal food.

" It knows not the wine of wantonness, nor the songs or riot.

" No corpses are to be seen in its streets, nor war, nor warriors.

" The tears of weeping women disturb it not.

" Revealer, who makest known the inmost secrets, have mercy upon us."

These are the simple rites of the Nazarines :—

" Assemble the faithful. Read to them the Scriptures. Pray to the Lord for His mercy, that His splendour may go before and His light follow after."

The fact that the disciples of the Baptist are called the Nazareens in the " Codex Nazaræus " is important. The Christians according to the Acts were called Nazarines, and the section of Christ's flock which kept close to the traditions of the Apostles was called the Nazarines for at least three hundred years. Pilate on the cross wrote up Ἰησοῦς ο Ναζαραῖος (Jesus the Nazarine). This in our Gospels is translated " Jesus of Nazareth," a place invented some think for the purpose. The "Encyclopædia" Britannica announces that there is no mention of this " Nazareth " outside the New Testament until Jerome and Eusebius seek to identify it with an insignificant village near the modern Nasira.

The Gospels announce that Christ was born in Bethlehem, but that he lived for some time in Nazareth, but a Roman Procurator in giving the name and crime of a condemned man would scarcely descend to such small facts in his biography. The prophecy, " He shall be called the Nazarine," wherever it comes from, has been literally fulfilled. Jews, old and modern, early Christians, Mussulmans, all the East, have used this title, and it is still used. " Nazarite " and " Nazarine " are the same word. " We are they," says Tertullian, " of whom it is written. Her Nazarites shall be whiter than snow."

And Tatian thus bitterly sums up the change of the Pauline party which converted an intuitive into a sacrificial religion. "Ye gave the Nazarite wine to drink, and commanded the Prophet saying, 'Prophesy not.'"

We must now consider a little more closely the contention that Christ and His disciples were orthodox Jews.

The main evidence for this is deduced from St. Paul's epistles, which assert roundly that the chief apostles "Cephas, James, and John" attempted to compel the new church to "live as do the Jews." They enforced the old laws about circumcision, the Sabbath, unclean meats, festivals, and holidays. They forbade any preaching to the Gentiles. In this last they were certainly backed by speeches put into the mouth of Jesus Himself in some of the Gospels. He commands His apostles to avoid the Gentiles and go to the "lost sheep of the House of Israel." They are not to give that which is holy to the dogs, or cast their pearls before swine. That the "dogs" mean the Gentiles is proved by Christ's dialogue with the woman of Samaria. And the following text is cited to clench the postulate that the earliest Christianity was pure Mosaism.

"Think not that I am come to destroy the law or the prophets. I am come not to destroy but to fulfil.

"For verily I say unto you, till heaven and earth pass, one jot or one tittle shall by no means pass from the law."

Now all this, it must be admitted would upset the main contention of this book, if by the word "law" Jesus and St. Paul meant the Mosaic law as interpreted by the dominant party.

Let us take St. Paul first. He is rather vague about the word "law," and uses it in more senses than one. Sometimes the word means the mere law of right and wrong. Sometimes it means the Jewish law as interpreted by the orthodox Jews; and sometimes as interpreted by the Essenes.

"For ye also have suffered like things of your own countrymen, even as they have of the Jews.

"Who both killed the Lord Jesus and their own prophets, and have persecuted us, and are contrary to all men, forbidding us to speak to the Gentiles that they might be saved."*

Here he plainly confuses the two together. He could never mean that it was the Essenes who killed Christ and the prophets, or that it was Caiaphus and the priestly party that forbid the Christians to spread Nazarine ideas amongst the Gentiles. The capital offence with them was preaching such ideas to the Jews.

Let us turn to the Epistle to the Romans. "The Church of Rome," says Renan, "was a Jewish Christian foundation in direct connection with the Church of Jerusalem."†

It was the chief stronghold of the Petrine party outside the Jewish capital. St. Paul in his epistle to this community attacks those who would be saved by "works," and he states explicitly that his own followers are only a remnant, that is a minority.‡ And the fourteenth chapter allows us to see the nature of the "works" relied on by the majority of the Christians in the Roman capital, the Petrine party, in point of fact.

They abstained from flesh meat, and were offended with those who preferred flesh meat to herbs.

They forbade the use of wine.

This completely shows that St. Paul's foes at Rome were Essenes. Killing and eating flesh meat, with

* 1 Thess. ii. 14*f*.

† "Conférences d'Angleterre," p. 67.

‡ Romans xi. 4, 6.

proper ceremonial, was a religious duty with orthodox Mosaism.

And other epistles show also that the "false Apostles," as St. Paul calls them, who opposed him in the church were Essenes. It could not be Jews of the orthodox Mosaism whom he accused of "forbidding to marry," or who had "each one a psalm, a doctrine, a tongue, a revelation."

It must be mentioned, too, that Origen in a translation of Josephus in the Philosophumena states that the Essenes insisted on circumcision, and that some of their more violent members "if they hear one discoursing of God and His laws if he be uncircumcised, one stands in watch for such a person when somewhere alone and threatens to slay him without he consents to circumcision."

That brings us to the first of our string of questions. Did Christianity know anything like early Buddhism and its Buddha?

Now certainly there was an early Christianity whose leader was a mere man. He is born of a woman, and has a line of human ancestors. He forsakes all to become a Nazareen, as Buddha desires to become a Yogi. He has his baptism, his fastings, his temptations by the spirit of evil. He sits in solitude to purify his soul, and render it a fit receptacle for the Spirit of God. He has human imperfections. He prays that the cup of death may pass away from him.

The Jewish Saint becomes full of the Spirit of God and goes forth to preach the Dharma Raj—the Kingdom of Justice. He denounces bloody sacrifices; and like Buddha, has his "Beatitudes," invoking blessings on altruism, a forgiving spirit, purity, the love of even our enemies. At the last supper a treacherous disciple dips into the dish of each. Both die like ordinary mortals; and a Magdalena washes the dead body of each with her tears.

The earliest account of this Jewish saint is contained in a Gospel called the "Gospel according to the Hebrews." The Bishop of Hieropolis, Papias, announces that "Matthew first in the Hebrew tongue wrote this Gospel, and each person translated it as he was able."

I will give a few quotations from this Gospel: I have only space for quite a few. Let us begin with the baptism of Jesus.

"And when the people had been baptised, Jesus also came and was baptised by John.

"And as he went up the heavens were opened, and he saw the Holy Spirit, in shape of a dove, descending and entering into him.

"And a voice from heaven said, Thou art my beloved Son. I have this day begotten thee.

"And straightway a great light shone around the place. And John fell down before him, and said, I pray thee, Lord, baptise thou me.

"But he prevented him, saying, Let be; for thus it is becoming that all things be fulfilled.

"And it came to pass when the Lord had come up from the water, the entire fountain of the Holy Spirit descended and rested upon him, and said to him—'My Son, in all the prophets did I wait thee, that thou mightest come and I might rest in thee;

"'For thou art my rest. Thou art my first-born Son for evet and for ever.'"

Two points are noticeable here. The Holy Ghost "enters into" Jesus. And the Voice from heaven makes an accurate quotation from the Old Testament.

"Thou art my beloved Son; this day have I begotten thee." This did not suit subsequent orthodoxy, and it has been altered.

Another passage has also been altered for the same purpose.

" And behold there came to him two rich men. And one said, Good master.

" But he said, Call me not good, for he that is good is one, the Father in the heavens."

I will give a few more quotations.

" I have come to abolish sacrifices, and if ye do not cease to sacrifice the wrath of God against you will not cease."

" Be ye approved money changers."

The transfiguration in this Gospel is very like Buddha's ascent to the Devaloca to meet his mother.

" Just now, my mother, the Holy Spirit, took me by one of my hairs and bore me up to the great mountain of Tabor.

" He that hath marvelled shall reign, and he that hath reigned shall rest."

Jesus figures as a prophet raised up from his brethren.

" I am he concerning whom Moses prophesied, saying, A prophet will the Lord our God raise unto you from your brethren even as me.

" Him hear ye in all things, for whosoever heareth not that prophet shall die."

It is to be mentioned also that the " locusts " eaten by John the Baptist are unknown in this Gospel.

" His food was wild honey whereof the taste was of manna."

Of a scene that is described as occurring on the night of the crucifixion, I will speak by-and-bye.

The church of Jerusalem had five characteristics :—

(1) They held Jesus to be " a man in like sense with all," as may be seen from Hippolytus (L. VII. 2).

(2) They rejected the writings of Paul, and indeed all other New Testament scriptures, except the Gospel according to the Hebrews.

(3) They refused to eat meat, like the Essenes.

(4) Like the Essenes also, they rejected wine, even in the Sacramentum. " Therefore do these men

reject the co-mixture of the heavenly wine, and wish it to be the water of the world only, not receiving God so as to have union with Him," says Irenæus (Hoer. v. 3) speaking of them.

(5) Like the Essenes they also insisted on the rite of circumcision. Here is another passage from Irenæus: " They use the Gospel according to Matthew only, and repudiate the Apostle Paul, maintaining that he was an apostate from the law. As to the prophetical writings, they endeavour to expound them in a somewhat singular manner. They practise circumcision, persevere in the observance of those customs which are enjoined by the law, and are so Judaic in their style of life that they even adore Jerusalem as if it were the House of God." (Hoer. iii. 1). Irenæus says also that their opinions were similar to those of Cerinthus, who held that Jesus was the son of Joseph and Mary, and that at His baptism the Holy Spirit came to Him.

But it is to be confessed that the Gospel according to the Hebrews has been assailed lately and pronounced later than the present St. Mark, of which it is affirmed to be an enlargement. In the Synoptics are found sprinkled about a number of passages nearly word for word the same, although the incidents and other speeches near these differ considerably. These facts have suggested that some earlier document was used by each Evangelist as a " Common Stock " ; and that if we take the special passages that are common to all three Gospels we shall get this document. It is held, too, that St. Mark being shorter and more free from miracles practically represents it, dating from the times of the Apostles.

There seem to me many weighty reasons against this last conclusion. Irenæus calls the second Gospel a Docetic Gospel.

Now a Docetic Gospel would naturally reject the

Virgin birth, or any birth at all, because the Docetœ viewed Christ as a Docetic Phantasm; it would also alter the account of Christ's death to suit its dogma, and this it seems to have done by inserting the doubt of Pilate and other touches, which have actually induced Huxley and other shrewd writers to argue that there was no dead body at all in the sepulchre owned by Joseph of Arimathea.

Certainly under these circumstances the greater brevity of Mark's Gospel is against its claims rather than a support. It is a stone statue, only half Docetic Phantasma, the other half honest Nazarine; and the strong torso shows where the mutilations have been made and the plaster added. Long ago Mr. Greg in his "Creed of Christendom," not having seen the passage in Irenæus, showed a "tendency" in Mark which seems to have induced him to throw overboard inconvenient matter. Matthew was the Gospel of the Jewish Christians, who held that Jesus was a mortal and the Jewish Messiah, whereas Mark was the Gospel of the Gentile converts. Says Mr. Greg:—"Matthew who wrote for the Jews, has the following passage in the injunctions pronounced by Jesus on the sending forth of the twelve Apostles: 'Go not into the way of the Gentiles, and into any city of the Samaritans enter ye not. But go rather to the lost sheep of the House of Israel' (x. 5). Mark, who wrote for the Gentiles, omits this unpalatable charge (vi. 7-13). Matthew (xv. 24) in the story of the Canaanitish woman, makes Jesus say: 'I am not sent but to the lost sheep of the House of Israel.' Mark (vii. 26) omits this expression entirely, and modifies the subsequent remark. In Matthew it is thus: 'It is not meet to take the children's bread and cast it unto the dogs.' In Mark it is softened by the preliminary: 'Let the children first be filled,' etc. Matthew (xxiv. 20): 'But pray ye that your flight be not in the winter, neither on the Sabbath day.' Mark omits the last clause.

"In the promise given to the disciples in answer to Peter's question: 'Behold we have forsaken all and followed thee, what shall we have therefore?' The following verse given by Matthew (xix. 28) is omitted by Mark (x. 28): 'Verily I say unto you that ye which have followed me in the regeneration when the Son of Man shall sit in the Throne of his glory, ye also shall sit upon twelve thrones judging the twelve tribes of Irsael.'" *

On the other hand Mr. Greg holds that there are passages in Matthew that were never in the written tradition at all, but are due to the pure fancy of the writer that put Matthew into its present form, such as the prophecy that a "Virgin shall conceive," the slaughter of the innocents, the flight into Egypt, the Magi who detected the star of the King of the Jews, the statement that Jesus as the Messiah is the "son of Abraham" and the son of David. But on one point here Mr. Greg is plainly wrong. The flight into Egypt was in the Nazarene version of the "Gospel according to the Hebrews," and so was the passage about Christ being born in "Bethlehem of Juda," and so was the passage "He shall be called a Nazarene." These three fragments are found in one chapter (Matt. ii.), which seems to authenticate the whole chapter, visit of the Magi, massacre of children, and all. And these passages are in Justin who used the "Gospel according to the Hebrews."

And this habit of Mark of wholesale crowding out for the purpose of spreading a later form of Christianity is of the highest importance to our narrative, as his main raid is against Essenism. Thus Mark throws out the scene with the money changers, which, if a real event, shows that Jesus far from being an orthodox

* "Creed of Christendom," p. 127.

Jew, knew little of Jewish customs, for the money changers and "doves" were a necessity to the Temple sacrifices, especially of the poor. But if our Mark knows nothing of this scene a writer who was in the in the field before him does, namely Justin. This is strong evidence that our present version of Mark does not represent the oldest tradition.

In Matthew we have this passage: "There be eunuchs which have made themselves eunuchs for the Kingdom of Heaven's sake. He that is able to receive it, let him receive it." This was the Essene doctrine that absolute continence was necessary for the higher life. And the doctrine is put more strongly (Matt. vii. 27). "Whoso looketh on a woman to lust after her hath committed adultery already with her in his heart."

This occurs when Christ is treating of adultery and divorce, and Mark with probably this passage before him, inserts this contradictory precept: "For this cause shall a man leave his father and mother and cleave to his wife, and they twain shall be one flesh" (x. 7, 8). As we see from the Apocalypse, the hundred and forty-four thousand of the sealed ones at the day of judgment have never been defiled with women at all, it is plain that this last passage was never in the early Gospel.

The Essenes had for a crucial object the removal of the plague spot in all religions, the sin offering. Twice Christ in Matthew (ix. 13; xii. 7) says He will have "mercy and not sacrifice." The language is stronger in the Gospel according to the Hebrews: "Except ye cease from sacrificing, the wrath of God abideth in you." Mark throws out all this because the Pauline Christianity had brought back the sin offering. Its motto was: "Without shedding of blood there is no remission."

Then in Mark the claim of Peter to leadership, and

the status of St. James, are also ignored. And an attempt has also been made to neutralise the strong speeches in Matthew and Luke about poverty and family renunciation. "Blessed are the poor!" and "Woe unto you ye rich!" are cut out. In Luke (xiv. 26) we have this passage:—

"If any man come to me and hate not his father and mother and wife and children and brethren and sisters, yea, and his own life also, he cannot be my disciple."

Now it is quite plain that Mark knew of this passage, and thus he explains it away:—

"And Jesus answered and said: Verily I say unto you there is no man that hath left house or brethren or sisters or father or mother or wife or children or lands for my sake and the Gospel's, but he shall receive an hundred fold this time, houses, etc. . . . and in the world to come eternal life" (Mark x. 29). No two precepts could more widely diverge. In the one a future in heaven or hell depends on complete renunciation. In the other this is made optional. A man who leaves his wife, say, if he can establish a plausible motive for the act, may go to paradise, but he may do so likewise if he clings to her and his lands, his house and shekels.

Mark (vi. 10) in giving an account of the sending forth of the Twelve which is word for word like that of Matthew, omits this passage where Jesus enjoins them to "inquire who is worthy" when they came to a city. The Essenes had brother initiates in each town, who were bound to entertain and conceal the wandering missionary at the risk of their lives; but the Pauline Christians evidently had not, hence the omission. But the command of Christ is infamously unjust without it. According to Mark's Gospel, Jews, and Gentiles too, are to be punished for ever in hell for refusing to entertain fanatic preachers of a religion about which most of them can know nothing.

Matthew (vi. 16) has a passage about the Essene fast, face washing, etc. The great fast is an important feature in the Codex Nazaræus. How does Mark treat all this? He not only banishes all about fasting from the sermon on the Mount, but he concocts a passage condemning "washings" and "pots and brazen vessels," and asserting that the disciples of Jesus always eat without washing their hands.

And there is a passage in Mark that tells still more strongly against the theory that the earliest Gospel was Pauline:—

"For false Christs and false prophets shall arise, and shall show signs and wonders to seduce if it were possible the very elect" (Mark xiii. 21).

Matthew (xxiv. 23) gives the same passage almost word for word, but we know from the "Gospel according to the Hebrews" that the words "False Apostles" were included in the passage at one time. "For there shall be false Christs, false prophets, false apostles." Justin also puts it in: "For many false Christs and false Apostles shall arise and shall deceive many of the faithful." This is of course a gird against Paul; and Renan urges that the "enemy who sowed tares" (Matt. xiii. 25) is also that teacher. "The enemy" was St. Paul's nickname with the early church.

All this militates also against the "Triple Tradition" of Dr. Abbott, in the "Encyclopædia Britannica," a theory that in seeking the source of those passages that are the same in the three Synoptics, seeks to substitute for the "Gospel according to the Hebrews" an alleged written "tradition" dating from the Apostles. But in this "Triple Tradition" the transfiguration and the two accounts of Jesus multiplying food must have figured. How is it that James, who did not die till A.D. 44 knows nothing about it and them. Had he known of those astounding miracles, he would certainly have made use of them to solemnise his episcopal injunctions. How, too, was it that Josephus who lived amongst the Essenes, had never heard of it ?—nor John, nor Peter ? And how is it that the earliest and most reliable Gospel, if it is represented by Mark, is a theological pamphlet fired off against the men that it admits in its own pages (Mark iii. 14), were specially commissioned by Christ to preach His Gospel. Paul thought that the teaching of these men was "beggarly elements," and avoided them. Mr. Greg has pointed out that no single word has ever been quoted by Paul as coming from the flesh and blood Christ. He gathered all he knew of Jesus from his visions, and despised "traditions of man" (Col. ii. 8), including the "triple" as well as the solitary. But supposing that the cart-before-the-horse exegesis is really right, and that Mark's Gospel is really the earliest and most authentic record of the life of Jesus, from this it would result that Peter, James and John knew nothing of His real thoughts, and that the astounding scheme of God Almighty descending to earth in human form and suffering an ignominious death to teach the world was an absolute failure. And it would show that Christ Himself has at any rate altered His ideas since His Ascension.

I may pause here to make a few remarks about a scripture which I think has been much undervalued, the "Gospel of the Infancy." This was believed by Origen to be written by Basilides. It was certainly known to Irenæus.* As he is the first to talk of the four Canonical Gospels, it thus receives an antiquity at least equal to theirs. But it goes beyond this, for the author only knows one Gospel, not four. He calls it the "Gospel of Perfection." And from the

* Migne, "Dictionnaire des Apocryphes," Tome I.

few meagre details that he gives, this seems to have been the "Gospel according to the Hebrews." Jesus was born in a cavern as in the copy of this Gospel used by Justin. Luke has plainly taken the account of Simeon from this Gospel, for the passage "to be a light to lighten the Gentiles" is not to be found in the hymn of thanksgiving in this Gospel. Early Christianity was a purely Jewish movement.

But what is most remarkable is the Buddhism. In Alexandria, as we have seen, some two hundred years before Christ there were a number of ascetics who believed that they could pass muster as Buddhist monks in a great Buddhist festival. Their experiment was quite successful. They were properly entertained on their arrival in Ceylon as real Buddhists. This fact proves that a life of Buddha of some sort must have reached Alexandria some two hundred years at least before the Saviour's birth. In that case, say about the year 100 A.D., we might expect to find a life of Buddha at Alexandria and a life of Jesus at Jerusalem, both describing the career of a holy Personage with somewhat similar details.

The Gospel of the Infancy is a band that seems to tie these two biographies together.

Let us recapitulate a few of these points that do this.

(1) The palm-tree bends down to Mary as the Asoka tree to Yashodara.

(2) The story of Simeon, the accounts of the bright light being almost word for word the same.

(3) The idol bending down to the Infant Jesus.

(4) The miracle of the sparrows restored to life.

(5) Judas Iscariot in early life attacked Jesus just as Devadetta, the Judas of Buddhism, attacked Buddha. A violent blow that Jesus received in the left side made a mark which was destined to be the exact spot that received the mortal spear-thrust at the Crucifixion.

(6) The whole story of the disputation with the Doctors seems copied servilely from the "Lalita Vistara."

(7) Buddhism had invaded Persia, and Maitreya, the coming Buddha, was expected five hundred years after Buddha's death—the Persian Buddhists called him Sosiosh. The Gospel of the Infancy explains the presence of the Magi, which in the Canonical Gospels is quite unintelligible. Why should Persians come with hysterical enthusiasm to greet a Messiah whose chief exploit was to be the slaughter of all Persians and all the other nations except Jews. The "Gospel of the Infancy" announces that Zoroaster had sent them. The Persians mixed up Sakya Muni, Buddha, Mithras and Zoroaster and were expecting Sosiosh at the time.

CHAPTER XII

MORE COINCIDENCES

Twelve Disciples—Love one another—Buddhist Beatitudes—The Sower—Blind Guides—Early Buddhism a religion of joy—Buddhist Baptismal Rites—Other Coincidences.

I HAVE shown certain curious points of contact between the Buddhist and the Christian scriptures. Here are a few more :—

"THEN WAS JESUS LED UP BY THE SPIRIT INTO THE WILDERNESS, TO BE TEMPTED OF THE DEVIL."

Comfortable dowagers driving to church three times on Sunday would be astonished to learn that the essence of Christianity is in this passage. Its meaning has quite passed away from Protestantism, almost from Christendom. The "Lalita Vistara" fully shows what that meaning is. Without Buddhism it would be lost. Jesus was an Essene, and the Essene, like the Indian Yogi, sought to obtain divine union and the "gifts of the Spirit" by solitary reverie in retired spots. In what is called the "Monastery of our Lord" on the Quarantania, a cell is shown with rude frescoes of Jesus and Satan. There, according to tradition, the demoniac hauntings that all mystics speak of occurred.

"I HAVE NEED TO BE BAPTISED OF THEE."

A novice in Yoga has a guru, or teacher. Buddha, in riding away from the palace, by-and-by reached a jungle near Vaisâlî. He at once put himself under a Brahmin Yogi named Arâta Kâlâma, but his spiritual insight developed so rapidly that in a short time the Yogi offered to Buddha the arghya, the offering of rice, flowers, sesamun, etc., that the humble novice usually presents to his instructor, and asked him to teach instead of learning.*

THIRTY YEARS OF AGE.

M. Ernest de Bunsen, in his work, "The Angel Messiah," says that Buddha, like Christ, commenced preaching at thirty years of age. He certainly must have preached at Vaisâlî, for five young men became his disciples there, and exhorted him to go on with his teaching.† He was twenty-nine when he left the palace, therefore he might well have preached at thirty. He did not turn the wheel of the law until after a six years' meditation under the Tree of Knowledge.

"AND WHEN HE HAD FASTED FORTY DAYS AND FORTY NIGHTS."

Buddha, immediately previous to his great encounter with Mâra, the tempter, fasted forty-nine days and nights.‡

"COMMAND THAT THESE STONES BE MADE BREAD."

The first temptation of Buddha, when Mâra assailed him, appealed to his hunger, as we have seen.

THE TWELVE GREAT DISCIPLES.

"Except in my religion, the twelve great disciples are not to be found."§ Speech by Buddha.

* Foucaux, "Lalita Vistara," p. 228.

† Foucaux, "Lalita Vistara," p. 236.

‡ "Chinese Life," by Wung Puh.

§ "Bigandet," p. 301.

"THE DISCIPLE WHOM JESUS LOVED."

One disciple was called Upatishya (the beloved disciple). In a former existence he and Maudgalyâyana had prayed that they might sit, the one on the right hand and the other on the left. Buddha granted this prayer. The other disciples murmured much.*

"GO YE INTO ALL THE WORLD."

From Benares Buddha sent forth the sixty-one disciples. "Go ye forth," he said, "and preach Dharma, no two disciples going the same way."†

"THE SAME CAME TO JESUS BY NIGHT."

Professor Rhys Davids points out that Yâsas, a young rich man, came to Buddha by night, for fear of his rich relations.

PAX VOBISCUM.

On one point I have been a little puzzled. The password of the Buddhist Wanderers was "Sadhu!" which does not seem to correspond with the "Pax Vobiscum!" (Matt. x. 13) of Christ's disciples. But I have just come across a passage in Renan,‡ which shows that the Hebrew word was "Schalom!" (*bonheur!*) This is almost a literal translation of "Sadhu!"

"A NEW COMMANDMENT GIVE I YOU, THAT YE LOVE ONE ANOTHER."

"By love alone can we conquer wrath. By good alone can we conquer evil. The whole world dreads violence. All men tremble to the presence of death. Do to others that which ye would have them do to you. Kill not. Cause no death."§

* Bigandet, p. 153.

† *Ibid*, p. 126.

‡ "Les Apôtres," p. 22.

§ "Sûtra of Forty-two Sections," v. 129.

THE BEATITUDES.

The Buddhists, like the Christians, have got their Beatitudes. They are plainly arranged for chant and response in the temples. It is to be noted that the Christian Beatitudes were a portion of the early Christian ritual.

The "long suffering and meek," those "who follow a peaceful calling," those who are not "weary in well-doing," are included in the catalogue.

Here is one verse :—

10 *Self-restraint* and *purity*,
The knowledge of noble truths,
The attainment of Nirvâna—
This is the greatest blessing.

THE ONE THING NEEDFUL.

Certain subtle questions were proposed to Buddha, such as :—"What will best conquer the evil passions of men ?" "What is the most savoury gift for the alms-bowl of the mendicant ?" "Where is true happiness to be found ?" Buddha replied to them all with one word "Dharma" (the heavenly life).*

"WHOSOEVER SHALL SMITE THEE ON THY RIGHT CHEEK, OFFER HIM THE OTHER ALSO."

A merchant from Sûnaparanta having joined Buddha's society, was desirous of preaching to his relations, and is said to have asked the permission of the master so to do.

"The people of Sûnaparanta," said Buddha, "are exceedingly violent ; if they revile you what will you do ?"

"I will make no reply," said the mendicant.

"And if they strike you ?"

"I will not strike in return," said the mendicant.

"And if they kill you ?"

* "Bigandet," p. 225.

"Death," said the missionary, "is no evil in itself. Many even desire it to escape from the vanities of life."*

BUDDHA'S THIRD COMMANDMENT.

"Commit no adultery." Commentary by Buddha: "This law is broken by even looking at the wife of another with a lustful mind."†

THE SOWER.

It is recorded that Buddha once stood beside the ploughman Kasibhâradvaja, who reproved him for his idleness. Buddha answered thus: "I, too, plough and sow, and from my ploughing and sowing I reap immortal fruit. My field is religion. The weeds that I pluck up are the passions of cleaving to this life. My plough is wisdom, my seed purity."‡

On another occasion he described almsgiving as being like "good seed sown on a good soil that yields an abundance of fruits. But alms given to those who are yet under the tyrannical yoke of the passions are like a seed deposited in a bad soil. The passions of the receiver of the alms choke, as it were, the growth of merits."§

"NOT THAT WHICH GOETH INTO THE MOUTH DEFILETH A MAN."

In the "Sûtta Nipâta" (chap. II.) is a discourse on the food that defiles a man (Âmaghanda). Therein it is explained at some length that the food that is eaten cannot defile a man, but "destroying living beings, killing, cutting, binding, stealing, falsehood, adultery, evil thoughts, murder"—this defiles a man, not the eating of flesh.

* "Bigandet," p. 216.

† Buddhaghosa's "Parables," by Max Müller and Rodgers, p. 153.

‡ "Hardy "Manual," p. 215.

§ "Bigandet," p. 211.

"WHERE YOUR TREASURE IS."

"A man," says Buddha, "buries a treasure in a deep pit, which lying concealed therein day after day profits him nothing, but there is a treasure of charity, piety, temperance, soberness, a treasure secure, impregnable, that cannot pass away, a treasure that no thief can steal. Let the wise man practice Dharma. This is a treasure that follows him after death."*

THE HOUSE ON THE SAND.

"It (the seen world) is like a city of sand. Its foundation cannot endure."†

BLIND GUIDES.

"Who is not freed cannot free others. The blind cannot guide in the way."‡

"AS YE SOW, SO SHALL YE REAP."

"As men sow, thus shall they reap."§

"A CUP OF COLD WATER TO ONE OF THESE LITTLE ONES."

"Whosoever piously bestows a little water shall receive an ocean in return."||

"BE NOT WEARY IN WELL-DOING."

"Not to be weary in well-doing."**

"GIVE TO HIM THAT ASKETH."

"Give to him that asketh, even though it be but a little."††

* "Khuddaka Pâtha," p. 13.
† "Lalita Vistara," p. 172.
‡ *Ibid*, p. 179.
§ "Ta-chwang-yan-king-lun," serm. 57.
|| *Ibid*, serm. 20.
** "Mahâmangala Sutta," ver. 7.
†† "Udânavarga," chap. xx., ver 15.

"DO UNTO OTHERS," ETC.

"With pure thoughts and fulness of love I will do towards others what I do for myself."*

"PREPARE YE THE WAY OF THE LORD!"

Buddha's triumphant entry into Râjâgriha (the "City of the King") has been compared to Christ's entry into Jerusalem. Both, probably, never occurred, and only symbolise the advent of a Divine Being to earth. It is recorded in the Buddhist scriptures that on these occasions a "Precursor of Buddha" always appears.†

"WHO DID SIN, THIS MAN OR HIS PARENTS, THAT HE WAS BORN BLIND?" (John ix. 3).

Professor Kellogg, in his work entitled "The Light of Asia and the Light of the World," condemns Buddhism in nearly all its tenets. But he is especially emphatic in the matter of the metempsychosis. The poor and helpless Buddhist has to begin again and again "the weary round of birth and death," whilst the righteous Christians go at once into life eternal.

Now, it seems to me that this is an example of the danger of contrasting two historical characters when we have a strong sympathy for the one and a strong prejudice against the other. Professor Kellogg has conjured up a Jesus with nineteenth century ideas, and a Buddha who is made responsible for all the fancies that were in the world B.C. 500. Professor Kellogg is a professor of an American university, and as such must know that the doctrine of the *gilgal* (the Jewish name for the metempsychosis) was as widely spread in Palestine A.D. 30, as it was in Râjâgriha

* "Lalita Vistara." Chap. v.

† "Bigandet," p. 147.

B.C. 500. An able writer in the "Church Quarterly Review" of October, 1885, maintains that the Jews brought it from Babylon. Dr. Ginsberg, in his work on the "Kabbalah," shows that the doctrine continued to be held by the Jews as late as the ninth century of our era. He shows, too, that St. Jerome has recorded that it was "propounded amongst the early Christians as an esoteric and traditional doctrine."

The author of the article in the "Church Quarterly Review" in proof of its existence adduces the question put by the disciples of Christ in reference to the man that was born blind. And if it was considered that a man could be born blind as a punishment for sin, that sin must have been plainly committed before his birth. Oddly enough, in the "White Lotus of Dharma," there is an account of the healing of a blind man. "Because of the sinful conduct of the man (in a former birth) this malady has risen."

But a still more striking instance is given in the case of the man sick with the palsy (Luke v. 18). The Jews believed, with modern Orientals, that grave diseases like paralysis were due, not to physical causes in this life, but to moral causes in previous lives. And if the account of the cure of the paralytic is to be considered historical, it is quite clear that this was Christ's idea when He cured the man, for He distinctly announced that the cure was effected not by any physical processes, but by annulling the "sins" which were the cause of his malady.

Traces of the metempsychosis idea still exist in Catholic Christianity. The doctrine of original sin is said by some writers to be a modification of it. Certainly the fancy that the works of supererogation of their saints can be transferred to others is the Buddhist idea of good karma, which is transferable in a similar manner.

"IF THE BLIND LEAD THE BLIND, BOTH SHALL FALL INTO THE DITCH" (Matt. xv. 14).

"As when a string of blind men are clinging one to the other neither can the foremost see, nor the middle one see, nor the hindmost see. Just so, methinks, Vâsettha is the talk of the Brahmins, versed in the Three Vedas."*

"EUNUCHS FOR THE KINGDOM OF HEAVEN'S SAKE."

In the days of St. Thomas à Kempis the worshipper was modelled on the Christ. In our days the Christ seems modelled on the worshipper. The Bodleian professor of Sanskrit writes thus:—"Christianity teaches that in the highest form of life love is intensified; Buddhism teaches that in the highest state of existence all love is extinguished. According to Christianity, Go and earn your own bread, and support yourself and your family. Marriage, it says, is honourable, and undefiled, and married life a field where holiness can grow."

But history is history; and a French writer has recently attacked Christ for attempting to bring into Europe the celibacy and pessimism of Buddhism. This author in his work, "Jésus Bouddha," cites Luke xiv. 26:—

"If any man come to me, and hate not his father, and mother, and *wife*, and children, and brethren, and sisters, yea, and his own life also, he cannot be my disciple."

He adduces also:—

"Let the dead bury their dead.

"Think not that I have come to send peace on earth: I come not to send peace, but a sword. For I am come to set a man at variance against his father, and the daughter against her mother, and the daughter-in-law against her mother-in-law. And a man's foes shall be they of his own household" (Matt. x. 34-36).

* Buddha, in the "Tevigga Sutta," I., 15.

"And the brother shall deliver up the brother to death, and the father the child; and the children shall rise up against their parents, and cause them to be put to death" (*Ibid*, ver. 21).

"So likewise, whosoever he be of you that forsaketh not all that he hath, he cannot be my disciple" (Luke xiv. 33).

The author says that all this is pure nihilism, and Essene communism. "The most sacred family ties are to be renounced, and man to lose his individuality, and become a unit in a vast scheme to overturn the institutions of his country."

"Qu'importe au fanatisme la ruine de la societé humaine."

Here also is a remarkable passage from an American writer:—

"The anticosmic tendency of the Christian doctrine," says Mr. Felix Oswald,* distinguishes it from all religions except Buddhism. In the language of the New Testament the 'world' is everywhere a synonym of evil and sin, the flesh everywhere the enemy of the spirit. . . . The gospel of Buddha though pernicious, is, however, a perfectly consistent doctrine. Birth, life, and re-birth is an eternal round of sorrow and disappointment. The present and the future are but the upper and lower tyre of an ever-rolling wheel of woe. The only salvation from the wheel of life is an escape to the peace of Nirvâna. The attempt to graft this doctrine upon the optimistic theism of Palestine has made the Christian ethics inconsistent and contradictory. A paternal Jehovah, who yet eternally and horribly tortures a vast plurality of his children. An earth the perfect work of a benevolent God; yet a vale of tears not made to be enjoyed, but only to be despised and renounced. An omnipotent heaven, and yet unable to prevent the intrigues

* "Secret of the East," p. 27.

and constant victories of hell. Christianity is evidently not a homogeneous but a composite, a hybrid religion; and considered in connection with the indications of history, and the evidence of the above-named ethical and traditional analogies these facts leave no reasonable doubt that the founder of the Galilean Church was a disciple of Buddha S'âkya muni'' (p. 139).

A propos of this "pessimism," is it certain that early Buddhism and S'iva Buddhism were quite in harmony?

Asoka certainly believed that Buddhism was an optimism. "On my subjects I confer happiness both in this world and the next." Buddha called his message "Subhashita" (the glad tidings), and declared that the man who was spiritually awakened had joy for his accompanying shadow. The Burmese are the happiest of God's creatures.

"THEN ALL HIS DISCIPLES FORSOOK HIM AND FLED."

It is recorded that on one occasion when a "must" elephant charged furiously, "all the disciples deserted Buddha. Ânanda alone remained."*

"IF THE RIGHT EYE OFFEND THEE."

Mr. Felix Oswald† announces, without, however, giving a more detailed reference, that according to Max Müller's translation of the "Ocean of Worlds," a young monk meets a rich woman, who pities his hard lot.

"Blessed is the woman who looks into thy lovely eyes!"

"Lovely!" replied the monk. "Look here!" And plucking out one of his eyes he held it up, bleeding and ghastly, and asked her to correct her opinion.

* "Fo-sho-hing-tsan-king, IV., 21.

† "Chinese Dhammapada," p. 51.

WALKING ON THE WATER.

Certain villagers, hard of belief, were listening to Buddha on the shore of a mighty river. Suddenly by a miracle the great teacher caused a man to appear walking on the water from the other side, without immersing his feet.*

"AND, LO! THERE WAS A GREAT CALM."

Pûrna, one of Buddha's disciples, had a brother in danger of shipwreck in a "black storm." But the guardian spirits of Pûrna informed him of this. He at once transported himself through the air from the distant inland town to the deck of the ship. "Immediately the black tempest ceased as if Sumeru had arrested it."†

"WHY EATETH YOUR MASTER WITH PUBLICANS AND SINNERS?" (Matt. ix. 11).

The courtesan Amrapalî invited Buddha and his disciples to a banquet in the mango grove at Vaisâli. Buddha accepted. Some rich princes, sparkling in emeralds, came and gave him a similar invitation. He refused. They were very angry to see him sit at meat with Amrapalî. He explained to his disciples that the harlot might enter the kingdom of Dharma more easily than the prince.‡

THE PENITENT THIEF.

Buddha confronts a terrible bandit in his mountain retreat and converts him.§

"THERE WAS WAR IN HEAVEN."

Professor Beal, in his "Catena of Buddhist Scriptures" (p. 52), tells us that, in the "Saddharma

* "The Secret of the East," p. 134.

† Burnouf, "Introduction," p. 229.

‡ "Bigandet," p. 251.

§ "Chinese Dhammapada," p. 98.

Prâkasa Sasana Sûtra," a great war in heaven is described. In it the "wicked dragons" assault the legions of heaven. After a terrible conflict they are driven down by Indra and the heavenly hosts.

"THE KINGDOM OF HEAVEN IS LIKE UNTO A MERCHANT-MAN SEEKING GOODLY PEARLS, WHO, WHEN HE HAD FOUND ONE PEARL OF GREAT PRICE, WENT AND SOLD ALL THAT HE HAD AND BOUGHT IT" (Matt. xiii. 45).

The most sacred emblem of Buddhism is called the maṇi (pearl), and in the Chinese biography a merchant seeking goodly pearls finds it, and unfortunately drops it into the sea. Rather than lose it he tries to drain the sea dry.*

THE VOICE FROM THE SKY.

This sounds often in the Buddhist narratives.†

FAITH.

"Faith is the first gate of the Law."‡

"All who have faith in me obtain a mighty joy."§

"THOU ART NOT YET FIFTY YEARS OLD, AND HAST THOU SEEN ABRAHAM?"

In the "White Lotus of Dharma" (chap. xiv.), Buddha is asked how it is that, having sat under the bo-tree only forty years ago, he had been able, according to his boast, to see many Buddhas and saints who died hundreds of years previously. He answers that he has lived many hundred thousand myriads of Kotis, and that though in the form of a Buddha, he is in reality Swayambhu, the Self-Existent, the Father of the million worlds. In proof of this

* "Rom. Hist., p. 228.

† See Beal, "Rom. Hist.," p. 105.

‡ "Lalita Vistara," p. 39.

§ *Ibid*, p. 188.

statement he causes two Buddhas of the Past, Prabhûtaratna and another, to appear in the sky. The first pronounces loudly these words: "It is well! It is well!" These Buddhas appear with their sepulchral canopies (stûpas) of diamonds, red pearls, emeralds, etc. Peter, at the scene of the Transfiguration, said to Christ:—

"Let us make here three tabernacles—one for Thee, one for Moses, and one for Elias." Why should Peter want to adopt a Buddhist custom and build tabernacles for the dead Moses and the dead Elias? Why, also, should Moses come from the tomb to support a teacher who had torn his covenant with Yahve to shreds?

"HE WAS TRANSFIGURED BEFORE THEM."

Buddha, leaving Maudgalyâyana and another disciple to represent him, went off through the air to the Devaloka, to the Heaven Tuśita, to preach to the spirits in prison and to convert his mother. When he came down from the mountain (Mienmo), a staircase of glittering diamonds, seen by all, helped his descent. His appearance was blinding. The "six glories" glittered on his person. Mortals and spirits hymned the benign Being who emptied the hells.*

In the "Gospel according to the Hebrews" is a curious passage which Baur and Hilgenfeld hold to be the earliest version of the Transfiguration narrative.

"Just now my mother, the Holy Spirit, took me by one of my hairs and bore me up on to the great mountain of Tabor."

This is curious. Buddha and Jesus reach the Mount of Transfiguration, each through the influence of his mother. But perhaps the Jewish writer did not like the universalism inculcated in the Buddhist narrative.

* "Bigandet," p. 209.

"HE BEGAN TO WASH THE DISCIPLES' FEET" (John xiii. 5).

In a vihâra at Gândhâra was a monk so loathsome and stinking, on account of his maladies, that none of his brother disciples dare go near him. The great Teacher came and tended him lovingly and washed his feet.*

THE GREAT BANQUET OF BUDDHA.

In the "Lalita Vistara" (p. 51) it is stated that those who have faith will become "sons of Buddha," and partake of the "food of the kingdom." Four things draw disciples to his banquet—gifts, soft words, production of benefits, conformity of benefits.

BAPTISM.

In a Chinese life of Buddha by Wung Puh,† it is announced that Buddha at Vaisâlî delivered a Sûtra entitled "The Baptism that Rescues from Life and Death and confers Salvation."

"AND NONE OF THEM IS LOST BUT THE SON OF PERDITION."

Buddha like Christ had a treacherous disciple, Devadatta. He schemed with a wicked prince, who sent men armed with bows and swords to slaughter Buddha. Devadatta tried other infamous stratagems. His end was appalling. Coming in a palanquin to arrest Buddha, he got out to stretch himself. Suddenly fierce flames burst out, and he was carried down to the hell Avîchi (the Rayless Place). There, in a red-hot cauldron, impaled by one red bar and pierced by two others, he will stay for a whole Kalpa. Then he will be forgiven."‡

* "Chinese Dhammapada, p. 94.

† See Beal, "Journ. As. Soc.," Vol. XX., p. 172.

‡ "Bigandet," p. 244.

THE LAST SUPPER.

Buddha had his last supper or repast with his disciples. A treacherous disciple changed his alms-bowl, and apparently he was poisoned.* Fierce pains seized him as he journeyed afterwards. He was forced to rest. He sent a message to his host, Kunda, the son of the jeweller, to feel no remorse although the feast had been his death. Under two trees he now died.

It will be remembered that during the last supper of Jesus a treacherous disciple "dipped into his dish," but as Jesus was not poisoned, the event had no sequence.

"NOW FROM THE SIXTH HOUR THERE WAS DARKNESS OVER ALL THE LAND UNTIL ABOUT THE NINTH HOUR."

The critical school base much of their contention that the Gospels do not record real history on this particular passage. They argue that such an astounding event could not have escaped Josephus and Tacitus. When Buddha died, the "sun and moon withdrew their shining," and dust and ashes fell like rain. "The great earth quaked throughout. The crash of the thunder shook the heavens and the earth, rolling along the mountains and valleys."† The Buddhist account is certainly not impossible, for the chronicler takes advantage of the phenomena of an Indian dust-storm to produce his dark picture. At Lucknow, before the siege, I remember a storm so dense at mid-day that some ladies with my regiment thought the Day of Judgment had arrived.

"AND MANY BODIES OF THE SAINTS WHICH SLEPT AROSE."

When Buddha died at Kusinâgara, Ânanda and another disciple saw many denizens of the unseen world in the city, by the river Yigdan.‡

* See Rockhill's, "Buddha," p. 133.

† "Fo-sho-hing-tsan-king," v. 26.

‡ Rockhill's "Life of the Buddha," p. 133.

The Buddhist baptism has striking analogies with that of the Christians. The Swastika Cross is the only cross in the Catacombs, and for this baptism a large Swastika cross is marked on the ground called Sastika Asan. On this sits the postulant, and holy water is sprinkled on his head. That head is shaved, a rope is put round his neck. His name is changed, and he is made to vow that he "will not amass property of any kind," nor "go near a woman," nor touch intoxicating liquors of any kind, nor animal food. He vows to devote himself to the worship of the Chaitya and the Trinity, Buddha (Spirit) Dharma (Matter), Sañgha, who is Padmapani, the Gnostic "Christos" as distinguished from Jesus.

"TO ANOINT MY BODY TO THE BURYING" (Mark xiv. 8).

The newly-discovered fragments of the Gospel of Peter give us a curious fact. They record that Mary Magdalene, "taking with her her friends," went to the sepulchre of Jesus to "place themselves beside him and perform the rites" of wailing, beating breasts, etc. Amrapalî and other courtesans did the same rites to Buddha, and the disciples were afterwards indignant that impure women should have "washed his dead body with their tears."*

In the Christian records are three passages, all due, I think, to the Buddhist narrative. In one, "a woman" anoints Jesus; in John (xii. 7), "Mary" anoints him; in Luke, a "sinner," who kisses and washes His feet with her hair. Plainly these last passages are quite irrational. No woman could have performed the washing and other burial rites on a man alive and in health.

* Rockhill, "Thibetan Life," p. 153.

"THEY PARTED MY GARMENTS."

The Abbé Huc tells us* that on the death of the Bokté Lama, his garments are cut into little strips and prized immensely.

"HE APPEARED UNTO MANY."

Buddha prophesied that he would appear after his death."† In a Chinese version quoted by Eitel,‡ Buddha, to soothe his mother, who had come down weeping from the skies, opens his coffin lid and appears to her. In the temple sculptures he is constantly depicted coming down to the altar during worship.

THE "GREAT WHITE THRONE."

Mr. Upham, in his "History of Buddhism," (pp. 56, 57), gives a description of the Buddhist heaven. There is a "high mountain," and a city "four square" with gates of gold and silver, adorned with precious stones. Seven moats surround the city. Beyond the last one is a row of marble pillars studded with jewels. The great throne of the god stands in the centre of a great hall, and is surmounted by a white canopy. Round the great throne are seated heavenly ministers, who record men's actions in a "golden book." A mighty tree is conspicuous in the garden. In the Chinese heaven is the "Gem Lake," by which stands the peach-tree, whose fruit gives immortality.

THE ATONEMENT.

The idea of transferred good Karma, the merits of the former lives of an individual being passed on to another individual, is, of course, quite foreign to the lower Judaism, which believed in no after life at all. In the view of the higher Buddhism, Sâkya

* "Voyages," II., p. 278.
† "Lotus," p. 144.
‡ "Three Lectures," p. 57.
§ See illustrations to my "Buddhism in Christendom."

Muni saved the world by his teaching; but to the lower, the Buddhism of offerings and temples and monks, this doctrine of Karma was the life-blood. It was proclaimed that Buddha had a vast stock of superfluous Karma, and that offerings at a temple might cause the worshipper in his next life to be a prince instead of a pig or a coolie. In the "Lalita Vistara"* it is announced that when Buddha overcame Mâra, all flesh rejoiced, the blind saw, the deaf heard, the dumb spake, the hells were cleared, and all by reason of Buddha's Karma in previous lives.

St. Paul is very contradictory about the atonement. This passage seems pure Buddhism.

"As by the offence of one judgment came upon all men to condemnation, even so by the righteousness of one the free gift came upon all men unto justification of life." (Rom. v. 18).

Contrast this with another passage:—

"Whom God hath set forth to be a propitiation through faith in His blood, to declare His righteousness for the remission of sins" (Rom. iii. 25).

* Chinese version, p. 225.

PLATE 15.

BUDDHIST MONKS.

CHAPTER XIII

RITES

The Abbé Huc on the close similarity of Christian and Buddhist rites—Confirmed by Fathers Disderi and Grueber—Rev. S. Beal on a Buddhist liturgy—Mr. Fergusson holds that the various details of the Christian Basilica have been taken from the temples of the Buddhists—On which side was the borrowing ?—Arguments *pro* and *con*.

I HAVE left myself little space to write of the many points of close similarity between the Buddhists and the Roman Catholics.

The French missionary, Huc, in his celebrated travels in Thibet, was much struck with this similarity.

"The crozier, the mitre, the dalmatic, the cope or *pluvial*, which the grand lâmas wear on a journey, or when they perform some ceremony outside the temple, the service with a double choir, psalmody, exorcisms, the censer swinging on five chains and contrived to be opened and shut at will, benediction by the lâmas, with the right hand extended over the heads of the faithful, the chaplet, sacerdotal celibacy, Lenten retirements from the world, the worship of saints, fasts, processions, litanies, holy water—these are the points of contact between the Buddhists and ourselves."

Listen also to Father Disderi, who visited Thibet in the year 1714. "The lâmas have a tonsure like our priests, and are bound over to perpetual celibacy. They study their scriptures in a language and in characters that differ from the ordinary characters. They recite prayers in choir. They serve the temple, present the offerings, and keep the lamps perpetually alight. They offer to God corn and barley and paste and water in little vases, which are extremely clean. Food thus offered is considered consecrated, and they eat it. The lâmas have local superiors, and a superior-general."*

Father Grueber, with another priest, named Dorville, passed from Pekin through Thibet to Patna in the year 1661. Henry Prinsep† thus sums up what he has recorded :—

"Father Grueber was much struck with the extraordinary similarity he found, as well in the doctrine as in the rituals, of the Buddhists of Lha Sa, to those of his own Romish faith. He noticed, first, that the dress of the lâmas corresponded to that handed down to us in ancient paintings as the dress of the Apostles. Second, that the discipline of the monasteries and of the different orders of lâmas or priests bore the same resemblance to that of the Romish Church. Third, that the notion of an Incarnation was common to both, so also the belief in paradise and purgatory. Fourth, he remarked that they made suffrages, alms, prayers, and sacrifices for the dead, like the Roman Catholics. Fifth, that they had convents filled with monks and friars to the number of thirty thousand, near Lha Sa, who all made the three vows of poverty, obedience, and chastity, like Roman monks, besides other vows. Sixth, that they had confessors licensed by the superior lâmas or bishops, and so empowered to receive confessions, impose penances, and give absolution. Besides all this there was found the practice of using holy water, of singing service in alternation, of praying for the dead, and of perfect

* "Lettres Edifiantes," Vol. III., p. 534.

† "Thibet, Tartary," etc., p. 14.

similarity in the customs of the great and superior lâmas to those of the different orders of the Romish hierarchy. These early missionaries further were led to conclude, from what they saw and heard, that the ancient books of the lâmas contained traces of the Christian religion, which must, they thought, have been preached in Thibet in the time of the Apostles."

In the year 1829 Victor Jacquemont, the French botanist, made a short excursion from Simla into Thibet. He writes: "The Grand Lâma of Kanum has the episcopal mitre and crozier. He is dressed just like our bishops. A superficial observer at a little distance would take his Thibetan and Buddhist mass for a Roman mass of the first water. He makes twenty genuflexions at the right intervals, turns to the altar and then to the congregation, rings a bell, drinks in a chalice water poured out by an acolyte, intones paternosters quite of the right sing-song—the resemblance is really shocking. But men whose faith is properly robust will see here nothing but a corruption of Christianity."*

It must be borne in mind that what is called Southern Buddhism has the same rites. St. Francis Xavier in Japan found Southern Buddhism so like his own that he donned the yellow *sanghati*, and called himself an apostle of Buddha, quieting his conscience by furtively mumbling a little Latin of the baptismal service over some of his "converts."

This is what the Rev. S. Beal, a chaplain in the Navy, wrote of a liturgy that he found in China:—

"The form of this office is a very curious one. It bears a singular likeness in its outline to the common type of the Eastern Christian liturgies. That is to say, there is a "Proanaphoral' and an 'Anaphoral' portion. There is a prayer of entrance (τῆς εἰσοδου), an ascription of praise to the threefold object of

* "Corr.," Vol. I., p. 265.

worship (τρισαγίον), a prayer of oblation (τῆς προσθεσεως), the lections, the recitations of the Dharani (μυστηριον), the Embolismus, or prayer against temptation, followed by a 'Confession' and a 'Dismissal!'"*

Turning to architecture, I must point out that Mr. Fergusson, the leading authority in ancient art was of opinion that the various details of the early Christian basilica—nave, aisle, columns, semi-domed apse, cruciform ground plan—were borrowed *en bloc* from the Buddhists. Relic-worship, he says, was certainly borrowed from the East. Of the rock-cut temple of Kârle (B.C. 78) he writes:—

"The building resembles, to a great extent, an early Christian Church in its arrangements, consisting of a nave and side aisles terminating in an apse or semi-dome, round which the aisle is carried. . . . As a scale for comparison, it may be mentioned that its arrangements and dimensions are very similar to those of the choir of Norwich Cathedral, and of the Abbaye aux Hommes at Caen, omitting the outer aisles in the latter buildings.

"Immediately under the semi-dome of the apse, and nearly where the altar stands in Christian churches, is placed the Dâgoba."†

The list of resemblances is by no means exhausted. The monks on entering a temple make the gesture that we call the sign of the cross. The Buddhists have illuminated missals, Gregorian chants, a tabernacle on the altar for oblations, a pope, cardinals angels with wings, saints with the nimbus. For a full account I must refer the reader to my "Buddhism in Christendom."

How is all this to be accounted for? Several theories have been started:—

* "Catena of Buddhist Scriptures," p. 397.

† "Indian and Eastern Architecture," p. 117.

PLATE 16.

THE BUDDHIST HIGH ALTAR

The first attempts to make light of the matter altogether. All religions, it says, have sacrifice, incense, priests, the idea of faith, etc. This may be called the orthodox Protestant theory, and many bulky books have recently appeared propounding it. But as these books avoid all the strong points of the case, they cannot be called at all satisfactory to the bewildered inquirer.

To this theory the Roman Catholics reply that the similarities between Buddhism and Catholicism are so microscopic and so complete, that one religion must have borrowed from the other. In consequence they try to prove that the rites of Buddhism and the life of its founder were derived from Christianity, from the Nestorians, from St. Thomas, from St. Hyacinth of Poland, from St. Oderic of Frioul.*

In the way of this theory, however, there are also insuperable difficulties. Buddha died 470 years before Christ, and for many years the Christian Church had no basilicas, popes, cardinals, basilica worship, nor even for a long time a definite life of the founder. At the date of Asoka (B.C. 260) there was a metrical life of Buddha (Muni Gâtha), and the incidents of this life are found sculptured in marble on the gateways of Buddhist temples that precede the Christian epoch. This is the testimony of Sir Alexander Cunningham, the greatest of Indian Archæologists. He fixes the date of the Bharhut Stûpa at from 270 to 250 B.C. There he finds Queen Mâyâ's dream of the elephant, the Rishis at the ploughing match, the transfiguration of Buddha and the ladder of diamonds, and other incidents. At the Sanchi tope, an earlier structure (although the present marble gateways, repeated probably from wood, are fixed at about A.D. 19), he announces representations of Buddha as an elephant

* See Abbe Prouvése, "Life of Gabriel Durand," Vol. II., p. 365.

coming down to his mother's womb, three out of the "Four Presaging Tokens," Buddha bending the bow of Sinhahanu, King Bimbisâra visiting the young prince, and other incidents.

A man who invents, let us say, a submarine boat, at once puts his idea to a practical test. Let us try and construct a working model here. Suppose that the present ruler of Afghanistan were paying us a visit, and, introduced at Fulham Palace, he were to suggest that the life of Mahomet should supersede that of Jesus in our Bible, and Mussulman rites replace the Christian ritual in the diocese of London. What would be the answer? The bishop, anxious to deal gently with a valuable ally, would point out that he was only a cogwheel in a vast machinery, a cogwheel that could be promptly replaced if it proved the least out of gear. He would show that the Anglican Church had a mass of very definite rules called canon law, with courts empowered to punish the slightest infringement of these rules. He would show that even an archbishop could not alter a tittle of the gospel narrative. Every man, woman, and child would immediately detect the change.

Similar difficulties would be in the way of St. Hyacinth of Poland in, say, a monastery of Ceylon. The Abbot there would be responsible to what Bishop Bigandet calls his "provincial," and he again to his "superior-général," and so on to the Achârya, the "High Priest of all the World," who, in his palace at Nalanda, near Buddha Gayâ, was wont to sit in state, surrounded by ten thousand monks. Buddhism, by the time that a Christian missionary could have reached it, was a far more diffused and conservative religion than Anglicanism. It had a canon law quite as definite. It had hundreds of volumes treating of the minutest acts of Sâkya Muni.

CHAPTER XIV

PAULINISM

St. Paul a puzzle—Was he an ascetic mystic, or the author of the theory of the "Atonement," "Original Sin," etc., in fact of priestly Christianity?—Up to the date of Irenæus there is no trace of his writings, nor even of his teachings—Did he convert Peter and James as described in "The Acts?"—James, Peter, John the Evangelist, and Matthew all Nazarites,—also Paul—Were they all instrumental in making the water drinking Essenes drink wine?—Valentinus—"Left-handed gods"—Early Zodiac of S'iva.

No problem is so difficult as the question of the Apostle Paul. Early Christianity, like other religions, had soon two sections, the religion of the individual and the religion by body corporate, the religion of the conscience and the religion of state ceremonial. It has been the fate of St. Paul to figure as the guiding spirit of both.

There are two Pauls, the one put forth by Catholics as the type of St. Vincent de Paul and Fénelon, as the ideal of the Christian ascetic. This Paul states that for the mystical life all men should be celibates. This Paul spent his life "in watchings often, in hunger, thirst, fastings" (2 Cor. ii. 27); "in tumults in labour, in fastings" (2 Cor. vi. 7). This Paul states that the spiritual drink of Christians in the Communion Service should be the water that flowed from the rock of Moses. This Paul had for motto "Walk in Sophia," a word with mystics for the interior life. He announces that he had as the resultant "spiritual gifts," "the inspired word," "healing," "miracle," "prophecy," the "discerning of spirits" (1 Cor. xii., *et seq.*). And as a crowning fact this Paul announces that he was a "Nazarite," separated from his mother's womb, that is, an Eremite vowed from birth to water drinking and desert communings (Gal. i. 15). The other Paul is credited with having brought back into religion under a new form the principle of forgiveness of sins by shedding of blood, which the Essenes and the Therapeuts were struggling hard to banish. He invented theories about "redemption," "expiation," "original sin." He induced the Essene celibates and vegetarian water drinkers to break their vows. This last feat is the more noticeable as we have seen that he himself was a Nazarite.

And these difficulties have much increased since modern scholarship has taken up St. Paul. Dr. Cheyne's "Encyclopædia Biblica" pronounces his epistles to be all spurious. Mr. W. J. Birch has written a clever book entitled "Paul an idea, not a Fact," which affirms that his theories are stolen bodily from Philo. The learned Dr. Giles maintains that there is no mention of the Pauline epistles in the authentic records of early Christianity until the date of Irenæus. This he says is very remarkable, as Justin Martyr can never have heard of them or he would certainly have used them in his attack on Marcion. Dr. Giles holds that the "most excellent Theophilus," mentioned by the author of the third Gospel and the Acts, must have been Theophilus, the sixth Bishop of Antioch, an opponent of Marcion. Mr. W. Glanville, in a powerful little work, "The Web Unwoven," has further damaged the Pauline theory. He holds that in chapters ix., x., xi. of the Acts we get a fictitious narrative intended to immensely ante-date the rise of what is now called Paulinism.

The story there narrated is certainly strange. The Maker of the hundred million starry systems visits earth in a bodily form to introduce an exceptional religion. He leaves behind him a trusted agent to carry on the great enterprise after his death. And yet in a few years this agent guided chiefly by a " dream " of a heathen, throws over all the regulations believed to be divine. Mr. Granville points out a certain shrewdness in the story. Peter is made to go to the house of a tanner, the most defiling of residences, in the mind of the Jews. The chief agent of the change, Cornelius, is made a Roman captain that the Roman magistrates might think that Christianity is an orthodox form of the Jew's religion, entitled in consequence to State toleration. The date of this great change is fixed at about the time of James's martyrdom (44 A.D.). Is there any historical proof that such a change then took place?

Mr. Newman, in his work " James and Paul," maintains that the former was plainly quite ignorant of what we now call Paulinism :—

In his Epistle " he has nothing about being good for example's sake. Concerning the Cross, or death, or blood of Christ we gather nothing from him, nor does Jesus appear as Saviour or Mediator." " It cannot be discovered that any acts of internal devotion towards Jesus were a part of James's religion."*

But a passage from Eusebius carries the matter a step further, and shows that James, like St. Paul, could not have accepted Paulinism without gross perjury, for he, too, was consecrated from his mother's womb to the water-drinking life of the Nazarite or Nazareen.

" He was consecrated from his mother's womb. He drank neither wine nor strong drink, neither ate

* Newman, " James and Paul," p. 18.

he any living thing. A razor never went upon his head. He anointed not himself with oil, nor did he use a bath. He alone was allowed to enter into the holies. He did not wear woollen garments but linen. And he alone entered the sanctuary and was found upon his knees praying for the forgiveness of the people, so that his knees became hard like a camel's through his constant bending and supplication before God, and asking for forgiveness of the people."*

There is also evidence that St. Peter was a Nazareen ascetic, subsequent to the dream of the Roman captain, Cornelius.

Says St. Peter in the "Clementine Homilies":—

"However such a choice has occurred to you, perhaps without your understanding my manner of life that I use only bread and olives and rarely pot herbs, and this my only coat and cloak which I wear . . . for those who have determined to accept the blessings of the future reign have no right to regard as their own the things that are here . . . with the exception of water and bread, and those things procured with sweat to maintain life."†

Epiphanius in commenting on the passage about James in Eusebius, adds the two sons of Zebedee to the list of water-drinking Nazarites; and Clement of Alexandria writes thus of St. Matthew:—

"It is far better to be happy than to have a demon dwelling with us. And happiness is found in the practice of virtue. Accordingly the Apostle Matthew partook of seeds and nuts and vegetables without flesh."

Up to the second century A.D. the early Christians were called "Nazareens" or "Nazarites"—Tatian, Tertullian and others treat the two words as identical.

* Eusebius, "Hist.," Eccl. ii. 23.

† Clem., "Homilies," XII., 6.

The Jews, the Moslem, the East generally, still employ the title Pilate wrote up on the cross, and all the early disciples were baptised by a Nazarite separated from his mother's womb. The Essenes and Therapeuts according to Philo and Josephus drank nothing but water, and we see from my present chapter that the most prominent of Christ's disciples, St. James, St. Matthew, St. John and St. Peter were water-drinking Nazarites, in deed as well as in name. How is it then that the Nazarite St. John has written a gospel which proclaims—according to its modern interpreters in Rome and Lambeth—that unless a Christian drinks wine at least once a year he will be punished everlastingly in the flames of hell. And the Nazarite St. Paul backs up the Nazarite St. John with an account—the earliest according to scholars—of the institution of the Sacrament of bread and wine by Jesus, an account which the Nazarite St. Matthew has copied into his gospel. All this points to a wholesale falsification rather than the chance modifications of a few zealous copyists. Irenæus, who first mentions the Fourth Gospel, tells us that it was the special gospel of the followers of Valentinus. Was he the falsifier?

This question will have to be probed from many points of view. One statement of Tertullian may here be mentioned. He announces that the Valentinians maintained that it was necessary to worship the "left-handed" deities* as well as the right-handed. Here we have the Vâmâcharîs of S'iva. These "left-handed" deities, were on the left side of the Zodiac.

I tried to show in an early work, "Buddha and Early Buddhism," that almost every mansion in the Buddhist Zodiac seemed intentionally to suggest the two great Serpents, the Father and the Mother. This

* Tertullian, "Adversus Valent," C. XXVI.

fact if it could be established, would be of far greater importance now that we are considering S'iva Buddha.

Fig. 1 Plate 17 is S'iva's Trisula. Outside of India it is called the Rod of Hermes. It is the holiest symbol of Buddhism, Mani, the Pearl.

Om Mani Padme Hum.

This Trisula of S'iva is everywhere. It is conspicuous on the summit of the great Sanchi Tope (Fig 3). It makes up the conventional head of Buddha (Fig. 4). It is on a charm in Tibet (Fig. 2). We see from the Catacombs the meaning of the descending dove (Fig. 5). Now this outline is plainly to be seen in the Crab, the Scorpion, the Taurine or Bull, and also the Scales which according to Ptolemy are simply the claws of the Scorpion.* Then the Serpent is certainly suggested in the tail of the Lion, and the trunk of the Elephant (Capricorn). An elephant and a serpent have the same name in Sanskrit—Nâga. Here we get eight serpent symbols, but two I completely overlooked in my early work. For the Twins (they are male and female in India), I give a design which I took from some Buddhist sculptures, given in the "Tree and Serpent Worship" of Mr. Fergusson, the male twin holds up a lotus (See Indian Zodiac (Plate 18) in next page). Plainly the outline purposely makes the head of a cobra, an Indian virile symbol. That I have not made a mistake is evident, for the same outline is repeated in the hand of Virgo, who again is S'iva the great Father-Mother. For the Ram there is a horse with two snakes on his head.† It is also from Fergusson's "Tree and Serpent Worship." In the Indian epic the Mahabharata there is an episode, the "Churning

* Arago, "Popular Astronomy," p. 204.

† Siva holds an Antelope in his hand, this may be the earliest form of the symbol. (Plate 19.)

PLATE 17.

1

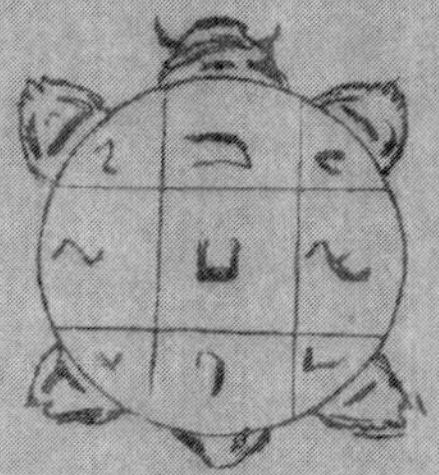

2

3

5

4

THE TRISUL OUTLINE.

PLATE 19.

S'IVA WITH ANTELOPE.

PLATE 18.

ZODIAC OF S'IVA.

of the Ocean." Almost all mythical poetry in all languages is a mixing up of astronomical signs, kaleidoscopical fashion. In this little story Nârayana, to gain for mortals the amrita or immortal drink, coils the Serpent Vâsukhi (the ecliptic) round the Mountain Mandar (the Kosmos) and makes it spin round and "churn" the ocean (unfashioned fluidic matter). In this little story the signs of the Zodiac are brought in a little clumsily.

The sign for the fish is Chakra.

What is Chakra?

The little myth, the Churning of the Ocean, answers the question.

"Beneath the trenchant Chakra he saw guarding the Amrita two immense and terrible serpents, strong, venom-darting, with fiery eyes and throats, and tongues of forked lightning."*

Here is another passage :—

"Here dwell two serpents the terror of enemies Arvouda and Sakravapi. Here are the sublime palaces of Swastika and Maninâga."†

Plainly Chakra, the Fish of the Zodiac, is the wheel called Swastika in India,‡ and Cancer the Serpents of the mani or pearl. And the palaces of these two are the black and white halves of the Zodiac.

It is, oddly enough, the only cross in the catacombs, and it was the only symbol on the drapery of the high altar when the Japanese constructed a model Japanese temple in Knightsbridge a few years ago. It is called the "Seal of the heart of Buddha."

In the Rig Veda, India's terrible Vajra or bolt is called Chaturasri (the four angled). This is plainly the Swastika.

* Mahabharata, "Adi parva," vv. 1500-1501.

† Mahabharata, "Sabha Parva," p. 806.

‡ See "Bhilsa Topes," p. 31.

(3) *The Twins.* This is the Sowing Festival, the Epoch of the Lesser Mysteries. Buddha, Rama, Krishna and the Sons of Pandu, of the Mahabharata, marry now, after showing their animal strength at its culminating point at Olympian games. Rama bends the bow of S'iva, a constellation that is shining at midnight at this very moment. The Asvins or Twins are sometimes male and female in the Rig Veda. Plainly if the S'ivan designs on the punch marked coins are zodiacal, we get here the "Jew's harp." It explains the splendid bas relief of the Marriage of S'iva and Durga at Elora. Opposite this marriage is "the Bow" in the sky, Life confronted with Death.

(4) *The Crab.* This is plainly the Maninaga of the Mahabharata, S'iva's Trisula, the trident which heads the yogi's staff as he treads along the mystical "way." Opposite is Ganes'a, the Elephant, the definite God, detaching himself from the Great Fish in the Great Ocean.

(5) *The Lion.* This is Durga's carrier, and her pet sign. The two together form the Sphinx, the great enigma which man must guess to live. Buddha on the lion throne near the tree of Knowledge was guessing it. Lions and sphinxes abound in Elora, and other rock cut temples.

(6) *Virgo.* We now come to the Virgin of the Sky, the "Mother who delivers the World" as the Buddhists call her, the much abused Durgâ who gave agriculture to Greece and Babylon, and sent her son Ganes'a to give it to the Romans. To this day she presides at the Festival of Plenty in India, and the Brahmin polytheists and her other theological opponents crowd to it quite as eagerly as her own votaries. Her symbol is also a tree—the tree of the ascetic.

(7) *Libra* is the Firebird and probably the dismembered S'iva. S'iva, Indra, Osiris, Saturn, were

all dismembered; and Durgâ in the Mysteries wailed and made the temples resound with her grief that the Kosmos had lost its productive energy. The legend of the flying Mahadeo burning up the Tripura, the three cities (Earth, Kailâs, and Pandemonium) means a starving Kosmos.

(8) *Scorpio.* It is plain, too, also, that Scorpio, or S'iva as Bhairava with a gaping mouth that breathes out flames, is the same destructive energy. He is the Ialdibaoth of the Gnostics, the inexplicable confusion in the world's harmony.

(9) *Sagittarius.* This sign is called the "Bow of S'iva" in the Ramâyâna, and the young Râma is the only competitor at the jousts that can bend it. The arrows that fly from that bow become serpents and kill their foes, and then return to the sender.

(10) *Capricorn.* The zodiacal signs sometimes represent the sun-god in his annual cruise, and sometimes his victims. Durga kills Mahishasura, and S'iva kills an elephant named Gaya, he kills Kâma (the Twins, the erotic principle), he kills Tripurasura (the Brahmanic hierarchy figuring as Scorpio), he dominates the serpent that is sent against him and the antelope (Aries) and seizes the Dwarf's "Club" (Virgo, the Tree), and he smashes the head of his own son, being angry that he was born as an elephant. Then, by a clumsy myth, he restores him to life, but the head being smashed an elephant's head had to be substituted. The Elephant represents the Holy Spirit in India. The Indian sign for Capricorn is an elephant emerging from a Makara, the definite from the chaotic, the Buddhist Padmapâni and the S'ivan Ganes'a from Îswara the Unthinkable.

The last two signs, the Yogi with the pot of immortal food (Aquarius) and the Chakra of Dharma (Pisces), terminate the career of the ideal man. At first the entanglements of the animal life—and then dreamland with its angels and hobgoblins, and the crucial puzzle of all philosophies and all religions, the origin of evil. The yogis of S'iva and Buddha when first united must have had many such dreams before the Cosmism of the Nirisvara school swamped up the Aiswarikas. I mention this here because in treating S'iva-Buddhism I am forced to consider chiefly the side that it shows to the world.

CHAPTER XV

TRANSUBSTANTIATION

Gibbon on the rites of the Agapae at Alexandria—Professor Horace Hayman Wilson discovers similar rites in the Indian books—The S'ri Ka Chakra in the Devî Rashya—The Sacrifice of the Year-God in the Kâlî Ka Purâna—Its analogy with the Roman Catholic Eucharist—Both sacrifices make-believe—Startling points of contact with the great Mystery-play in Tibet—Description of the "Sacrificial Body of the Dead Year"—Stabbed and cut to pieces—Great scramble for the fragments—New Year as in Alexandria represented by a baby covered with flour.

MR. MEREDITH, in his "Prophet of Nazareth," tries to discover the origin of the Roman Catholic doctrine of Transubstantiation. He traces it to the rites of the Agapæ mentioned by Jude. These had to be modified as time went on. Gibbon thus describes them.

"There were many who pretended to confess or to relate the ceremonies of this abhorred society. It was asserted that a new-born infant entirely covered over with flour was presented like some mystic symbol of initiation to the knife of the proselyte, who unknowingly inflicted many a secret and mortal wound on the innocent victim of his error; that as soon as the cruel deed was perpetrated the sectaries drank up the blood, greedily tore asunder the quivering members, and pledged themselves to eternal secrecy by a mutual consciousness of guilt. It was as confidently affirmed that this inhuman sacrifice was succeeded by a suitable entertainment, in which intemperance served as a provocation to brutal lust, till at the appointed moment the lights were suddenly extinguished, shame was banished, nature was forgotten, and as accident might direct the darkness of the night was polluted by the incestuous commerce of sisters and brothers, of sons and of mothers.

"But the perusal of the ancient apologies was sufficient to remove even the slightest suspicion from the mind of a candid adversary. The Christians, with the intrepid security of innocence, appeal from the voice of rumour to the equity of the magistrates. . . . Nothing, it should seem, could weaken the force or destroy the effect of so unanswerable a justification unless it were the injudicious conduct of the apologists themselves who betrayed the common cause of religion to gratify their devout hatred of the domestic enemies of the church. It was sometimes faintly insinuated and sometimes boldly asserted that the same bloody sacrifices and the same incestuous festivals which were so falsely ascribed to the orthodox believers were in reality celebrated by the Marcionites, by the Carpocrations, and by several other sects of the Gnostics. . . . Accusations of a similar kind were retorted upon the church by the schismatics who had departed from its communion, and it was confessed on all sides that the most scandalous licentiousness of manners prevailed amongst great numbers of those who affected the name of Christians."

Gibbon instances Tertullian who, when he became a Montanist, turned against his former comrades.* Mr. Meredith, enlarging on this difficult question, comes to a conclusion that a doctrine so utterly repugnant to reason as the Roman Catholic doctrine of Transubstantiation must be a survival of something that once had a logic. He urges that it is a modifi-

* "Decline and Fall," Chapter XVI.

cation of something that had to be softened down. If he had had access to Indian literature, he would have found this view confirmed.

The great Orientalist, Horace Hayman Wilson, was startled to find in the S'ivan books scenes described very like those attributed to the Christian Agapæ. The tântrika rites ought properly to be called the Left-Handed Tantrikas (Vâmâcharîs) when applied to certain rites which the celebrant, as Mr. Wilson puts it, "dare not publicly avow." In the mysteries of the Durgâ-pûjah, the great festival of nature's powers of reproduction, the Vâmâcharîs had a Bacchantic rite which they called S'rî Ka Chakra (the "Wheel of S'rî"). The upper vests of the women were taken off and put in a basket, and the males present each took one of these, and this accident indicated to him his partner in the coming debauchery. A naked female presided at the great mystery. She was Durgâ in person; and the males were called Bhairavas and the women Bhairavîs. Each in fact was supposed to be S'iva himself, the great giver of life, or his other half.

. The Devî Rashya, a Hindu work which treats on the subject, settles that the women must be "a dancing girl, a female devotee, a harlot, a washerwoman or barber's wife, a female of the Brahmanical or Indra tribe, a flower-girl or a milkmaid." The members of the sect were enjoined to preserve their mystery a complete secret. Exactly at the hour of midnight the rampant orgy was to take place.

I will turn to another Indian work. It is called the Sanguinary Chapter of the Kâlî ka Purâna, and a translation of it is given by Mr. Blacquiere in Volume V. of the old "Asiatic Researches." The God S'iva tells in person how the divine favour is to be obtained, and announces that it is "though sacrifices that

* H. H. Wilson, "Asiatic Researches," Vol. XVII.

princes obtain bliss, heaven and victory over their enemies." His wife Kâlî is particular in her tastes, and the animals that she likes are enumerated. Thus the blood of a wild bull gives pleasure for a year; but "a bird whose throat is blue and head red and legs black with white feathers" is quite her favourite. And the Rohita fish gives her pleasure for three hundred years.

But it is when we come to warm human flesh and blood that we see her real sentiments.

"An oblation of blood which has been rendered pure by holy texts is the Ambrosia (amrita)."

One special sacrifice is described at length.

The victim must be willing and must be a person of good appearance. He must be prepared by ablutions and requisite ceremonies such as eating consecrated food the day before. He must be adorned with chaplets of flowers and besmeared with sandal wood. Death should be given with the Chandrahasa, a sort of axe. The sacrificer's face must be towards the North, and the victim's towards the East.

Then the sacrificer is called upon to worship the several deities presiding over the different parts of the victim's body. Let him worship Brahmâ in the victim's Brahmâ Randhra (a cavity in the skull). Let him worship the earth in his nose, saying Medenyaiah Nâmah, and casting a flower; in his ears Akasa, the subtle æther, saying Akasaya Nâmah. Let him worship Fire on his left cheek, Death on his throat, the Moon on his forehead, and the Serpent King in his belly.

Then let him make the following invocation:—

"O best of men! O most auspicious! O thou who art an assemblage of all the deities, and most exquisite! Bestow thy protection on me, save me thy devoted. Save my sons, my cattle and kindred, preserve the state, the ministers belonging to it and all my friends. And as death is unavoidable, part with thy life doing an act of benevolence. Bestow upon me, O most auspicious, the bliss that is obtained by the most austere devotion, by acts of charity and the performance of religious ceremonies; and at the same time, O most excellent, attain supreme bliss thyself. May thy auspices, O most auspicious, keep me secure from Râkshasas, Piśâchas, terrors, serpents, bad princes, and other evils. And death being inevitable, may they charm Bhâgavatî in the last moments by copious streams of blood spouting from the arteries of thy fleshy neck."

It is plain from all this that the victim is an impersonation of S'iva, and this fact is not concealed.

"When this has been done, O my children, the victim is even as myself, and the guardian deities of the ten quarters take care of him. Then Brahmâ and all the other deities assemble on the victim."*

Now if we compare all this with the transubstantiation rites of the Roman Catholic Church, we find a close analogy. In each a God under one aspect of himself sacrifices himself to another aspect of himself, that his faithful followers may drink that mixture of human blood and spirits which the ancients believed to be the meat and drink of immortal life.†

But it might be said that Victim, Priest and God were all united.

Also in each we find that the sacrifice was a make-believe, all the adoration and prayer being made not to the God but the victim.

It seemed to me, too, on first reading the passage from the Kâlî ka Purâna that it was a description of S'iva dying at the end of the year.

* Blaquiere "Asiatic Researches," Vol. V.

† "Himself the Victim and Himself the Priest" is a verse of a hymn based on Heb. vii. 27.

A perusal of the Great Mystery Play of Tibet fully confirmed me.

In the matter of devil dancing and sorcery, Tibet takes the lead. Witness its great mystery play, which might be called the "Great Apocalypse of Sorcery." Man, according to the Lâmas, is surrounded by hordes of man-eating devils who vex him with diseases and accidents. These demons infest the air, the earth, the water, and are ever seeking to destroy him. Against this endless persecution he can himself do nothing, but the great S'iva benignly comes to his aid and places at his disposal charms, spells, talismans which are wielded by the good spirits or Lâmas; and these aids can be obtained by a proper attention to Lâmaic rites, and above all Lâmaic offerings. In the drama I am considering, millions of fiends battle together, and brief victories occur, to the good sometimes and the bad sometimes, for the effect of Karma or magical energy is transient.

"And only for a time," says Surgeon-Major Waddell, "can this relief from persecution endure for all the exorcisms of all the saints are of little avail to keep back the advancing hordes. The shrieking demons must close in upon the soul again."*

The great "Miracle-play" or "Mystery" of Tibet is called "The Sacrificial Body of the Dead Year," and it "is acted on the last day of the year by all sects of Lâmas," as Surgeon-Major Waddell tells us.

Strictly analysed it has two parts, and two distinct plots or motifs.

(1) To set forth the importance of Tântrika rites, charms, etc.

(2) To reveal the mighty secret of the old world, immortal life through drinking the blood of S'iva, impersonating the dead year, and being sacrificed for the purpose.

* Waddell, "Buddhism in Tibet," p. 523.

These sections are plainly of different dates; indeed, if you saw the play acted for the first time, your first question would be—"What has all this to do with the dead year, and where is its body?"

The first part is a tedious and overdone battle between demons white, red, and black, who assail one another with charms and magic weapons. The plot is a confused plot telling a local story of the Lâma, who assumed the disguise of a "black-hatted devil-dancer" to assassinate King Lan Darma.

Then comes the part that most interests the modern reader.

Four ghouls bring on an object wrapped in a black cloth. These ghouls are called the "Four Cemetery Ghouls." They place the object on the ground, and dance round it "with intricate steps." They raise the cloth and discover a large dough statue of a man. Organs representing the heart, lungs, liver, brain, stomach, intestines, etc., are inserted into it, and the heart and the large blood-vessels and limbs are filled with a red-coloured fluid to represent blood. Plainly in the original version of the play a real man was killed. This is confessed. Cannibalism was an ingredient in the play until the great Tibetan saint, Padma Sambhava, in the ninth century substituted a man of dough for a victim of human flesh.

Then comes a great procession of pantomime gods and devils, naked figures with the heads of tigers, serpents, horses, bulls, with "demoniac Brahmâs" and Vishnus and Indras, and even "demoniac Buddhas," for every being, divine or otherwise, in S'ivism, has two aspects like the divine chief. These are followed by the fiendesses, including the "twelve Tan-ma" under Devî. Tom-toms sound, and cymbals and large trumpets eight or ten feet long, and wooden tambourines, and a portentous and long-drawn whistling "with the fingers on the mouth."

Now comes on the chief fiend, the "Religious King-devil," with the head of a bull, holding in his right hand a dagger and in his left the pas'a or Thug-noose. This character can only be assumed by a monk of the purest morals. The Emperor of China on one occasion rewarded him with a dress of great price. There is no great secrecy in this Mystery about the identity of this Demon King. The more intelligent Lâmas admit that he is S'iva as Mahâkâla,* and that the stage of this mighty drama is S'iva's hell.

Now for the great climax. After more devil-dancing the Demon King draws a swórd and stabs and hacks the figure of dough, ringing a bell all the time, assisted by his devils, who tear the figure to pieces. These are collected in a huge silver basin, shaped like a skull and carried in a procession to the Demon King, who eats a small portion and then throws the rest into the air. "They are fought for by the other demons, who throw the pieces about in a frantic manner. Then a sacrifice of apparently the same figure in papier maché is made, with blood and arak in a human skull."

Now if we put this description side by side with that of the victim in the S'ivan mystery, we find that they mutually explain one another. The dough figure in Tibet is the "Sacrificial body of the dead year:" the name explains everything. And so is the Victim described in the Kâlîka Purâna. And the scraps of flesh and the skull with blood and spirit are the immortal food scrambled for by the gods and men in the old mysteries. Tibet in the old days reeked with cannibalism. "At the new year in Tibet," says an ancient Chinese manuscript, deciphered by Dr. Bushell, "the Tibetans sacrifice men, or offer monkeys."†

* Waddell, "Buddhism in Tibet," p. 531.

† "Journal R.A. Society's New Series XII.," p. 440.

"Up to the Middle Ages," says Dr. Waddell, "cannibalism is reported, and vestiges survive in the dough images, the sacrifice of which form an essential part of the Lâmaist daily worship." He mentions, too, that so great is the craze for human flesh even now that the Tibetans chew a portion of the human skin when preparing the human thigh bone for a "bone trumpet." Also we learn from him that the neighbours of the Lâmas in the Tsang Po valley are cannibals to this day.*

A minor scene in the great Miracle play must not be omitted. A figure of a child in dough is brought in, and naked skeletons something like S'iva as a skeleton, at Elora, dance round it and make believe to attack it with long spears. Then, to solemn chanting, low music and the swinging of censers, a stately procession comes through the porch of the temple and slowly descends the steps. Under a canopy borne by attendants comes a tall form in beautiful silk robes, wearing a large mask representing a benign and peaceful face. "As he advanced, men and boys dressed as abbots and acolytes of the Church of Rome," prostrated themselves before him and addressed him with intoning and pleasing chanting.† There are doubts whether this figure is Padma Sambhava, a popular local saint and indeed local Buddha, or Buddha himself. The demons flee away with loud shrieks. A more important question arises:—Was this little child the new year? The pontiff covers him with flour to render him safe against the fiends of hell. This reminds one of what was alleged of the Gnostic sects in Alexandria. They, too, covered a child with flour, at the date of the new year. But why was he sacrificed? This seems to have been his fate both in Alexandria and in Tibet. Logically, the big dough

* Waddell, "Buddhism in Tibet," 518.

† Waddell, "Buddhism in Tibet," p. 526.

figure is the old year and the little dough figure is the new year. What is the white flour ? plainly the white ash of the men and gods and systems that remorseless Mahâkâla has swept away.

Mr. Meredith urges that even the phraseology of the Roman Catholic Eucharist bears traces of a real sacrifice. The word "Sacramentum" in old days could only have meant an oath, the oath, in fact, of the early Christians not to reveal their mysteries under the pain of death. Then the word "host" meant a sacrificial victim and not a piece of bread. And what is still called the "altar" must have been a real altar up to the time when the ninth and tenth Canon of the Council of Nice imposed upon the Christian priests degradation if they sacrificed any more."* And the word "mass" from "Ita missa est" was also pagan. Certainly, the Catholic and the Tibetan "mysteries," and their modifications seem to have run on the same lines.

But how terribly important is all this to our special investigation, cannibalism and Bacchantic licentiousness forced into the Holy of Holies of the religion of the blameless, vegetarian, water-drinker S'âkya Muni.

* Meredith, "The Prophet of Nazareth," p. 527.

CHAPTER XVI

CEYLON

Hiouen Thsiang, the Chinese traveller, on the religion of the Island in his day—" Followers of the Great Vehicle "—Bishop Copleston combats this—Three hundred Great Vehicle monks at Kânchapura—Wytulian heresy—Kappooism—S'iva as Saman Deva Râja supreme in the Island—Dewales and Buddhist Viharas in the same enclosures—Cure of the sick officially handed over to the Kappooists—Sekkraia (S'iva as Indra) a man, half-man, half stone—S'ivan mystery—the " Inebriating Festival of the Buddha "—Legend—Temple women—Kattragam or Karttikeya—His power and popularity.

WE have seen that a crowd of monks from Alexandria were feasted in Ceylon in the year 160 B.C. on the occasion of the opening up of the Great Tope at Ruanwelli. As these holy men were treated like orthodox Buddhist monks it would help us if we could know exactly what was Cingalese Buddhism at this particular time, for Ceylon had plainly much to do with the passage of Gnosticism from India to the West.

On this point we have evidence of quite exceptional importance from the Chinese traveller, Hiouen Thsiang. It is quite plain from him that what we call S'iva-Buddhism was the religion of the island.

Bishop Copleston, in his work " Buddhism," combats this, and he begins with as, it seems to me, a slight mistake. He says that Hiouen Thsiang " describes a school of Mahâyâna existing as far south as Ceylon."* This is not at all what the Chinese traveller says.

* Copleston " Buddhism Primitive and Present," p. 11.

"In Ceylon," he declares, "are about ten thousand monks who follow the doctrines of the Great Vehicle"; and the context shows that he believed that the change had affected the whole island.

And why should all the testimony of Hiouen Tsiang be at once "set aside," as the Bishop phrases it. Hiouen Thsiang was a sort of Lord High Commissioner, selected by the Head of the Buddhist Church to conduct the great convocation of King Sîlâditya, which was summoned especially to consider the dispute between the disciples of the Great Vehicle (Mâhâyana), and the disciples of the "Little Vehicle."

The Chinese traveller says, moreover, that the controversy raged fiercely for a time before the Great Vehicle was successful over the Little Vehicle. He tells us that one of the Chief Apostles of the Great Vehicle was Devi Bodhisatwa, a Cingalese. He announces that the early Buddhists called the Great Vehicle the "Carriage that drives to Nothingness," and that it came from the followers of S'iva and not Buddha at all.

At Kânchapura, the Chinese pilgrim came upon three hundred monks who had just fled across the water from Ceylon to escape the anarchy and famine consequent on the death of the king there. This stopped his visit. The Bishop "sets him aside" because he never reached the Island at all,* but supposing that Dr. Pusey was visiting the Isle of Man to see if "Church" ideas had reached the clergy of that island; and supposing that the steamer were wrecked but the passengers rescued by another steamer, coming from the Isle of Man, and having on board thirty clergymen hastening to an Anglican conference, surely these clergymen could tell him quite as much about the religion of the Island as he could acquire by an actual visit.

* Copleston, "Buddhism," p. 11.

In point of fact, history supports the Chinese traveller. The Râjaratunacari announces that a great heresy arose with the advent of one Wytulia. What it was is a little vague, but it "sought to subvert by craft and intrigue the religion of Buddha." It was put down summarily. The books of the Wytulians were burned. But by-and-bye a fresh heretic arose in the person of one Sanghamitta, who was profoundly versed in the religion of the Bhûtas (demons).

"It is probable," says Sir Emerson Tennant, "that out of the Wytulian heresy grew the system which prevails to the present day by which the heterodox Dewales and halls for devil dancing are built in close contiguity to the temples and Wiharas of the orthodox Buddhists, and the barbarous rites of demon worship are incorporated with the abstractions of the national religion."*

What was the devil dancing? A very able work will help us here. In the year 1829 Mr. Edward Upham published a work on "Kappooism," or the Demon Worship of the Island. It is enriched with forty-three plates, crude, untouched, fresh from a Cingalese bazaar, and therefore most valuable. They are from a collection brought home by Sir Alexander Johnson, a Ceylon Chief Justice.

Mr. Upham, with his plates, gives us a very good idea of the "Kappooism" or the "devil worship" of Ceylon. He was astonished when reading the work of Mr. Hodgson "to find how close was the resemblance in the matter of the metempsychosis, the heavens, and the divine agencies" between the Buddhism of Ceylon which is generally pronounced the Hînayâna or Little Vehicle, and the Buddhism of Nepal, which we call S'iva-Buddhism.

Let us inquire first who is deemed the Supreme God? or to put it in the language of the country,

* Sir Emerson Tennant, "Ceylon," Vol. I., p. 380.

what Deity possesses the mighty "Stone of Supremacy," the Minne Phalange? As the accounts are very contradictory, we must see if the legends and the plates can throw any light upon it.

There was a Serpent King, Samana Deva Râja, Lord of Hell, who lived in a palace called Nangewenodenneye. This Serpent King sent an invitation to Buddha, who came to his palace through the air, and by a miracle created a darkness so thick that all the "nâgas" subject to this sovereign fled in consternation. This allowed Buddha to occupy the Minne Phalange or Seat of Supremacy; and fire issued from the four points of the compass which frightened the "devils," as Mr. Upham calls them, still more. But Buddha released them from hell, preached to them and comforted them, and handed over to them the wood called Jak-girre for their abode.*

Two points are prominent. The legend is intended to give an account of the religion of Buddha superseding that of Samana Deva Râja, or S'iva with his Nâgas. Buddha, by his superior miracles, takes from him the Minne Phalange; and transfers his crew from hell to a pleasant wood, Jak-girre, miraculously erected. It is called an island in the Mahâwanso.

A second legend announces that Buddha at his death handed over the Minne Phalange to Deva Râja. I do not see that this can mean anything except the advent of S'iva Buddhism, with the date purposely mis-stated (p. 130). Deva Râjah is S'iva, and S'iva now rules once more.†

* The legend is taken from the Mahâwanso where is an account of Sumano Devah Rajah and of Buddha frightening the Yakkos in the garden of the Great Serpent by making his "carpet of skin fringe" fling forth flames in all directions. See "Mahâwanso," Turnour's translation, p. 3.

† Deva means the Deva of Devas, S'iva (Benfey's "Sanskrit Dictionary").

Plate 20.

SEKKRAIA SINKING INTO THE STONE.

But there is a third claimant for the "Stone of Supremacy," Sekkraia (Sanskrit—Śakra or Indra).

To those who have not studied S'ivism, this claim gives rise to many contradictions apparently purposeless. But S'ivism being a rigid Pantheism, its god has two faces, that of the god of what men call "evil," as well as the god of what men call good.

Though the name Sekkraia and some of the facts concerning him indicate the god Indra (Plate 20), there is much more of S'iva in his composition.

Sekkraia has in the Devaloka a most wonderful tree, the Tavateinza Tree. Its stem is a pillar of silver. It flowers only once in a thousand years, and produces most delicious fruit. In order to get this fruit the gods assemble in crowds for a hundred years before it ripens, and for one whole year they dance and sing, accompanied by drums and other musical instruments. Having eaten of that fruit they become inebriated for four entire months. Immediately the tree has flowered, Sekkraia is informed of the fact, and he mounts the great Elephant Erravum to hurry to the festival.

"Erravum" is Indra's famous elephant, Airâvana, but the Stone of Supremacy is the lingam. On it Sekkraia stands when he administers justice: that is when he is S'iva as Yama. If the accused is guilty, the god sinks partly into the stone. It does not want Plate 20 to tell exactly what that means. Man, stone, and spire-shaped crown make up an unmistakeable Lingam.

The gods of Kappoism are worshipped in erections, chiefly rude, called Dewales (devalayas?), and Dr. Davy is cited by Mr. Upham as announcing "that it is not uncommon to see a Dewale and a Wihara (Buddhist Temple) contiguous, or under the same roof."* The Dewales have for presiding genius the

* Upham "Hist. Buddhism," p. 130.

Goddess Pattinee. She is described as "the most mischievous fairy in Ceylon" (p. 50), and seems to correspond with Major Waddell's "She Devil Devî." Her likeness shows her to be Durgâ. Above her head as a crown is a head of S'iva without the upper jaw. A clergyman named Fox, wandering in a jungle at night with one native attendant, came accidentally across a scene of devil dancing. The native was wild with fear when he found that his master was going to try and probe such tremendous mysteries.

"We came at length to a temporary hut (which they call a maduwa) adorned in front with cocoa-nut leaves and about sixty lamps made of coarse clay. I saw shadows of men, but they disappeared; and on my approach I only saw the Kappooa dancing before the place, with hollow bangles on his arms filled with stones to make a jingle. Inside the maduwa was a sick man, near his feet was a wicker basket. This I lifted up. It contained a live cock smeared all over with soot.*

"The man who acts the part of the devil is dressed in a garment of dried grass or rushes which reaches to the ground. His arms and his feet are concealed, a white country cloth covers his shoulders. Round his head and under his chin are two or three cotton handkerchiefs. The face is frightful. The mouth and nose are black. Two large teeth project far beyond the lips. A row of coarse shells is bound over the eyes. On the head is a red cap which reaches four or five feet in height."

Now here we get the Buddhism of the North, as it is called, face to face with the Buddhism of the South. In the Tântrika Rites of Nepal, as Mr. Hodgson calls them, offerings of flesh and spirits and warm blood are made to the "Balis." A mummer

* Upham, "Hist. Buddhism." p. 121.

PLATE 21.

BALI DEVIL-DANCER.

in a mask of Bhairava impersonates the god. Here also is a mummer impersonating the "Bali." The word "Bali" means literally a sacrifice, but in Nepal and also in Ceylon it is used to denote the sorcerers as well. The "devil" in Nepal is called Bhairava. In Ceylon he has two enormous teeth, and turning to Mr. Upham's plates I find that the demon so furnished (See Plate 21) is called Coola Kumara. Kumara is S'iva's son, and dancing before the altar a S'ivan rite.

All the Cingalese, including the Buddhist hierachy, admit that above Buddha there is a superior God, Saman-deva-râja. This God, says Mr. Upham, is called Saman from Samane Galle (Adam's Peak), "where he is now living with his deities with power over Ceylon" (p. 51).

There he stands upon the Minne Phalange or Seat of Supremacy given to him at the death of Buddha. There grows the immortal Tavateinza Tree. Around him are myriads of "divine nâgas of mighty power," rendered orthodox formerly by Buddha, and he has moreover the sacred White Elephant which is Buddha reincarnate.

These "devas" watch to cure the sick and to preserve men from incurring losses in their goods, and are represented as residing on the peaks of their high mountains whence they inspect, govern and exercise a tutelary superintendence over their favourite districts. The Buddhist Church make a virtue of necessity and officially adopt the devils, in the matter of the cure of disease. They say that Buddha gave that faculty to Kumara.

"The natives of Ceylon," says Mr. Upham, "show the demons honours and make offerings, because they fear that demons can visit human beings with sickness; and therefore they in cases of sickness invoke them and make offerings of money, also of boiled and unboiled meats, and cause the throat, arms, legs and body of the sick to be tied by the Bali conjurers with necklaces or threads (amulets) dyed yellow with saffron water" (p. 66).

It must be remembered, too, that Bhairava judges the dead and consigns some to the jewelled palaces of his Kailâs, and others to regions which, as depicted in Mr. Upham's book, show red demons beating sinners with red-hot clubs and hammers, as they lie in beds of flame. All this scarcely describes a few belated Nâgas beating tom-toms and selling gambouge amulets in sly corners. If the Buddhists of Ceylon turn to S'iva and his Devas in business, in sickness, in affliction—if they use him to direct their happiness on earth and their hope in the hereafter—there is little wonder that the altars of the Devalayas are thronged, and those of the Buddhists are deserted.

And now let us pause and take stock of what we have discovered in the Island of Ceylon. Simply that there, as in other Buddhist countries, the religion is the religion of S'iva-Buddha. S'iva is the acknowledged divine Ruler. The foul rites of the Vâmâcharîs, the left-handed Tântrikas, are the only rites that any of the Cingalese seem to care anything about.

Now there are two explanations of all this, the one furnished by Hiouen Tsiang, the Chinese Buddhist, namely that the Great Vehicle (or S'iva Buddhism) effected a complete revolution in the religion of S'âkya Muni in Ceylon about the epoch of the Christian era. The second is that the religion of Ceylon is the pure and unadulterated religion of S'âkya Muni, but as popular superstitions are difficult to completely eradicate some of the old Nâgas, or Serpent Worshippers, who were supreme in the island before its conversion by Buddha, still perform on the sly some of their ancient rites.

In fact, once more upsprings the Barnacle theory, the Nâgas are mere barnacles quite outside the ship.

Plate 22.

SESH DISGUISED AS BUDDHA.

But are they outside the ship? Plainly one of the barnacles has taken command of it. Bishop Copleston notices the "Wytulian heretics," and their attempt to mix up Buddhism and the religions of the South of India. And he tries to account for this heresy:—

From early times hordes of Hindus have fled to the island from their oppressors. Also the native kings have sought their brides in India, and selected Tamil soldiers for their body-guard. And in point of fact the civilisation of Ceylon itself was due to India. But with all due respect to the learned Bishop I think he scarcely appreciates the puzzle. It is not whether individuals on the Island of Ceylon in the old days had, or had not, opportunities of studying other religions besides the official creed. The puzzle is that a powerful hierarchy, for according to the French Bishop Bigandet, Ceylon had a hierarchy as effectively organised, and very like that of the Christians; the puzzle is that this hierarchy should have allowed their beatified Saint to be pushed off his pedestal, and a novel god to be placed there, and that god to be worshipped with human sacrifices, cannibalism, and Bacchanalian orgies, the very rites that S'âkya Muni had spent eighty years in trying to eradicate.

Such a vast change must have come from above, not below. Hierarchies are accustomed to turn a deaf ear to the reasonings of individuals. At Nalanda, near Buddha Gâya, was the Âchârya, the acknowledged pope of the Buddhists—the Mahâwanso calls him the "High Priest of all the world." Now the invaluable Hiouen Tsiang gives us a hint of what might have occurred. He says that Kanis'ka wanted to adopt high-handed measures with his convocation or council, and force this high priest to let it sit at Nalanda, though that prelate and his ten thousand monks were strongly opposed to the proposed changes. But

Parsvika, the prime minister, suggested caution and urged that it was safer to hold the convocation in his own dominions.

"Many conflicting opinions will be expressed, and we shall not have time to answer and refute them. The whole convocation is attached to this kingdom. Why compose S'âstras? Your realms are defended on all sides by high mountains under the guardianship of Yakshas."*

Is it stretching a point to say that the high-handed monarch, although he yielded on this occasion, still exerted a pressure which was by-and-bye successful?

In point of fact, the religion of Ceylon is a vast cosmical amalgamation. A and B, let us say, are carrying C in a rickshaw. A has been a shining Deva in Tavateinza, wearing a golden crown shaped like the pinnacle of a temple, but his Karma being exhausted and his moral nature deteriorated, he has come to earth as a punishment. B was a banker in one of the stars that whirls round a distant sun in the Milky Way, only just discernible with the largest telescope at Greenwich. But certain faults in his accounts have brought him likewise to the Karma of carrying heavy people about in rickshaws. C in his last rebirth was in hell, and was beaten by red demons with heavy clubs, but he bowed to the Chaitya, or Lingam, several thousand times, and the Karma of this good action makes him now an elegant young prince receiving the saalam of the crowd as he passes along. There is no death, only change. The Kosmos is a vast penitentiary. Buddha, it is said, was once a Yaksha, a foul corpse-eating ghoul. And as Mr. Upham tells us, he was once Sekkraia, the God Indra, and he "ruled the Tavateinza heavens with thirty-two Nat-devas as his Counsellors."† Then again he was

* "Memoires de Hiouen Tsiang," Vol. I., p. 174.

† Upham, "Buddhism," p. 62.

plainly Yama-râjah, the Lord of Hell, in the splendid parable of the plague-stricken pig. In fact, in Ceylon, as elsewhere, S'ivism deals very cavalierly with Indian gods. S'iva in one legend knocked off one of Brahma's four heads; and in the life of Buddha, Brahmâ, with a funny parasol, is made into a comic character, during Buddha's great struggle with Mâra the tempter.

"Maha Brahmâ offers flowers to the cloth that cleans my feet."* Dr. Rhys Davids tells us that Buddha had been six times on the earth as Brahma, and the Tibetans have "Buddha devils" in their hells. In point of fact, the lines that mark off hell from heaven, and a corpse-eating Yaksha from a bright Deva with a golden crown have been a little obliterated by time. Saman Deva Râjah, although he is Bhairava, or what we call "evil" in the divine economy, sits in a palace at times in the Tavateinza Heavens amongst the elect, and Sekkraia, who is Nature in her most benign aspects, has to put on the mask of Yama-râjah, the Lord of Hell, and judge the dead.

But we now come to a graver question. What is the "Inebriating Festival of the Buddha?" (p. 56). Mr. Upham himself is aghast at this question, and although he knows nothing of our S'iva-Buddha theories, visions of foul Bacchantic mysteries in Babylon and Eleusis float before his eyes.

Indians prefer fables to Athanasian Creeds for religious instruction. The story runs that Deva Râjah, the Lord of Hell, cast his eyes on a man of renowned probity named Mâga, and was astounded to note that this man with thirty-two followers was constantly levelling the roads for the Great Buddha, Dipankara, to pass—an infallible token that he was about to become the new Buddha himself. To frustrate this the demon hatched an infamous plot. He

* Hardy's "Manual," p. 185.

invited him to the initiatory Bacchantic Festival, that afterwards got to be called the "Inebriating Festival of the Buddha." A "Japani" (some mess of rice) was prepared, steeped in the juice of the inebriating tree. Mâga, who was S'âkya Muni, came with his thirty-two followers, but scenting the deceit, only made a pretence of eating, and made Deva Râjah and his followers blind drunk. He then drove him and his Yakshas out of hell. Here we have, without doubt, Buddha's descent into Hell, an experience which was a prominent point of all the old Bacchantic Mysteries. It is added that Buddha being compassionate, caused a floating island called Jak Girri to come, and upon that he installed the Yakshas.*

I will show later on from five bas reliefs of the Amarâvatî Tope now at the British Museum, that this story must have been much valued in the Buddhist Kingdoms in touch with Nalanda. And Mr. Upham shows plainly that Tappooism, even when supervised by English or Dutch magistrates, had pregnant secrets. Why did Mr. Fox's native attendant show such fear when his master proposed to approach the Devil dancers? Why did those gruesome ghosts fade away into the enshrouding night?

At Galle, in December, 1817, Kali Singar-Karegay Gerrensoe, a tom-tom beater, was examined by a sort of commission then sitting. These are some of his answers:—

Q.—Who are the people that sing and prepare the Bali?

A.—There are only two castes—Berewaya and Olia.

Q.—Who are the people who dance the devil's dances?

A.—*I am not able to tell, as the Kappoerales will know it.* (This answer Mr. Upham properly prints in italics.)

* Upham "History of Buddhism," pp. 22, 59. See also "Asiatic Researches," vi. 207.

Q.—What are the four deities—who act as priests to the four deities—and who worship the four deities?

A.—This also I am unable to say, but the Kappoerales will know it.

Q.—For what sickness, or what reasons, are the devil dances?

A.—The Kappoerales are the people who make them.

Q.—Do they dance the devil-dances for the same purposes as they make the Bali?

A.—This also the Kappoerales will know.

All this points to vows of secrecy and gruesome rites. And Mr. Upham's drawings, selected at hazard, show that the goddess Pattinee and her corpse-eating subordinates were as fond of human blood in Ceylon as they were on the other side of Adam's Bridge, and also in Alexandria. Thus the "Giant Rirey" (Plate 40 in Upham's Book) has a woman's head in one hand and a knife in the other. Whilst the "Demon Ammoosihon" seems to prefer entrails, as he is depicted tearing them from a human victim.

The Rev. John Colloway gives us a translation of a Cingalese masque. It is a very different affair from the outspoken "Body of the Dead Year" in Tibet, but in the presence of Dutch and English magistrates a poet had to be cautious. The grotesque masks seem much the same in the Kolan Nattanawa, the Cingalese masque, as those who figured on the Tibetan stage, being chiefly versions of S'iva and Durgâ. And there is absolutely no plot to the drama: the characters come on one by one and describe their masks. But one point struck me. A bevy of handsome women, nearly naked, support each other in the air and make up a pyramid, the apex being crowned with a "cup." The native poet says frankly that all this is intended to excite the animal passions of "gallants."* Now the Tibetan mystery gives the

* Calloway, "Kolan Nattanowa," p. 46.

cannibalism of the known S'ivan rites and the "Inebriating Festival of the Buddha" gives the drunkenness. The Ceylon masque certainly adds the third ingredient, the erotic stimulant. I have more to say about the pyramid of women in the next chapter.

And even in Ceylon there are hints of human sacrifices. Images of human beings in rice are used in Ceylon mysteries. This fact, of course, like the dough images of Tibet, points to repressed cannibalism.

And Spence Hardy writes thus:—

"Europeans are not allowed to enter the dewâles, and it is difficult to ascertain the exact nature of the rites therein performed."*

That difficulty might have been overcome if the writer had studied the religion of S'iva as clearly as he shows in his admirable work that he has studied the religion of Buddha. The Devalayas are temples of Deva or S'iva, and on the other side of Adam's Bridge the missionaries could have shown him plenty of them, and told him gruesome secrets. Material for S'ri's sensuous "Chakra" would be ready in plenty in these Temples in the shape of the "Servants of the God" the "Brides of the God." Miss Wilson Carmichæl, a missionary lady, gives a pathetic picture of a sweet little Hindu child that she knew, very affectionate and prettily petulant. She sang to her one day some Christian verses, and the little lady with a pout replied in the Indian sing-song manner with an Indian psalm, declaring that she liked hers best, as her religion had been in existence hundreds of years before that of Miss Wilson Carmichæl. Two days afterwards she saw the child in the hands of two grave men, "dignified, educated men." What were they doing to her?

The men laughed. "We are taking her to the Temple, there to marry her to the god."

* Spence Hardy, "Eastern Monachism," p. 201.

"The child had one hand free," says Miss Carmichæl. "She waved it to me and smiled, and then the dark trees hid her from me."*

The little thing had joined the bands of temple women who dance and sing in the processions and feasts. Some are carried off like this, even when they are five years old. A phrase used in the south shows how difficult it is to get clear of S'iva symbolism. These Brides of the God are said to be "tied to the Stone."

In Tibet, women see nothing immoral unless the offending party is a married woman. Polyandry still exists there. "In Ceylon," says Sir Emerson Tennant, "the lower classes exhibit a licentiousness so shocking and practices so inconceivably vile as would scarcely obtain credence."

We learn also from him that polyandry is winked at by the Buddhist priests.†

Apropos of human sacrifices. Mr. M. Conway gives a story from Ceylon which is very instructive. There was a Cingalese King whose wife had several miscarriages. The King consulted the Kappooists, and they told him that a demon named Bahirawa lived in a mountain near Kandi, and that she could never have a son unless she sacrificed a "virgin" to this demon once a year. This was done until the Queen was an old woman. Then the sacrifice was stopped, but so many diseases fell upon the royal family that the sinister remedy was renewed until the arrival of the British in Kandi in 1815.‡ If all this was done openly as late as that, what may have been done and may be doing even now in secret?

Sir Emerson Tennant affirms that for magical purposes children were slaughtered when he was in

* Amy Wilson Carmichael, "Things as they are," p. 218.

† Sir Emerson Tennant, "Ceylon," II., 428.

‡ M. Conway, "Demonology," Vol. I., pp. 260, 266.

the island. In 1849, a case came before him of a sorcerer who was accustomed to cut off the heads of young children. The little skull was scraped, and denuded of the flesh, and cabalistic figures were drawn upon it, and the name of a person whose death was desired was inserted on it. Then it was taken to a graveyard, and for forty nights the evil spirits were invoked to destroy the proposed victim.*

These skulls the "Tamil Doctor" obtained, sometimes by murder, at others by the baby farming of his wife. The man got away, but left behind him a book containing various charms and invocations, all addressed to "S'iva the Destroyer," suitable for every imaginable purpose.

The festival of the "Perahar" described by the sailor Knox, shows how completely the religion of S'iva reigned in his day supreme in the Island.† A branch of a tree covered with flowers was the chief object of worship (S'iva as the Tavateinza tree). This paraded the streets on a magnificent elephant, with many drums and trumpets; and S'iva's son, Cottaragom (Kattragam or Karttikeya), and Potting Dio (Pattinee ?) on other elephants shared the honours. Maskers as giants (the Yakshas are all gigantic), and about fifty elephants were in the procession. "Thousands of ladies and gentlemen" and "all the beauties of Zelone" (Ceylon) turned out. And it used to be a custom of the King and his Court to come. One king tried to stop the show and in the year 1664 there was no Perahar; but a rebellion in consequence promptly caused the monarch to restore it.

The three chief gods have each a separate pagoda. Knox tells us that the Cingalese worship as a chief

* Sir E. Tennant, "Ceylon," II., 428.

† Knox, "Relation of Ceylon," p. 157.

PLATE 23.

From Amarāvatī.

DURGĀ AS A GIANTESS.

god " Ossa polowa maupt dio (the Creator of Heaven and Earth," and neglect " Buddou."

And modern travellers tell the same story. Professor Rhys-Davids tells us that in the quadrangle of almost every Buddhist temple is a dewale—a shrine to the Devas.

And Spence Hardy and Sir Emerson Tennant tell us that in the Mahâ-Dewayo Wihara Durgâ as Pattinee, and Saman Deva Râjah (S'iva) with his son Kattragam (Karttikeya), have their statues in the temple itself.*

I conclude this chapter with a design very popular in Ceylon. Is this the model from which the Java of Mr. Crawfurd received its jawless S'iva ?

* Spence Hardy, p. 203.

CHAPTER XVII

ALEXANDRIA

Adi Buddha described by Hodgson—Abrasax described by Matter—Close points of contact—Mithras—His death and burial at Easter—Abrasax an individual, and also the whole body of the faithful, like Sangha, and also St. Paul's "Christ"—Points of contact between Kattragam and the Logos of Philo—Abrasax has two serpent legs—So has Padmapâni in the sculptures of Jemalgiri—Close analogies between Sekkraia and Serapis—Each is half man, half stone—Description of the advent of the Son of Man in the Gospels, quite different from what was expected, but quite in harmony with S'iva's Pralaya.

I WILL open this chapter with a noteworthy description of the Supreme Buddha as conceived in the Buddhist books that came from Nalanda to Nepal. It is given to us by Brian Hodgson. I will then quote what Matter tells us of the God of Basilides. Linked together, the passages read curiously.

According to Hodgson the Buddhists hold that "Ishwara, the Supreme God, the Absolute, is Nirvritti, and Nirvritti is this: to know the world to be a mere semblance, unreal, and an illusion,—and to know God to be one, and Pravritti to be the opposite of this sublime science, and in fact the practice and notions of ordinary men. Therefore, according to Nirvritti Âdi Buddha is the author and creator of all things, without whom nothing can be done, whose care sustains the world and its inhabitants, and the moment he averts his face from them they become annihilated, and nothing remains but himself."*

* Hodgson, "Religion of Nepal," p. 46.

Now from Matter we learn that the God of Basilides was "unborn, unmanifested, nameless—He who hides himself in the plenitude of his perfections."

When he manifests these they take the form of countless beings, all analogous to himself. Each of these is not a mythical fancy without substance. Each is really God; and without him they and their worlds fade away into nothingness.

In connection with these emanations, Matter details what he considers a curious piece of letter puzzle, the "Abrasax." These letters make up three hundred and sixty-five, and Abrasax is the God that rules the Pleroma, the manifested world, the Indian Pravritti, as distinguished from the unmanifested, the Gnostic Buthos, the Indian Nirvritti. Abrasax is plainly the year-god.

In this letter puzzle the mightiest mysteries were said to be concealed.*

Matter tells us also that Μειθρας, the Persian Buddhist divinity, has a name whose Greek letters also make up three hundred and sixty-five, and who is also called the "Word." Tertullian said of this god that it imitated the "Mystery" of the Resurrection. Fermicus, a Christian controversialist who lived in the fourth century, tells us what that "mystery" was. Every year Mithras was supposed to die at Easter. In the form of a stone he was buried with great pomp in a cave. Then in a day or two he rose again with much rejoicings and illuminations.

But the most important of the ideas recorded by Matter as held by Basilides, I take to be this:—That Abrasax was at once a single divine being, and also the entire body of the Emanations that were manifested (la totalité des intelligences qui composent le Pleroma).* Does not this bring strangely together the Buddhist and the Christian Vice-God? Sangha

* Matter, "Histoire du Gnosticisme," p. 413.

also is at once one individual and all the congregation of faithful souls. And St. Paul held the same idea that the " Christ " was the body of all the faithful :—

" For in him the Pleroma of Divinity wholly dwelleth " (Col. ii. 9).

Whilst Christianity remained Jewish all art illustration was impossible, as Mr. King in his " Gnostics " points out. This gives an importance to the Gnostic gems which filtered in as talismans.

Matter tells us the certain stones (les pierres de Basilides) were viewed with special importance. These are plainly what in England we call the " Gnostic Gems."

Plate 24 gives some of the most important.

They throw much light on our special subject.

Epiphanius tells us that certain " heretics " even in his day had a god with serpent legs, " and they called it Abrasax." Tertullian also attacks certain Christians " who have taken unto themselves gods with wings, or with the heads of dogs, or of lions or serpents from the legs downwards."

Basilides died A.D. 136, and Epiphanius lived about A.D. 400, so Abrasax (see Pl. 24, fig. 1) must have been the symbolised representation of the manifested Supreme, the Logos, for a considerable time.

" Philo," says Keim, " described his god as a simple entity. He disclaimed for him every name, every quality, even that of the Good, the Beautiful, the Blessed, the One. Since he is still better than the good and higher than the Unity, he can never be known as—— but only that he is. His perfect name is only the four mysterious letters J. H. V. H.—that is pure being. It was the problem of theology as well as religion to shed the light of God upon the world and lead it again to God. But how could this being which was veiled from the world be brought to bear upon it. By Philo, as well as by all the philosophy

PLATE 24.

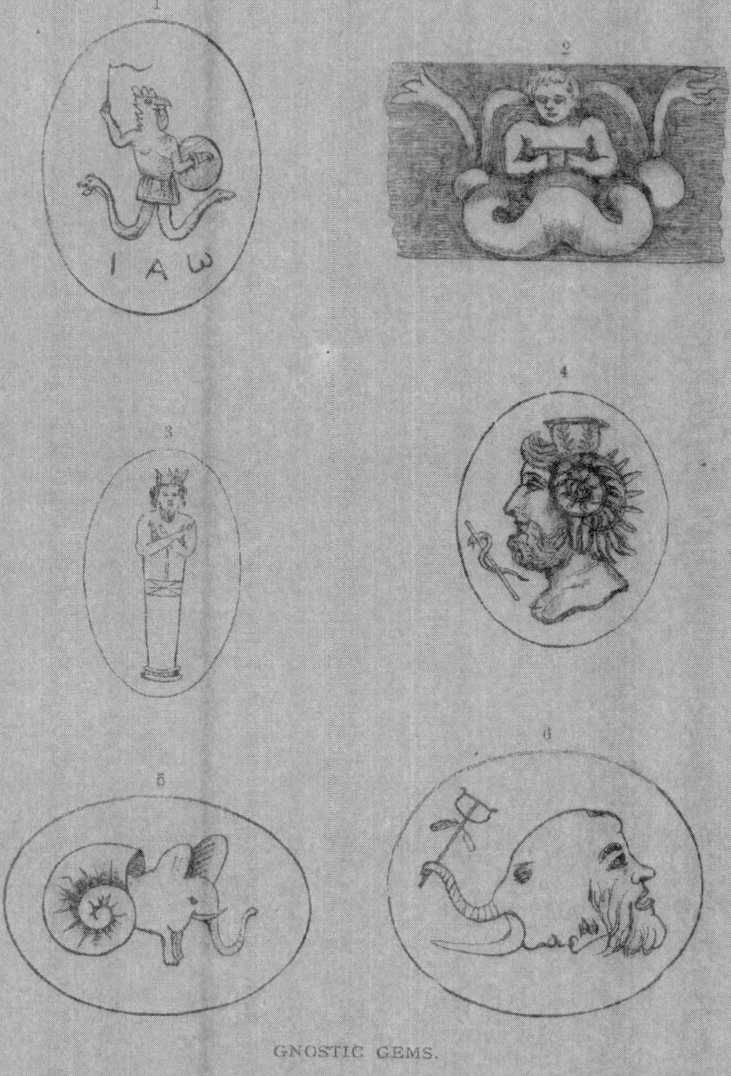

GNOSTIC GEMS.

of the time, the problem could only be solved illogically. Yet by modifying his exalted nature it might be done. If not by his being, yet by his work, he influences the world. His powers, his angels, all in it that is best and mightiest, the instrument, the interpreter, the mediator and messenger of God, his pattern and first-born, the Son of God, the Second God, even God himself, the divine Word is Logos, communicate with the world."*

The popular idea is that Philo got all his ideas about the Logos from Plato, but in Alexandria at Philo's date there were ideas added that could not have come from that source. The Yoga S'âstra of Patanjali was the chief Bible of the Mahâyâna Buddhists as we have seen, and in that work the inconceivable, the Great Absolute, took no interest in mortal affairs. This doctrine was transferred to Alexandria, and even to the Christians for a French wit has styled Tertullian's "Placid" God a "Dieu inutile"; but Plato's rigid logic would not probably accept such a God, for if we can know nothing about the Great Absolute, how can we know that he takes no interest in mortal affairs? Then again the Word by the Gnostic Kabbalists was practically interpreted to mean the letters J.H.V.H., made into a divine being. This was plainly derived from the A.U.M. of the Yoga S'âstra. A third question that arises is this—Did Philo know anything of the Cingalese god Kattragam, and had Kattragam (or Kârttikeya) connection with the Gnostic time god, Abrasax. Kârttikeya as the God of War was very popular in Ceylon for the seaman Knox tells us that the shrines of the Dewales bristled with weapons, but the Wiharas were quite without them.

Kattragam (like Abrasax) used the cock for a symbol. It figured on his banner. His temple was more

* Keim, "Jesus of Nazara," Vol I, p 281.

honoured than the wihara erected for the worship performed by the King. He received from Buddha the chief power to cure the sick, "especially those of royal blood"; also to perform miracles; to assist men in distress; and to do good to animals. Once a year he had in Ceylon a magnificent festival. All Ceylon assembled, and also Hindus from the Malabar and the Coromandel Coasts. On the tallest of elephants, seated in an ivory howdah profusely be-gemmed, the god passed along, accompanied by drums, and lighted torches. The festival lasted fifteen days. Then with much mystery a golden sword was carried in a palanquin to the nearest river to "cut the water" (arrest its flow). The gold sword was apparently as much honoured as the god, and was carried back carefully to the Temple.* This gold sword explains much of the popular enthusiasm for Kattragam. Ignorant natives, in abject terror of the thousands of evil spirits around them, would seek a protection in the gold sword. As it is stated, that Kattragam was the Son of S'iva and his wife Pattinee or Durgâ and was, moreover, the God of War, what better safety?

Now Abrasax and Padmapani, the Buddhist "Præsens Divus" according to Hodgson,† have each two serpents for legs. (See Fig. 2, Pl. 24 of Padmapani, taken from a bas relief of the sculptures of Jemalgiri). And the ritual of the followers of S'iva, when scrambling for the flesh and blood of S'iva as the dying year, seems certainly to have reached the Buddhists, for we find this amongst Hodgson's quotations:—‡

"From between his (Padma Pani's) shoulders sprang Brahmâ, from his forehead Mahâdeva, from his two eyes the sun and moon, from his mouth the

* Upham, "History of Buddhism," p. 52.

† Hodgson, "Religion of Nepal," p. 88.

‡ Hodgson, "Religion of Nepal," p. 88.

air, from his teeth Sarasvatî," and so on and so on.* Remember that from the belly of the S'ivan Victim sprang the Serpent King. Abrasax was certainly two serpents from the belly downwards.

Let us now compare Kattragam and the Logos.

"The Logos is the son of God the Father," says Philo (De Profugis). Kattragam is also the Son of God, the God whose followers started all the subtleties about the Logos.

"The Logos is superior to all the Angels" (De Profugis).

Kattragam as the god of war commands all the Devas.

"The Logos is the Physician that heals all evil." Kattragam in Ceylon is the chief healer as well as the chief fighter, practically identical functions when healing means battling with evil spirits. Hence the importance of Kattragam's gold sword, and the big shield of Abrasax.

Says Philo :—"The just man when he dies is translated to another state by the Logos, by whom the world was created; for God by his said Logos, by which he made all things, will raise the perfect man from the dregs of this world, and exalt him near himself." (De Sacrificüs).

Abrasax has a whip which makes him the Lord of Hell and supreme judge. The Christos of the Gnostics had the same function. Also he brought not peace but a sword, and could summon more than twelve legions of angels.

All this sheds a flood of light upon the Gnosticism of Alexandria. It was Buddhism filtered through the Kappooism of Ceylon. Samana Deva Râjah and his Nâgas is reproduced in Ialdibaoth, a serpent God with his seven serpent-headed sons. Then the Goddess Pattinee is equally prominent. It was the aim of Philo, one of the Gnostics, ever to be the "Ser-

* Cited by Hodgson from the "Gunakaranda Vynha," p. 88.

vant of Sophia," the inspirer of all that is good. The most holy book of the Alexandrine version of the scriptures is called "The Book of Wisdom." (Sophia), in the same way that the tractates of the higher mysticism of the Buddhists are called Prajñâ Pâramitâ, the "Wisdom of the other Bank."

But Pattinee is also the Gorgon, a popular Gnostic gem. She is the Serpentine Durgâ.

Another plagiarism is noteworthy. Sekkraia, the god, half stone, half man, sits on his stone in one of Mr. Upham's drawings, and has in his hand a cup of wine. Now the chief god of Alexandria was Serapis, and his conventional head (Pl. 24, Fig. 4) is crowned with a wine cup and tree markings, the wine of the Tavateinza Tree. His hair is a coiled serpent.

This gives a meaning to one of the most popular of Gnostica mulets. Here is Sekkraia, the god, half man, half stone. In the mysticism of the Kabbala the "Cup of Libation" designates the fourth or highest grade in the progress of the mystic. Some trace a version of this idea in the legend of the Sangreal. Another gem (Pl. 24, Fig. 3) shows the god half man, half stone, still more clearly. He figures as a King and also a Yogi. King's "Gnostics" gives several specimens of this design. Each has the long hair of the Yogi and the Nazarite. Each has a beard; each also has his arms crossed. Mr. King dates the rise of Serapis from the building of Alexandria. The earliest statue—that at Sinope—had Proserpine (Durgâ) for his wife. Serapis has two faces like S'iva in India, and Janus at Rome. He was called Soter (the Saviour), as Tertullian* tells us, for he healed body and soul. But Mr. King says that in his earliest form he was the Lord of Hell, and Judge of the dead; these conflicting functions have been worked into Christianity. Tertullian talks of the

* Adv. Valent. Chap. xxv.

" three natures " of Soter. The gems throw a light on this. Fig. 6 gives plainly the Trinity of S'iva-Buddhism: One—the Yogi with a beard (Tertullian's " Unmanifested Supreme "). Two—the wife, the Buddhist Dharma, the Gnostic Sophia; and the third emblem is the Elephant with the Rod of Hermes, two Symbols of the Spiritual life. Fig. 5 makes this still more plain. Here we see the Elephant, like Buddha, coming from Nirvritti to the manifested Plenoma.

Herodotus, who speaks in a very circumstantial manner of the deities, and of the religion of the Egyptians, makes no mention of Serapis, His worship was not introduced to Rome until 146 A.D. Serapis is described as a sort of Jupiter-Æsculapius. In the second century his temples in Egypt, called Serapes, numbered forty-three, at which great cures were effected. His symbol was the Serpent, and he was pronounced one of the infernal gods; and Jacobi in the " Dictionnaire Mythologique " says that his statue, which Ptolemy replaced with that of Sinope, was a block of granite rough and formless.

And the reader will perhaps remember Gibbon's account of the Serapion at Alexandria whose pompous colonnades, upraised on a vast artificial mound one hundred steps above the city, glittered with golden statues like the Mahâdewayo Vihara in Ceylon; and possessed " arches, vaults, and subterranean apartments,"* presided over by the goddess Anaitis, the special patroness of the Brides of the God.†

* Gibbon, " Decline and Fall," Chap. XXVIII.

† Mr. King tells us that the Serapion was of a style " totally different from the native Egyptian or Grecian model," but exactly agreeing with that of the Hindu Temple of S'iva in Tanjore. He cites a curious letter from the Emperor Hadrian to Servianus. " Those who worship Serapis are also Christians; even those who style themselves the Bishops of Christ are devoted to Serapis. The very Patriarch himself, when he comes to Egypt, is forced by some to adore Serapis, by others to adore Christ." (" The Gnostics," pp. 68, 69).

At Sinope, an early statue of Serapis with three heads marked the rise of the Nile, and also, like Trailinga Is'wara, the Past, the Present and the Future.

Mr. Moncure Conway, commenting on the exceptional concealments of the body of Serapis, likens them to similar veilings when the body of the Bambino of Aracœli is exhibited. But the mythology of Ceylon sufficiently explains the matter. If a portion of the body of a god is sometimes of flesh and sometimes of stone it would not do to show too much of him.*

The ideas which we call Messianic, which were in existence just before the epoch of Christianity, were derived from many sources. From the prophet Micah, the Jews had been taught to expect an earthly conqueror, who was to destroy all the enemies of Israel and to set up the Chosen Race upon the "Mountain of the Lord" resplendent with the "gains" (Micah iv. 13) of his conquests. This Messiah was certainly a man, for according to Daniel he was to be cut off. Then came the influence of a very old Persian book, the Bundahesh. In it Soshios or Soshyans comes with his angels to effect a general resurrection, and to send the wicked to eternal suffering with Ahriman in hell.†

A work, the "Apocryphal Book of Enoch" seems a version of this work Judaised, with Jehovah for Ormuzd and Satan for Ahriman. A similar resurrection and a judgment is there described, but Soshios is an angel, and the leader of the heavenly host in the "Book of Enoch" is Jehovah in one part of the book, and "Messiah," the "Son of Man" in another. This work is quoted by St. Jude, and it was viewed as part of Scripture by Tertullian.‡

* Conway, "Demonology," I., 338.

† See Bundahis C. XXX. "Sacred Books of the East," V., p. 120.

‡ Compare Chap. I., verse 4, with Chap. CCLXI., 4, 10, etc. Laurence's translation.

A fifth influence must be mentioned, overlooked for a long time, but now held by scholars to have had great influence with the Gnostic societies at that time abundant.

"Five hundred years Ânanda," said Buddha, in the Culavagga, "will the doctrine of the Truth abide." It is urged that this prophecy must have excited the Gnostics, for Buddha's death is fixed at 477 B.C., and a new Buddha would be due exactly at the time of the coming of Christ. Now it is a noteworthy fact that each of these five descriptions is radically unlike the "Coming of the Son of Man" as depicted in the three first gospels. For his coming was to effect a complete destruction of the earth, and the million billion star-systems of the Kosmos :—

"The sun shall be darkened and the moon shall no more give her light, and the stars in heaven shall fall, and the powers that are in heaven shall be shaken" (Mark xiii. 25).

Heaven and earth were to pass away, and a new heaven and a new earth were to come down from heaven. Under such circumstances all the descriptions of eternal punishment in a cave under the earth with Ahriman or Satan must be more recent additions. If the Son of Man of the Gospels were really to come as described, there would be no Cave in the centre of the earth, no Satan, no wicked at all, and the verse in Mark more than implies that the celestial cohorts would have come to an end. It is true that these descriptions in modern pulpits are made to refer to the taking of Jerusalem, on the strength of an interpolated passage in Luke, but that is quite irrational. The epistles, which were much earlier than the Gospels, announce that the heavens being on fire shall be dissolved at the coming of the day of God (2 Peter iii.

* Cited by Oldenburg, "Buddhism," p. 327, also Beal, "Romantic History," p. 16.

12). That phenomenon was not observed at the taking of Jerusalem.

Now if we turn to the Buddhism of Ceylon we may find a possible explanation :—

It was believed that S'iva at stated periods effected the complete destruction of the Kosmos, and annihilated both men and gods. Then he created a new Kosmos. This idea had come on to S'iva-Buddhism.

In the Mahâwanso "Kappos" (Kalpas, Sansk.) are constantly mentioned, periodical destructions that come like a thief in the night. Their arrival, says Mr. Turner, can be no more calculated upon than a man can guess how many mustard seeds there are in a mountain one yogana in height made up entirely of mustard seeds.*

"It," says Mr. Upham, writing of Ceylon Buddhism, "is philosophically described as a circle. The universe arises in beauty and excellence, and enjoys a golden age of excellence and peace. It deteriorates as it passes through a determinate series of changes from its brightness and glory; the stature of its inhabitants diminishes; and the perfection of its fruits and every other natural quality become proportionately lessened and impoverished by stated degrees, until the arrival of the period of their destruction, for which three agents are periodically assigned, namely fire, water and wind. Each of these causes has its exact limits. The last is the final and grand cataclysm, which sweeps the whole system into general destruction."†

Matter believes that the chief battle in the early stages of Christianity was between the Old Testament dualism derived by the Jews from Persia, and Gnosticism. It was said of Basilides that he made the devil a divinity. Readers of this work will see the falsehood

* Turnour "The Mahâwanso," p. 12.

† Upham, "Buddhism," p. 3.

of this: indeed, Matter refutes it from the Gnostic's own writings. But much of the Christianity of the priest, which was totally different to the Christianity of Christ, seems to be a compromise between these two antagonistic forces. The fate of the wicked, as I have shown, to be confined for ever and ever with Ahriman in the flames of hell, would be an impossibility to Basilides, who believed that the Supreme God burnt up the systems from time to time. On the other hand the idea of two omnipotent gods, different and yet the same, one-half much concerned for, and the other entirely callous to, the fate of mankind their offspring, which is the basis of the Logos and also the Trinity idea, would be pronounced utterly irrational except in regions where the philosophy of the followers of S'iva prevailed.

In point of fact, an atmosphere of Cingalese Buddhism was battling with Jewish influences in those early Christian days. Take the ideas concerning the punishment of the wicked and the rewards of the just. Each of these is now held to be eternal; but in one passage of scripture Satan and the sinners are described as being shut up in the fiery pit for a thousand years. Also the bliss of the just in the new Jerusalem, like that of saintly natives of Ceylon in the palaces of Tavateinza, is also limited to "reign with Christ a thousand years."

Another point seems to connect Alexandria and Ceylon—the action of "devils" in causing disease, and the action of the disciples of Serapis and Jesus in curing it. Tertullian, in speaking of the first, says that they "inflict on the body diseases and many grievous mishaps, and violently visit the man with sudden and extraordinary aberrations."

And he says of the healers they are "Sorcerers also truly in respect to the cure of diseases," and that they often cause the diseases magically before they proceed to cure them.§ In St. Luke's Gospel (x. 17) we learn the great success of the seventy who were sent forth to "heal the sick."

A passage from Professor Harnack may be here cited, dealing with Christian times.

"The whole world and the circumambient atmosphere were filled with devils. Not merely idolatry, but every phase and form of life was ruled by them. They sat on thrones. They hovered around cradles. The earth was literally a hell, though it was and continued to be, a Creation of God."*

A graver point is the question of sex. The women of the Nicolaites, the Prodiciens, the Carpocratiens and others, proclaimed that the laws of chastity were not binding; and an influential female leader, a woman named Agape, enunciated ideas very similar to those current in a temple of S'iva; and she persuaded a large bevy of Agapetes to become in all innocence and zeal "Brides of the God."†

One point more. It was held in Ceylon that between the earth and Mienmo the fabled holy peak, corresponding to the Jewish Zion and the Greek Olympus, were millions of Spirits. The space was called the "Jugandere." Had these spirits any affinity with those of the Archon of St. Paul (Eph. ii. 2) who had the domination of the air. Hippolytus tells us that the Great Archon, Abrasax, had three hundred and sixty-five heavens.‡

§ Tertullian "Apology," Chap. XXII.

* Harnack's "Expansion of Christianity," Vol. I., p. 161.

† Matter. "Hist. Gnost," Vol. III., pp. 33, 34.

‡ Hipp. Haer, VII., 14.

PLATE 25

THE BURNING OF THE NAGA'S PALACE.

CHAPTER XVIII

OPHIS AND THE SERPENTS

Sepent symbol everywhere in S'iva-Buddhism—Unknown in early Buddhism—Legend of Buddha burning the palace of the Nâga king—On a bas relief of the Sanchi Tope—The Serpent and the Lotus leaf—Valentinus—Dhyâni Buddhas—Saktis or Wives of the Dhyâni Buddhas—Gnostic Aeons—They also have their Saktis—Violent attack of Tertullian on these Saktis—Tertullian and Fourth Gospel—Valentinus and Serpent Worship—The Gnostic Kristos a Serpent—Cainites and Naasseni—The "Thousand-eyed (Dasasatanayana)" in Alexandria.

In S'iva-Buddhism the serpent symbol is everywhere ; on the miniature Chaitya-domes, on the heads of Buddha, in all the temple sculptures, on the altar. It is a striking and immensely important fact that on the early topes, Sanchi and Bharhut, there is no Serpent worship. One exception is noticed in Mr. Fergusson's Tree and Serpent Worship. I reproduce it. (Pl. 25). This bas relief is to be seen at Sanchi. Sir Alexander Cunningham denies that it is Serpent worship, but Mr. Fergusson points to the altar, and he makes one very noticeable observation. The worshippers are not like the other Buddhists of the sculptures. They have different dresses and different caps. Mr. Fergusson calls them Dasyus.

I think if these writers had come across the legend of the burning of the palace called Nangewcnodenneye in the Cingalese records, their conclusions would not have been antagonistic. I have given this story already. Buddha visits Samana Deva Râjah in his palace in hell. He frightens all his Nâgas to death by making fire issue from four sides of the palace. The Nâgas are the ancient rulers of Ceylon, and the Nâgas are to this day a sect of S'iva. Probably in early times it was a generic title. The five-headed serpent (Pl. 25) is the Serpent King, with his fire altar and crowd of bullocks and other victims, which include I fear, two little boys. There is wood piled, and a second brazier is in the corner. Buddha's object, we must recollect, was to secure the Minne Phalange, or "Seat of Supremacy." In one corner of the Plate is Buddha working his magic under a Pan-sil. The Kûsa grass mat of the ascetic was called the Throne of the Bodhi (Bodhi mandi).

The Fourth Gospel is judged by scholars to be much more recent than the other three. Irenæus calls it the Gospel used by Valentinus and his followers. He tells us that there were four Gospels used by the church; Matthew's, which was the Gospel used by the Ebionites; Mark's, the Gospel used by the Docetæ; Luke's, the Gospel used by the Marcionites; and John's, the Gospel used by the Valentians! Does this mean that each of the four principal sects had a version of the early Gospel, the "Gospel according to the Hebrews," and that these were each altered by them to suit their teachings?

Valentinus is placed by Matter at the head of the Gnostics.* He became prominent in the Church about A.D. 136 on the death of Basilides.†

In our last chapter we dealt with the distinction drawn by the Gnostics between the visible and invisible portions of the universe. Valentinus seems to have gone beyond Basilides, he made Buthos (the unmani-

* Matter, "Hist. du Gnosticism," II., p. 37.

† *Ibid*, II., p. 38.

fested portion) into a God. Now one section of the Indian Swâbhâvikas also worshipped a space turned into a God. The Prâjnikas, says Hodgson, made Nirvritti into a God. And the other section of the Swâbhâvikas went nearly as far. There was nothing, they said, but matter. It was called Swayambhu (the Self-existent).

The Mortal Buddhas who ruled this space in S'iva-Buddhism, were changed into Dhyâni Buddhas, that is, Buddhas that have never lived on earth at all. This was, of course, nonsensical, but the strict pantheism of the second school required all divine beings to descend in an unbroken chain from Îs'wara. Valentinus took over these Dhyâni Buddhas, and called them Æons (Eternals). With both they were "virtues," "powers," "emanations." Also they increased and multiplied like mortals, for each had his sakti, or female energy.

I will give the names of the Five Dhyâni Buddhas. They helped Î'swara to build up the universe.

Attributes.	Dhyani Buddhas.	Saktis.
Suvisuddha Dharma Dhâtu (Purifying Eternal Law).	Vairochana (Sunborn)	Vajra Dhâteswarî (Goddess of Eternal Elements).
Adarsana (Invisibility)	Akshobhya (Immovable).	Lochanâ (Eye Goddess).
Prativekshana (Eyes that sleep (not).	Ratna Sambhava (Born of the Jewel).	Mâmakhî.
Sânta (Calmness).	Amitâbha (Diffusing infinite light).	Pândarâ (Pale Goddess).
Krityânushthâna (Strict to rites).	Amogha Siddhi (Unfailing aim).	Tarâ (The Star).

Now let us turn to the five chief Æons of Valentinus and their wives or saktis.

SUPREME GOD.

THE ABYSS (BUTHOS).

AEONS.	WIVES.
Buthos.	Ennoia (Thought).
Monogenes (Only-begotten Son).	Aletheia (Truth).
Logos (Word).	Zoe (Life).
Anthropos (Man, Adam Kadmon, Purus'a of India).	Ecclesia, (Higher Humanity, Buddhist Sangha).
Phos (The Light).	Pneuma (Spirit).

Tertullian attacks these emanations of Valentinus, and their ever-increasing list, in the writings of Secundus and Marcus. He derides their "Fraternal nuptials,"* and their "conjunctions of execrable and unseen embraces"; and he makes much fun of the changes in conditions and alterations of domicile of the various beings, human and divine, at the end of an age—Achamoth restored to the Pleroma; the "Demiurge" promoted from the celestial Hebdomad to the higher regions"; and the just of the earth" dispersed amongst the angels"—without anyone being allowed to carry away any of the matter of the earth for a body.† Does he not picture here the constant shuffling of cards in the Ceylon Pantheon, and remind us that in the Mahâyâna there are at least seventeen distinct Devas who each created the world? "With humorous irony," as the two clerical translators put it, Tertullian describes how a "wonderful puppet, Soter (the Saviour) is formed out of these Gnostic emanations, although St. Paul practically says the same thing. Tertullian specially attacks the gross deeds of "Sophia" and "Achamoth" called "left-handed" deities‡ he tells us. Noteworthy is the fact that with these Gnostics Soter the Saviour had three natures: the carnal or left-handed; the right-handed

* Tertullian, "Adversus Valent.," VII.

† *Ibid*, C. XXXI.

‡ Tertullian, *Ibid*, C. XXV.

balanced between the carnal and spiritual; and third, the spiritual.* This seems to show that the differention between the active god and the Unmanifested Supreme, or as Tertullian puts it, the "placid" and "stupid" divinity,† was not as closely insisted on as it is now. Padmapani wears his mask loosely, and allows Trailinga Ī'shwara's head to peep out. Serapis was also called Soter.

Although the Buddhists and Gnostics differ in the choice of the virtues and qualities with which they christen their Æons and Buddhas, the analogy between them is sufficiently close.

Is there anything like all this in the Gospel that, according to Irenæus, was viewed at one time as the Gospel of Valentinus.

"No man hath seen God at any time. Monogenes, who is in the bosom of Propator, he hath declared him" (John i. 18).

Propator is "The Father" of the Fourth Gospel, and according to Matter, Proarche (the Beginning) is another name for him. Then we see that Monogenes made the world (John i. 3). He is the Phos, who lights up the Pleroma, as Padmapâni lights up the Pravritti (John viii. 12). And the names of other Æons, Zoe, Aletheia, Logos, Ecclesia, figure in the narrative.

Now this seems the teaching of Valentinus in epitome,‡ but here comes a bewilderment: Neander calls St. John's Gospel an attack on the Gnostics.

This is a little remarkable. According to Irenæus, Valentinus at one time believed that this gospel set forth his philosophy and teaching, and yet at a subsequent time a writer, not without shrewdness,

* *Ibid,* C. XXV.

† Tertullian, *Ibid,* C. VII.

‡ That is the opinion of Tertullian ("Adversus Valent.," C. VII).

can see nothing in the gospel but a fierce attack on Valentinus. It seems plain that these two observers cannot have seen the same document—or at any rate, the same document in the same condition.

Did Valentinus know anything of Serpent-Worship? Irenæus declares that he held that the mighty Sophia, the Dharma, the Wisdom of the Gnostics had for mother the Serpent Ennoia, and for father Buthos, the void.

Ennoia brought forth two emanations—one perfect, the Christos, the other imperfect, Sophia Achemoth. She descending into Chaos lost her way, and became ambitious to create a world entirely for herself.

Sophia, as I have said, parented Ialdabaoth, and Ialdabaoth parented Ophiomorphus, who had six sons :—Sabaoth, Adonai, Eloi, Oraios, Aslaphaios, Iao.

"Ophis," says Matter, "was at once with the Ophites both Satan and Christos."* The Pneumatics cited John iii. 14, 15, to prove the identity of the Saviour and the Serpent Ophis.† "Serpentem magnificant intantum ut illum etiam Christo prœferant," says Tertullian.‡ The Ophites outdid the serpent petting of Nâgpur in India :—

"They bred in their sanctuaries living serpents, and these were so trained that during the celebration of the Holy Communion these creatures issued from their cages, and came and "blessed" (by licking it) the consecrated bread exposed on the holy table."§ When the Ophites and Marcionites joined forces, and no live serpents were available, they had to be content, according to Theodoret, with a brass serpent in their churches.||

* Matter, "Hist. du Gnosticisme," Vol. II., p. 152.

† *Ibid*, Vol. II., p. 163.

‡ "De praeser," p. 250.

§ Matter, "Hist. du Gnosticisme," Vol. II., p. 375.

|| *Ibid*, Vol. II., p. 395.

Amongst the Gnostics there was a good serpent and also a wicked serpent. The Sethians and Paratæ worshipped a good Serpent. The Cainites worshipped an evil Serpent, and so did the Ophites, according to Matter, but Hippolytus identifies the latter with the Naasseni who professed to have received their teaching from James, the brother of the Lord. They held that "Jesus" represented three principles, the angelic, the psychical and the earthly, in fact that he was apparently Trailinga Ī'shwara. Here is another curious point. According to Hippolytus the Naasseni and Phrygians called the Father "the many named, thousand eyed, Incomprehensible."* Here we have Dasasatanayana's name literally translated. S'iva as Sesh is the "thousand-eyed" (Dasasatanayana).

Here is a passage in a hymn of the Naasseni :—

"Evoe, evan ! Thou art Pan as thou art Bacchus, as thou art Shepherd of brilliant stars."†

The Shepherd of the brilliant stars must be S'iva as Sesha, the shepherd of the spangled serpents in the sky.

Also S'iva is the Bacchus and Pan of the Greeks.

CISTA, FROM A ROMAN COIN OF ADRAMYTTIUM.

* Hippol., "Haer," v. 4.

† "Hippol. Haer," v. 4.

CHAPTER XIX

DESCENT INTO HELL

New evidence—Five bas reliefs of the Amarâvatî Tope—They illustrate Buddha's Descent into Hell—Details of Amarâvatî Tope imitate details of an early tope—Tree Worship—Tree stem a lingam—Cairn Worship—Cairn a lingam—Roman Catholics maintain that their rites give the life of Jesus in epitome—Question examined—Not the life of the Jesus of the first three gospels—A "willing victim"—Suffers at night—Herod Antipas, the "King of the Jews"—An originality of Luke—Why brought in—His dress the same as that of a Catholic Bishop—The "Amice" the Hood-winking rag of the Freemasons—The spear thrust—Blood and water—Baby New Year in Alexandria and Tibet—Covered with flour—Tertullian on "Eleusinian dissipations."

FROM Tibet and from Ceylon we have obtained evidence that there was in S'iva Buddhism a sacrifice of the year-god of a S'ivan type. Is it corroborated? On this point I have accidentally come across some very startling matter and evidence, given by the sculptures of the Amarâvatî Tope in the British Museum. I came upon this evidence only very recently, but I do not regret the position it occupies in my little work, as without these last three chapters its full importance would not be made evident. It completely confirms all I have said about the Tibetan Mystery of the "Sacrificial Body of the Dead Year," and also the "Inebriating Festival of the Buddha"; for five bas-reliefs, which I shall reproduce, represent that festival seriatim.

The large topes were developed from the sepulchral cairn; and have for ornament a handsome railing and four gateways all covered with bas-reliefs and stone emblems. The Amarâvatî Tope stood on the banks of the Kistna in Guntoor. It is believed to be the Dhanakacheka visited by the Chinese traveller, Hiouen Thsiang. It is believed also to be the Temple erected on the "Golden Sands" when the tooth of Buddha was brought back to India from Ceylon, after many romantic adventures in which the Princess Hemachala figured as a heroine. The celebrated Sanchi Tope and the Amarâvatî Tope, before it was broken up, must have presented at a distance a similar appearance. The dates of these Topes are very uncertain. Mr. Fergusson fixes the four gateways of the great Tope at Sanchi "within the limits of the first century A.D."; and Sir Alexander Cunningham—from 19 to 37 A.D.; but the last authority holds that the mound was set up as early as 500 B.C. The Amarâvatî Tope, in the view of Mr. Fergusson, might have been erected any time between 200 and 300 A.D. One fact in my mind throws it further back in the past than some folks suppose. Comparing this tope with the Sanchi Tope, a monument of early Buddhism, I was startled to find that the Amarâvatî Tope was of fell purpose constructed to exhibit the rites and legends of a Second Buddhism that proposed to supersede the first. It wore a masquerade dress borrowed from early Buddhism, which points to an epoch when such disguise was necessary.

That Buddhism was Saint Worship. There were seven great Saints or Buddhas. Each had his Saint's day like the Saints of the Roman Catholic Church. The rites were simple as we have shown, and centred round the Cairn where the relics of the Saint were deposited. Each had for symbol a tree in the forest; and received his flowers, food offerings, and adoration. This was the blameless Buddhist substitute for cannibalism and bloody sacrifices. With these simple rites the sculptors of both the Sanchi and the Amarâvatî Topes covered slab after slab, holy men adoring trees and holy men adoring relic cairns.

Now S'iva Buddhism sought to wreck this reform, and re-introduce cannibalism and the bloody altar. And if you narrowly scrutinise the Tree Worship of Amarâvatî (Pl. 26), you see that it is not real tree worship. The tree is the Tavateinza Tree, already described, that has a stem of silver. In other words, it is the worship of the Columnar Lingam of S'iva.

A second plate (Pl. 27) shows this very plainly. Here we get the worship of this Columnar Lingam, and a few branches are put at the top to suggest the Tavateinza Tree, the Tree of S'iva and his intoxication, the Soma Tree (*Æsclapius acida*). There are five or six large slabs at Amarâvatî exhibiting this worship of the Columnar Lingam. Mark, too, at the base of the smaller Lingam in this plate, the Charan or impress of Buddha's feet. Plainly, it has been cleverly converted into a grinning head of Avalokitishvara, the balls of the feet are his everlasting eyes, and the toes his terrible teeth.

In Chapter five I have already dealt with the dome-shaped lingam. Ornamental models of it are everywhere at Amarâvatî. On them is usually the five-headed Serpent; and often five Columnar Lingams, the five Dhyâni Buddhas, are sculptured on the little dome and present the appearance of the barrels of a cathedral organ. Why they are always five is a puzzle. The five Indrayas (five senses), the five Bhûtas (five material elements) have been suggested. Hodgson tells us that they are at the base of every Mahâ Chaitya (Lingam Temple) in Nepal.

It is a very important gain if we can show that at the date of the Amarâvatî Tope the story of the "Inebriating Festival of the Buddha" was in the

PLATE 26.

WORSHIP OF THE SILVER TREE-STEM.

PLATE 27.

LINGAM WORSHIP.

PLATE 28.

THREE SCENES IN THE INEBRIATING FESTIVAL.

PLATE 29.

THE CUP.

ritual of the Buddhism on the mainland of Hindustan, —somewhere about 150 A.D.; and that it is depicted in ineffaceable characters on five slabs of one of its temples. I commence with slab One (See bottom of Pl. 28).

"On the left," says Mr. Fergusson, "a chief seated on a throne is listening to the animated eloquence of a warrior who seems addressing a youth seated cross-legged on the ground." The second, he thinks, shows the King on an elephant with his army; the third the enemy fly without striking a blow."

My interpretation is different. It seems to me that the man that Mr. Fergusson takes to be an orator is about to strike off the head of the young man by him with a weapon very like the Kukri of the Nepaulese, a weapon that can sweep off a buffalo's head at one blow. The victim is tied to a post. A darikhâna, with jewelled throne and costly cushions, is hardly the place for a commonplace execution; and the young man is handsome and calm. This suggests a willing victim, as was required in the S'ivan mysteries. In fact, we have here the great Inebriating Festival.

When Sakya Muni as Mâga went down to hell and cleared out those regions of suffering, after the manner of Buddhas, the Nâgas became very drunk, and they fled from the kingdom without striking a blow. (Slab 3). The White Elephant in the second plate shows that their pursuer was Buddha in person, and the mighty "Cup" on the fourth bas-relief (Pl. 29.) shows the mixture of blood and spirit, the immortal drink. The framer of this wierd story of Buddha-Silenus thought to make it a little less preposterous by announcing that Buddha himself only pretended to drink. But he forgot that to take in Nâgas you must imitate their favourite rites to the letter. The warm blood from a human victim requires that that victim be slain on the spot. To avoid making Buddha a toper he is made treacherous and an assassin. Mr. Fergusson thinks that the vessel holding the drink that the assembled multitude is calling for in their corybantic frenzy is Buddha's alms-bowl, but would an alms bowl be as big as a sitz bath, and require five or six people to hold it up?

In the fifth of these tablets (Pl. 30) we have a startling piece of corroborative evidence making plain that this group of bas-reliefs really tells the story of Mâga. In the Cingalese Masque, the Kolan Nattanawa, as translated by the Rev. John Calloway, a pyramid of scantily clothed women supporting each other in the air is a prominent factor.*

Here is a similar pyramid, six women. The Cingalese group consisted of five.

Matter declared that it was held in the old days that the word "Abrasax" contained tremendous mysteries. The Roman Catholic priest with his amice, his wafer, his bell, his ornamental bandages, professes to give in epitome the whole story of Christ. This may be so but it is certainly not that of the Jesus of the first three Gospels, but it may be that of Abrasax.

To begin with, Jesus prayed that the "cup" might be passed away from him, whereas the S'ivan Year-god was a willing victim. Jesus was crucified in the daytime. Abrasax requires imposing tenebræ, the Φωτισμὸς, "Paschal Candles," "New Fire." He suffers at night.

Commonplace occurrences may acquire in the process of time tremendous meanings. The sun sinks into the sea in the evening. It rises again in glory in the morning, having passed through, in that interval, portentous and unknown terrors in the bowels of the earth. The ancients believed it passed through hell. The story of Sita, the story of Ceres, the story of

* See page 257.

PLATE 30.

PYRAMID OF WOMEN.

Buddha, all hinge on this; and we saw that hell was also the theatre of the "Religious King Devil" in Tibet. Deva Râjah, too, in Ceylon was in hell, and the mighty darkness with which Buddha frightened his Nagâs, and the miraculous flames that issued from the "carpet of skin" on which he sat, can certainly claim cousinship with the tapers that are miraculously lighted in Christ's sepulchre in Jerusalem, when the Patriarch of the Holy City goes into it at Easter, and then brings them out as a prize for his zealous but combatant congregation, who wrestle for them wildly.*

The death of the year-god by all ancient nations was fixed at the Spring equinox. He died always on March 25th. This gives a much graver aspect to the change of date introduced in the Fourth Gospel (John xix. 14). From the three first gospels we learn that Jesus was upon the cross from 6 p.m. to 9 p.m. on Saturday. He ate the Passover with His disciples the day before, and he appeared to James on the night of the Crucifixion. This we learn from St. Jerome, who gives us a passage from the "Gospel according to the Hebrews."

"The Lord, after giving his shroud to the servant of the High Priest, went forth and appeared unto James. Now James, since he had drunk in the cup of the Saviour, had made oath not to eat bread until he had seen him risen from the dead. The Lord then said, 'Bring me a table and some bread.' And when he had received that which he commanded he took the bread and blessed it and brake it, and gave it to James saying, 'My brother, eat this bread, because the Son of Man has risen from the dead.'"

From this two facts emerge:—

(1) It confirms our contention that Jesus was a water-drinking Nazarite, for James, who according

* Picart, "Ceremonies, etc.," III. p. 143.

to Eusebius was a Nazarite, bound by solemn oath to abstain from wine for life, could not have drunk out of the Lord's cup unless it was water only.

(2) That he was crucified on the day after the Passover and not on the day of the Passover, as John would make us believe.

Jesus is arrested by a vast "multitude armed with swords and staves." They include the "chief priests, the captains of the Temple, and Elders." They accuse him of calling himself the King of the Jews, and hand him over to Pilate, who learning that this offence took place in Galilee transfers Him to Herod Antipas. And now in the splendid palace of the Tetrarch a strange scene occurs. Jesus is dressed up in royal robes, and a white bandage blinds His eyes. Then all the soldiers of the palace, headed by the sober Tetrarch himself (Luke xxiii. 2) indulge in a sort of game of the "Blind Man's Buff" pattern. Individuals slyly pinch and hit Him, and cry,—"Prophesy unto us who is it that smote thee"; and the farcical dressing up is carried into the solemn hall of judgment of Pilate, the representative of the most powerful monarch in the world. This officer, instead of severely punishing the soldiers for their mistimed buffoonery, joins in the mirth; and sets up a burlesque description on the Cross, although quite convinced of the innocence of the accused. And the chief priests are found even there, mocking him and "wagging their heads" (Matt. xxvii. 55). Ever since the arrest in Gethsemane they seem to have been amongst the mob. The same must be said, I think, of the "great company of women" that knew him in Galilee (Luke xxiii. 49). They seem ever present; indeed, He halts on His last fatal journey to preach to them, and even from the cross addresses an exhortation to His mother, though the buffooneries of the chief priests who were "wagging their heads" there would have prevented her from hearing most of it.

Now do we get here sober history or a drama like the "Sacrificial Body of the Dead Year." Is this Tertullian's "Mystery" of the Resurrection? We see many characters dressed up—kings, chief priests, centurions, soldiers, thieves, multitudes,—actors remaining on the stage when they should be off it, and speaking set speeches in most unlikely places. And also as in the "Sacrificial Body of the Dead Year" we see a crowd of women, for according to Philo dancing and concerted song were prominent features in the nocturnal feasts of the Therapeuts.

In the midst of all this hurly-burly one prominent fact emerges. The "Christ" in the hall of Herod Antipas is not the historical Jesus. If it were really true that Pilate had found that he had no jurisdiction, and that he had handed over the prisoner to be judged by Antipas—the judgment pronounced by that ruler would, of course, have been final, and Jesus would have been at once released. But Strauss has shown that this "Herod" is a phantom due to the genius of the not very honest "Luke." Neither the first two gospels, nor the traditions that they drew from, knew anything of this "Herod," and the Fourth Gospel also ignores him.

And the puzzle, if probed at all, shows many new difficulties. Herod Antipas, the "King of the Jews," is a creation of mere fiction, and yet he is the keynote of the mystery. The dress that he wears, the dress that he hands over to the sacramental "King of the Jews," is apparently the same dress as the dress of the Roman Catholic bishop when performing mass. A little official catechism, sold broadcast for two pence, at the Roman Catholic libraries, tells us that the "alb," or white tunic that descends to the feet of the priest, "represents the white garment that Herod put on our Lord." It tells us also that the " Chasuble " represents the purple garment with which Jesus was clothed in derision as a mock king, the " amice " is the white rag that blinded His eyes, the " girdle, maniple, stole " are the cords that bound Him. The Eastern Church call the circle of hair left on the monk's head after the tonsure the " Crown of Thorns." Give to the bishop in addition to all this his pastoral staff which is imperative when he performs mass, and we have—Herod Antipas.

Now, premising that we have proved that the " Herod " of the Crucifixion story is a creation of fiction, several questions crowd upon us. Why is Herod Antipas dragged in at all? Why, too, is he dressed like a Catholic Bishop? Is " Herod " God Almighty handing over His dress (divine powers) to a mortal representative? If so, why is he placed in the camp of Baal-zebub? Why is the " amice " (the most ignoble part of the story) so highly prized? Has it any connection with the hood-winking rag of the Freemasons, who indulge in Bacchantic horse-play whilst the postulant is blinded?

All is a puzzle. To settle what was in the fourth Gospel at the date of Valentinus and what has been added since seems hopeless. If the proposition were presented for arbitration to—say an intelligent native of Japan—he might hold doubts whether the Jews were dealing with an evildoer who had earned the death penalty, or a man so blameless as to be able to claim the " glorification " of personating the Year-god at Easter.

" Take ye him and crucify him, for I find no fault in him " (John xix. 6).

This astounding *non-sequiter* of Pilate is capped by Caiaphas, who in the first three Gospels wants to kill everybody who dares to read the sacred books except in the most literal manner. In the Fourth

Gospel, however, this cruel old bigot seems to have quite adopted the explaining away of the Alexandrian Jews, and even their sacrifice of the Year-god.

"It is expedient for us that one man should die for the people" (John xi. 50). And the reason he gives is still more strange. He wants to make Israel into one camp. What camp? Plainly the camp of those who believed in the Year-god Abrasax.

It is a curious fact to start with, that "Herod" and his dress, if it were that of a Catholic Bishop, must have figured on the stage of a Buddhist Mystery play quite two hundred years before A.D. 30, for the French naturalist, Victor Jacquemont, who saw a Lâma performing a "Buddhist mass" in Tibet, declares that his dress was exactly that of a Roman Catholic Bishop in the same ceremony. And in the Tibetan play we saw bishops, priests, acolytes all properly dressed, and a Pope under a silken Baldachino.

Then the bell in a Buddhist country is a summons to gods to a feast, and in Tibet the "Religious King Devil" sounds his directly he begins to stab the "Sacrificial Body of the Dead Year." The Roman Catholic priest also sounds his bell directly he begins to immolate the wafer, as a summons to a feast. The body is already dead in Tibet, and there comes from it red wine which is lifted high in the air in a "cup." To John's Gospel has been added the account of a spear thrust delivered to the dead Christ, from whom comes blood and water, an incident that cannot be historical if the body were dead. But death by exhaustion, which is the result of a crucifixion, is inappropriate if we want a "cup" full of the fresh blood of the victim, for ceremonial purposes. This might be the reason why the spear-thrust was added by John. As in Tibet the Catholic priest lifts the cup into the air. It is sacramental "blood" and water, for a drop of the last has been added to signify Christ's mortal as well as His divine nature. Other points may or may not have significance.

Herod and his host pursuing the little infant suggest the "corpse devils" in Tibet, stabbing at the baby New-year with their spears.

Then the arrest is all unreal in John's Gospel. "Father, the hour is come, glorify thy son," says Jesus, and He gives Himself up and seems to desire the proceedings to be hurried along. Before Pilate He refuses to plead, and in the Gospel of Nicodemus He declares that Moses and the Prophets have foretold His passion and resurrection, and He speaks like a fatalist.

One point more seems to have suggested a difficulty. Jesus in the three first gospels rises up a full-grown man, but Abrasax, as his name implies, is an infant when the New Year begins. That may explain the invention of Simon of Cyrene. Valentinus declared that he perished instead of Christ.

There is one point more. The Jesus of the first three Gospels had, according to His disciples, a concise formulary.

"Repent and be baptised for the remission of sins" (Acts ii. 38).

The Christ of Valentinus had one equally short.

"Verily, verily, I say unto you, Except ye eat the flesh of the Son of Man and drink his blood, ye have no life in you" (John vi. 53).

Now the interpretation of this in the Roman Church is that all who fail to drink the blood of Christ sacramentally every Easter will be punished everlastingly in hell fire. No two schemes of perfection could be more antagonistic. One sought to train the conscience of the individual by making him dwell over his own short-comings. The other would have him ponder not on his own sins, but on an arbitrary condemnation that he might incur for neglecting a shameful savage rite. For one hundred years, at least, the first was the only "remission of sin" of the rising church. This is proved by the recently discovered Didache which gives the words of the early eucharistic rite as used about the year 130 A.D. The cup is called the "holy vine of David thy Servant." There is nothing about the body and blood of Christ. The allusion is to Psalm lxxx. 8, where Palestine is called a fruitful vineyard.

In Tibet the New Year, as we have seen, was a baby, and Buddha, under a baldachino of satin like the pope in the old days of Rome, comes in attended by priests and acolytes with orthodox chasubles, and albs, and he protects the little infant with a coating of flour, or, as I suggest, S'iva's white ash. Now one fact stands out in the troubled water of early Christian controversy, and that is that some sects in Alexandria, whether followers of Christ or Serapis is here unimportant, introduced a baby covered with flour in their occult rites.

There is nothing about a descent into hell in the story of Jesus as read in the first three Gospels, or even in the earliest version of the Apostle's Creed. Again we can separate the Gnostic Christ from Jesus. But without doubt Origen, Clement of Alexandria, Augustine, Cyril and others believed in this descent, and even debated such horrible questions as whether Jesus felt the torments of the flames, and whether like Buddha he cleared out hell or only took away the orthodox.

In the old days in France on Rogation Sunday a great dragon went before the Cross in the procession with a long tail filled with chaff. This chaff represented the souls in hell. And the third day, for the festival lasted three days, the tail was empty, "by which it was understood," says Hone, "that the first two days the devil reigned in the world, but that on the third day he was dispossessed of his kingdom."*

* Hone, "Ancient Mysteries described," p. 134.

This short interval in ancient days was depicted on the stage with the most abominable and licentious orgies even in Christian churches. Smooth apologists deny this, but we know historically that up to the Reformation such scenes did occur in Christian edifices. Hone in his "Mysteries" describes these "Bacchanalian and Calendary rites," monks disguised as mummers, mummers disguised as monks, the Paternoster read backwards, a donkey brought up to the Communion Table and a mock litany pronounced with imitation of a donkey's braying, "demoniacal dances," "ballads borrowed from the streets and brothels."

The Therapeuts, according to Philo, represented Miriam and Moses on the stage with elaborate part-singing and solemn dances, and the Buddhists had their Inebriating Festival.

Philo, an initiate of the Religion of Serapis, living in Alexandria, describes these "impure mysteries."

"Indecency approaches and insults the most holy temples." He tells us of "devotees performing unhallowed sacrifices," "offering victims that ought not to be offered." He talks of an "impure piety, a debauched service."*

The worship of Serapis reached Rome 146 A.D.; "but the Senate soon found," says Jacobi ("Dictionnaire Mythologique") "its rites so licentious that they were forced to forbid them."

Tertullian assails the "Eleusinian dissipations" of the followers of Valentinus, who imitated the oaths of secrecy, the long initiations, the reticences and pious falsehoods of their model.

"All the divinity lies in their secret recesses. There are revealed all the aspirations of the fully initiated, the entire mystery of the sealed tongue, the symbol of virility."†

* Philo. "Cain and his birth," sect. 28.

† Tertullian. "Adversus Valent." cap. 1.

GLOSSARY AND INDEX.

A

Abrasax, a figure with Serpents for legs, 264; represented the Christos in the early church according to Tertullian, 264; is S'iva as the year god who dies at Easter, 263; has affinities with Philo's Logos and the Cingalese god, Kattragam, 267.

Aditî, the Vedic Universal Mother,

Âdityas, Sons of Aditî, the months deified,

Aishwarikas, Buddhists guided by Patanjali's Yogi Sâstra, the theistic school,

Amitâyas, the Buddha of immortal life,

Amarâvâtî, Tablets from, reveal Bacchantic mysteries in Buddhism, 283.

Amrita, Pâli Amata, immortality, "bread of life," 101; the food of the sacrifice after consecration,

Arhat, one emancipated from rebirths, an Adept,

Arûpaloka, the heavens where form ceases,

Asoka on "God," the future life, prayer, mysticism, etc., 85 *et seq.*; his attitude towards Buddhism, 97 *et seq.*

Avalokitishvara, Down-looking S'iva. Also S'iva's head on the monuments, 129; brought Buddhism to Tibet, 119; incarnate in each Dalai Lâma, 119.

Avîchi, the "rayless place," hell, purgatory,

B

Baal-Phœnician, a form of S'ivism, 11.

Bacchantic rites, see Somnâth.

Baptism, the Buddhhist rite of, 112.

Beal, Rev. Samuel, first suggests the occurrence in the past of a S'iva-Buddhist union, 2.

Bhagavat, lord, god, a title applied to Buddha, and S'iva.

Bhikshu, beggar, one who has adopted the religious life. He is called also Parivrâjika (wanderer), Muni (silent one), Sramana (vile one), Son of Buddha, Son of Sâkya, Son of Dharma, Man of Pure Life, Smâsânika (dwelling amid tombs), Houseless one, etc.,

Bigandet, Bishop, on the Buddhist hierarchy, 122, 216.

Bimbisâra, advised to destroy the infant Buddha, 51.

Bodhi, gnosis, knowledge of the laws of spirit, annihilation of the ego, and mystical union of the soul with the non-ego, or God,

Bodhisatwa, one about to obtain the Bodhi in his next rebirth. Also a gloss of S'iva Buddhism to get rid of the early worship of the Buddhas of the Past. They are changed to Bodhisatwas of the Past; and Bodhisatwa Maitreya rules the Kosmos,

Brahma, the Great Spirit, the ineffable,

Brahmâ, the anthropomorphic god,
Brahmacharins, Seekers of Brahma, name for Buddha's early disciples,
Brahmajnâni, an Adept,
Büchner, Ludwig, derives Christianity from Buddhism, 1; Metempsychosis, on the, 17.
Buddha, esoterically God, exoterically Sâkya Muni. *See* Sâkya Muni.
Burnouf Emile, derives Christianity from Buddhism, 1.

C

Carpet (kûsa mat) of Brahma, a mystic state,
Ceylon, vast pretensions claimed for scriptures of, 92 *et seq.*, 245
Chaitya, sepulchral mound, dolmen,
Chaitya Lingam, a lingam disguised as a Chaitya, 109.
Chakravartin (lit. "he who turns in the Zodiac"), a king of kings,
Child, covered with flour, a feature in the Buddhist and also the Christian mysteries, 243.
Clement of Alexandria, on India,
Colebrooke, Henry, on the theistic Sankhya, 16; on the atheistic Sankhya, 16; derives the philosophy of Pythagoras from Buddhism, 171.
Copleston, Bishop, bases his onslaught on Buddhism on the Mahâyâna literature of Buddhaghosa, 245.

D

Dharma, the laws of spirit personified as a divine woman,
Dhyâna, the trance of extasia,
Durgâ, has many names and many functions. She is the Tree goddess, the pestilent breath of the jungle, 30; patroness of the Thugs, a foul witch, the "She Devil Devî," 112; but also the Dharma of the Buddhists, the Sophia of the Gnostics, the "Church," and the Virgin, 89.
Descent into hell, Cingalese legend explaining, 285; in the Catholic Mass, 286; in the death of S'iva as the year-god, 287.

E

Elora, Fergusson's date, Rock-detached temples, 750 to 950 A.D., 143; Ati-Brahman's Cave, 149.
Elephant, its meaning, 233; Buddha's descent as one, 48.
Essene rites, 167.

F

Fa Hian cited, declares that Nalanda, the Rome of Buddhism at the date of Buddhaghosa, held the Great Vehicle teaching, 94.
Fasting, Buddha's forty-seven days',
Fergusson, James, on Indian Architecture, 141 *et seq.*
Foucaux, Philippe Edouard, his translation of the "Lalita Vistara" cited, 46 to 69.

G

Gandharva, a cherub,
Ganeśa, the son of S'iva, gives civilisation to Rome as Janus, 18; parallel between these two gods drawn by Sir William Jones, 19.

Gâthâ, a poem, a verse,
Girnar Rock, Asoka's inscription, declares that his missionaries converted Egypt, 163.
Gopura, Early Pyramid of S'iva; afterwards a pyramidal gateway to S'ivan Temple,
Grueber, Father, on the similarity of Buddhist and Christian rites, 220.
Guru, a spiritual teacher,

H

Hadrian, the Emperor, sees little difference between the Christians and the worshippers of Serapis at Alexandria, 269.
Huc, the Abbé, on the similarity of Buddhist and Christian rites, 219.
Hiouen Thsiang, states objections of earlier Buddhism to Agnostic School, 246; on the Convocation of Kaniska, 253; Buddhism of Ceylon belongs to the Great Vehicle, 246.

I

Inebriating Feast of the Buddha, the form that the Bacchantic S'iva Buddha festival takes in Ceylon,
Isâna, God, on the Asoka stones,

J

Jerusalem, Church of, its earliest offshoot, in Rome, water-drinking vegetarians, 186.
Jina, a conqueror of his lower nature, a Buddha,
Jones, Sir William, draws a parallel between Ganeśa and Janus, 19.

K

Karma, the effects of sins or good deeds, which are supposed to land the doer in the hell Avîchi or the heavens of the Devaloka, and detain him until the said Karma is exhausted. He is then born once more into the world, his Karma influencing the new birth, 207.
Kellog, Professor, on the Metempsychosis, 206.
Kailâs, Rock-detached Temple. See Elora.

L

Lâma, the Grand, the high priest of Tibet, descended most probably from the Âchârya of Nalanda,
Lightfoot, Bishop of Durham, considers Christ's movement anti-Essene, 174; on the festival at Ruanwelli, 174.
Lingam, sex symbol, S'iva,

M

Mahâbâlipur, Rock-detached temples and pyramid, very ancient. Fergusson's date fifth and sixth century A.D.,
Mahâdeo, a monolith or menhir, "Great God," a name of S'iva as the Lingam, 10.
Mahâkâla, S'iva as Time.
Mahâkâla Sanhita, gives the rites of S'iva's yearly death as the Time god. These have descended to S'iva Buddhism in the "mystery" of the "Sacrificial Body of the Dead Year," 139.
Mandala, mystic ring,
Mantra, prayer, charm,

Manushi (mortal), Buddhas, seven, 100 *et seq*.
Mâra, the Buddhist Satan,
Megasthenes on India, 102, 105.
Monks from Alexandria accepted as genuine Buddhist monks in Ceylon, at the festival to inaugurate the Ruanwelli Tope, B.C. 160-174 *et seq*.

N

Nairanjana, the Buddhist Jordan, 67.
Nirvâna, heaven, emancipation, also annihilation.

O

Oldenburg, Dr., rejects second convocation, 98.

P

Palâsa, *Butea frondosa*.
Pâramitâs, the ten, the "qualities of the Other Bank."
Parivrâjika. *See* Bhikshu.
Pârsvika, a leader in the Agnostic revolution in Buddhism entitled the "Great Vehicle," 127.
Prajnâ Pâramitâ, the "Wisdom of the Other Bank"; Wisdom personified by a woman,

R

Rajendra Lala Mitra shows that the philosophy of the "Great Vehicle" was plagiarised from the Sunyavâdi, 128.
Râm Râz, Hindu Architect, 149.
Rishi, prophet, man of God,
Rosny, Léon de, derives Christianity from Essenism and Buddhism, 1.

S

Sâkya Muni, results of his movement, 69; comes down to earth as a white elephant, 48; miraculous birth, 50; marriage, 56; the four presaging tokens, 56; leaves the place, 65; sits under the tree of Knowledge, 66; on the Brahma religion, 72; his reform, 75; begins to preach 68; the historical Buddha, 79, 89; death of, 81.
Samana Deva Râja, S'iva as worshipped in Ceylon, 113.
Sekkraia, Chief God in Ceylon, half a Lingam, half Indra or Sakra. He came on to Alexandria as Serapis, like him a god, half man half stone. He is a mask for the benevolent aspect of S'iva,
Serpent Symbolism. Not in early Buddhism, 276 *et seq*.
Sesh, Symbol of S'iva, also starry heavens, 26.
S'iva, Pantheistic god, two faces, 241; cultus rises higher and sinks lower than that of all early creeds, 13; Invents Yoga or mysticism, 13; invents the Logos idea, 18; invents Heaven and Hell.
Skandhas, the five (lit. "bodies"), usually applied by Buddhists to the animal nature of man,
Somnâth, S'iva as inventor of first intoxicant, 139; as Bacchus, 139; he figures as a drunken Silenus at the modern festivals, 139.
Southern account of Buddha's movement, 92; drawn up by Buddhaghosa, 93 *et seq*.; shameful dishonesty of, 94 *et seq*.
St. Matthew an Essene, 228.

St. James an Essene, 228.
Stambha, upright monolith, menhir.
Sunya, the void, the "Great Nowhere."
Sunya pushpa, the "Carriage that drives to the Great Nowhere;" a nickname for the Agnostic or innovating school of Buddhism, the Buddhism of the "Great Vehicle,"
S'iva-Buddhism, Forced addition to early Buddhism of the worship of the left-handed, or evil, divinities, 107; identical with the Mahâyâna movement, 108 *et seq.*
Sûtra, discourse,
S'iva-Linga, the holiest form of lingam,
Swayamvara, marriage by athletic competition (lit. "her own choice"),

T

Tapas, self-torture (swinging on hooks, etc.) to gain magical power,
Tathâgata. *See* Śakya Muni.
Tïrthas, tanks, shrines,
Tope, a dolmen, or sepulchral mound,
Tusita, the highest heaven to be reached by unemancipated spirits.

U

Upham, Edward, in the Kappooism of Ceylon, 247; pro-
Upham, Edward—*continued.* nounces the Buddhism of the North and South identical, 247.

V

Vaitarani, the Brahmin River of Death,
Varshâ, the rainy season, the Buddhist Lent,
Vihâra, a monastery,

W

Williams, Sir Monier, pronounces Buddhism atheistic, 89; it ignores all "spiritual aspirations," 69; general denunciation, 89.
Wilson, Professor, Horace Hayman, detects S'ivan rites in the Christian Agapæ described by Gibbon, 237; S'iva's mythology neglected, 9.
Word of Glory—Indian Logos, 18.

Y

Yoga (lit. "union"), the conjoining of heaven and earth, spirit, and matter, the annihilation of the ego and merging of one's will with the divine will. Magical powers were conceived to be a result of this "union." Hence Yoga also means white magic, 15.